BAD TO BLUE

BAD TO BLUE

THE TRUE STORY OF A
CHINATOWN GANGSTER
TURNED NYPD DETECTIVE

MIKE MOY

BLACK
STONE
PUBLISHING

Copyright © TK
Cover and book design by Kathryn Galloway English

All rights reserved. This book or any portion
thereof may not be reproduced or used in any manner
whatsoever without the express written permission
of the publisher except for the use of brief quotations
in a book review.

This book is a memoir. It represents the personal
experiences and recollections of the author, as well as
the author's perspective of these experiences. Some names
and identifying details have been changed to protect the
privacy of individuals.

Printed in the United States of America

Biography & Autobiography / Personal Memoirs

Blackstone Publishing
31 Mistletoe Rd.
Ashland, OR 97520

www.BlackstonePublishing.com

I dedicate this book to my late kau fu, *Uncle William Cheung Kung, and my* po po, *Grandma Choy Fong Kung. These two people showered me with love and affection during my childhood, nurtured my humanity, and enabled me to hold on to what remained of my emotions during my difficult adolescent years. Without them, I would have been an empty soul devoid of feelings.*

AUTHOR'S NOTE

When I realized that a vital piece of history would soon dissipate into the mists of time without someone to tell the stories of Chinatown during the height of the Asian gangs, I felt a passion to take on this important task. This drive went counter to my quiet nature as someone who never aspired to be in the limelight. I rarely engage in idle conversation, speaking only as necessary and when I have something pertinent to say. I prefer to make things happen from behind the scenes. My greatest contentment comes from being alone, hidden from the public's attention. But here I was, spearheading a YouTube channel called Chinatown Gang Stories, documenting the events and interviewing the major players of this turbulent and colorful era. I was interviewed for a CNN article and approached by producers and filmmakers. Given the public's interest and excitement, I knew that to bring those who hadn't lived it—and even those who had—into this world viscerally, I had to tell my personal story.

That would mean going against my introverted nature to give readers context behind my decisions to join a gang and then the New York City Police Department (NYPD). In this book, I share some brutal stories from all the phases of my life with the stoicism baked into my DNA, along with my upbringing and the survival tactic of never allowing my feelings to overrun—and endanger—me and those with me, no matter what was happening. I share this so that you, the reader, will understand my point of view as we go on this harrowing journey together.

INTRODUCTION

GOOD COP/BAD COP

I was mere months from graduating from the police academy, a turning point that I hoped would change my life for the better, when detectives from the NYPD Sixty-Eighth Precinct knocked on my mom's door. Detective Donahue and his partner told her they wanted to question me regarding a possible homicide case. She calmly told them she would relay the message to me, then sent a panicked message to my pager.

Even as I told her not to worry, that it was no big deal, questions bombarded my mind: What did they want? Had they cracked open a cold case and somehow connected me to it? Had they found out my dark secret?

I called Detective Donahue during my meal break while in police training in Manhattan. In a well-modulated voice, he cleverly answered my questions without disclosing much information.

My worst fears might finally be coming true: Throughout training, I had a nagging unease that my unresolved past could surface at any moment. I pictured myself being led out of the academy in handcuffs. I'd managed to dodge close calls to this point in my life, but I was far from sure that my luck would hold out indefinitely.

After my training session, I drove straight to the precinct. Detective Donahue and his partner escorted me into the interrogation room. Looking around its bare walls and sparse furnishings, I imagined that in a few years, I'd be the one questioning persons of interest in rooms like this one. But if I didn't make it onto the police force and stayed on my current course, I'd be in prison like most of my friends. Or dead.

As it turned out, I *would* question suspects in this chamber in the future. But today I was a person of interest left to sit in the stark, windowless room. The longer I sat, the more I stressed over the looming interrogation. Later I learned that letting me stew was a trick to get me to talk, one I'd use countless times on suspects.

Years ago, my Italian friend and mentor, Uncle Louie, had advised me to always lawyer up in situations like this. I'd kept that in mind.

When the detectives finally came in to start the questioning, I sized up Donahue. A typical white detective in a suit and tie, he had a full head of hair and a medium build.

"Your former business partner, Keith, is dead," Donahue stated with a solemn-but-icy edge.

"Keith is dead?" I repeated in a hushed voice, not hiding my shock.

"We found his body floating off Caesars Bay."

A sense of relief washed over me, not because I wished Keith harm but because I knew I had nothing to do with his death. At least this was not something from my past catching up to me. Like a sped-up movie reel, I imagined the cops recovering Keith's body under intense floodlights, a chilling figure floating in shimmering black water.

Both Detective Donahue and his colleague started out by playing good cops, but when I didn't confess, Donahue dove into "bad cop" mode. Leaning into my space and pounding on the table, he bellowed, "Keith owed you twenty thousand dollars. You have twenty thousand reasons to kill him!"

I was a new police recruit being interrogated by a detective with a fiery, piercing gaze, his over-the-top accusation an obvious attempt to unravel me. I was worried that any investigation into Keith's death would inadvertently reveal my past. Or worse, that I'd be arrested for a crime I didn't commit. My future was on the line.

My name is Michael Moy.

For nine years, I was a gang member in New York City's Chinatown. I hid that secret from the NYPD for twenty-six years and nineteen days. My police uniform covered a dragon tattoo, a symbol denoting my untold history. In those early days, I also hid my plan to be a law enforcement officer from my former gangmates. I hid both identities from my family. Now I'm finally ready to reveal the truth about myself.

My life has come full circle, from a life of crime to a life's work of crime fighting. Back when I pledged my allegiance to a Chinatown gang, it had felt like the right thing to do. But taking my oath to be an NYPD officer in the Brooklyn College auditorium at midnight on June 30, 1995, disentangled me from that life, which felt even more right.

As I stood amid the announcements and applause with over two thousand other rookie cops, I had flashbacks of my gangland years in the streets of Lower Manhattan and Brooklyn. The same hand I raised to pledge the oath that night had committed crimes. When I wasn't on the streets engaging in gang wars, I was selling drugs or counterfeit money or unlicensed guns. I extorted money from business owners, ran illegal gambling dens, and committed assaults and robberies. Possessing unlimited cash and a sense of power had been gratifying for a kid who'd grown up in poverty. Being involved in the dangerous underworld had provided a thrilling adrenaline rush. My gang family made me feel safe.

Even so, at the time I'd reflected on the treacherous journey before me: a world in which gang leaders drove their crews toward their versions of power and success, regardless of cost.

The incredible story of one police officer's heroic forgiveness opened my mind to a new way of seeing myself, my past, and my life trajectory. After experiencing the freedom and chaos of gang life, I longed for structure, discipline, and normalcy, even the mundane act of going to work like regular people did. Mostly, though, I discovered I liked the feeling of doing the right thing. While doing the wrong thing had made me a lot of money, I realized that doing good felt even better.

While putting together this memoir, I spent long hours interviewing my elders as they recalled their journeys from China to America in the 1960s. I saw how Asians struggled to survive in a city immersed in the socioeconomic and racial problems of that era. They were determined to build better lives through both lawful and unlawful means.

I reconnected with former gangmates and revisited the streets where we'd fought our battles. With weary eyes and an aching back, I scoured online newspaper archives, studying decades-old articles about the Asian gang wars that had plagued Chinatown. In the New York Public Library, I pored over microfilm of old newspapers. Studying the gang situation from this distant viewpoint, I now saw that at its core stood a group of iron-willed people whose backgrounds, childhood trauma, and desperate poverty had influenced their decisions.

Their leaders' authority extended everywhere, with followers hanging on their every word. These formidable men also harbored the seeds of their own destruction. As their empires grew, hubris and internal conflicts undermined their foundations. Each leader's downfall or imprisonment dealt a devastating blow to their gang, plunging them into uncertainty, which in turn propelled them to act in desperation.

Marked by darkness, violence, and betrayal, the stories of these architects of chaos have been etched into New York's Chinatown criminal history while also serving as cautionary tales: Even the most powerful can fall victim to insatiable desires.

Joining the NYPD allowed me to make amends for past mistakes. I also faced numerous risks and threats inherent to the job. I developed World Trade Center–related illnesses due to exposure to toxins during 2001's Ground Zero rescue and recovery operations. I took an oath to serve and protect, which I did until my retirement in 2021.

America is about second chances, though many former gangmates of mine did not take advantage of their second chances, getting imprisoned, killed, even buried somewhere in a forgotten wasteland. But those, like me, who overcame their pasts reflect this American ideal, emerging from checkered pasts with newfound purpose.

Somehow, I survived the odds, both on the streets and in the police force, which must be for a reason—perhaps to write this story of determination and redemption.

Here is how I turned from *bad to blue*.

CHAPTER ONE

TAISHAN TO EAST BROADWAY

On September 3, 1969, I let out my first cry in a delivery room at Brooklyn's Kings County Hospital. I am an American-born Chinese.

That same year Richard Nixon took the oath as the thirty-seventh president, and the United States landed a man on the moon. Around four hundred thousand hippies gathered on a farm near Woodstock, New York, while the upheaval against the Vietnam War divided America. But those epic events of the sixties might as well have never happened for families like mine who lived in New York City's Chinatown. Chinese immigrants, focused on a daily fight for mere survival, didn't even notice the decade's turmoil and excitement.

I spent my first five years in a tiny apartment on the top floor of a six-story, ten-unit building at 26 East Broadway on the Lower East Side of Manhattan. Because the tenement building's cramped staircase was usually unlit, we often had to feel our way up and down the five flights.

Eleven of us crammed into the narrow apartment, including my mom, dad, younger sister, grandmother, three uncles, two aunts, and a distant relative of my grandmother's. Without an air conditioner, the place was like a sauna in August. We had one bunk bed, a full-sized bed that my grandmother slept on, and one mattress on the floor. Everyone else used bamboo mats on the living room floor. I preferred sleeping on a mat since it was cooler, but because I was her favorite, Grandma—who I called *Po Po*—insisted I sleep beside her on the more comfortable bed.

Surrounded by snoring adults honking out a disquieting chorus, I often stared at the dark ceiling, awaiting the nightly show: an army of cockroaches emerging from the crack in the wallpaper. They'd scurry all around the room, and I felt their little legs skittering over my skin as I lay in bed. I didn't mind though; I was used to them being part of my life. When we switched on the lights, they scattered in all directions. To amuse me, Uncle William—who I called *Kau Fu*—taught me a cockroach-catching game. He and I would snatch the roaches with our thumb, index finger, and middle finger. The one who caught the most in this "kung fu style" won. Bedbugs—they were the real nuisance. In the mornings I sometimes found clusters of them, fattened on my blood. When I squished them, they spewed out a red substance with a distinctive woodsy smell.

Our family owned a black-and-white television with a rabbit-ear antenna and a broken dial. I needed an adult's help to change the channel because the pliers we used to turn the knob were too big for my hands. In the middle of the night, garbage trucks collected trash along our street. Although I became inured to their noise, the foul smell woke me up. On the upside, our apartment offered the perk of providing a great view of parades and lion dances during Chinese New Year celebrations.

After working long hours, my parents came home too

exhausted to spend time with me and my sister. My mom rarely paid me attention unless it was to reprimand me. Even the slightest infraction or misstep irritated her. At just four years old, if I failed to identify Chinese characters, she would strike my hands with a duster's bamboo handle.

As I became rebellious and indulged in all sorts of mischief, my mom disciplined me without restraint, often leaving me with a swollen rear and legs. She sometimes made me kneel for hours before an altar of Wong Tai Sin while holding each of my earlobes. Many Chinese parents employed this punishment to remind their children to use their ears to listen to their elders. Often I would fall asleep, then wake up, wondering how I'd moved from kneeling to looking up at the ceiling.

Po Po called my mom *lo fu la*, meaning "tigress."

"Behave yourself, *lo fu la* is coming!" she cautioned when I grew too mischievous. I would quickly straighten up.

I resented how little time and attention I got from either of my parents. Looking back, I understand the circumstances that compelled my mother to be a tiger mom. She barely had time for us, much less for herself, and the immense pressure of providing for the family weighed heavily on her and my dad's shoulders. I didn't consider her cruel; I simply saw her punishments as shortcuts to discipline me when my antics became another of her many problems.

Admittedly, sometimes I deserved it, as I would purposefully annoy her out of retaliation. Within me lurked a rebel yearning to break free. Mostly, my mischief was a product of curiosity and the natural restlessness of a child eager to explore and experience new things. In hindsight, I am grateful to her for the way she raised me as I feel it made me stronger, although I did end the cycle of physical punishment with my own children.

Before I started attending school nearby on Mott Street, I

spent most of my time with my *po po*. Choy Fong Kung was born on April 28, 1927. As a fourteen-year-old, she barely survived the Japanese troops raiding and plundering their Taishan village in southwestern Guangdong, China.

I often begged *Po Po* to tell me the details, tantalized by the little bit I knew about her daring escape. At first, she gave me mere snippets of how they survived the Second Sino-Japanese War. She wanted to forget that traumatic, painful episode of her life, but I was too young to see that. My curiosity pushed me to pester her for the entire story, and she eventually conceded to telling me her war experiences as bedtime stories. I would close my eyes and imagine the events unfolding. In time, I was able to piece together her unforgettable story.

When the Japanese army attacked her village in 1941, the watchmen rang the alarm. After grabbing whatever belongings they could hold on to, the villagers and their children ran for their lives. They'd heard about the cruelty of the Japanese army, such as throwing children in the air and catching them with bayonets and burning villages to the ground.

"The Japanese soldiers went from house to house with their bayonets, looking for anything of value," *Po Po* recalled. "They hacked and shot anyone in sight."

An officer with several soldiers barged into the house of my great-great-grandfather, Chin Wui Man. The seventy-year-old had been too weak to leave, so he'd remained there with his wife. The officer pointed a bayonet at his face and asked him questions in Japanese about the photograph of my grandmother on the wall.

Annoyed that he could not understand, the officer hit Chin's head with the rifle. He reeled from the blow and fell to the floor. A soldier continued questioning him while pointing to the photograph. Only then did Chin realize that the Japanese were looking for young girls to rape. Using gestures, he said that she was dead.

Enraged by his answer, they broke a glass bottle and made Chin kneel on the shards. To mock him further, the soldiers forced him to bow to them while his wife looked on. They pressed him to disclose where their valuables were hidden.

A soldier weighed down on the old man's shoulder, so the broken glass cut deeper into his knees. Another pressed his boot with spikes on Chin's leg until it bled. At that point, he was ready to die. Having gotten their loot, the soldiers finally left.

Outside, Japanese soldiers chased villagers through the fields, hunting them down. *Po Po*'s brother, Edward, froze in terror as they ran amid the hail of bullets. *Po Po* hoisted him onto her back and, fueled by the adrenaline coursing through her body, ran toward a river in the distance. Fellow villagers fell dead as gunfire and screams filled the air all around them.

As they approached the river, her heart sank. The water was deep, and she knew it would be nearly impossible to cross. But she had no time to dwell on it with their pursuers closing in. She pushed her brother down onto the muddy riverbank, lay down on top of him, then smeared mud all over their bodies. She told him to play dead alongside the dozens of lifeless people around them.

The Japanese soldiers checked the bodies strewn across the area, likely looking for any that still showed signs of life. One soldier stood over my grandmother. She pleaded in her mind: *Brother! My brother! Do not make a sound or move one bit, or we will die!* Seconds ticked by, marked by a pounding heart she feared the soldier could hear. He kicked her to see if she reacted. Fortunately, or perhaps out of this soldier's humanity, the toe of his boot scraped the mud before it hit her, blunting the force. She heard him say something in Japanese to another solider, possibly confirming that she was dead. The soldier walked away to join his troop.

Grandma and her brother remained motionless for hours, long after the soldiers left, just in case someone watched and waited for survivors to emerge from the banks. She heard nothing but leaves rustling against the wind.

At one point, she believed she was indeed dead. Her body was so numb that she couldn't move. When she finally opened her eyes, all she could see was darkness. The sun had gone down by the time she finally staggered to her feet. She pulled Edward up from the ground and hugged him tightly. *We survived!* But they still had a long way to go.

They walked through a sea of corpses, searching for survivors while trying not to vomit. She recognized several familiar faces and cried. They followed the river until reaching a waterfall.

Po Po and her brother waded through the water toward a small cave behind the waterfall. They entered through a curtain of falling water to hide. Shivering and still in shock, they could do nothing but lie on the wet, rocky ground. They were too scared to return to their village, so they stayed in the damp cave for several days.

One morning, they heard someone calling out for survivors and screamed for help. *Po Po* was too weak to move due to fever and starvation, and both had to be carried out of the cave.

Back in the village, *Po Po* witnessed the destruction wrought by the Japanese soldiers. She and her brother reunited with their ailing grandfather and grandmother. *Po Po* tended to her grandfather's knee and leg wounds, but unfortunately, he died shortly after due to an infection.

There was nothing to eat because the Japanese had taken everything, down to the last grain of rice. *Po Po* roamed the fields to the other side of the river, scouring for anything edible to sustain our family. She chanced upon a Chinese villager dumping sacks of severed heads into the waters. Then, she realized where the vendors got the cheap meat they sold in the market.

As I grew older, I recognized how the war had traumatized her. She experienced severe emotional distress each time something reminded her of that harrowing episode. Her flashbacks would bring her to tears, and it pained me to see her suffer.

Po Po brought the same resilience, determination, and quiet strength when she immigrated from China to New York in 1966 with my mom. Had she made the slightest sound or reaction when the Japanese soldier kicked her on that riverbank, she would have lost her life—and with it, the lives of her future children and grandchildren. How profound that my entire existence hinged on that single split-second moment.

My clan became part of the US Chinese migration statistics when they arrived in America in the 1960s. The first wave of Chinese migrants came as early as 1815, the majority being men. However, in 1834, Afong Moy became the first female Chinese immigrant to the United States, and I often wonder if she is part of my family's roots since she came from the same village as my dad.

My great-uncle, whom I call *Ah Gung*, that little boy who played dead on the riverbanks of Taishan, later designed rockets and spacecraft for the National Aeronautics and Space Administration (NASA).

I have always looked up to my tall, bespectacled *Ah Gung*, whom I often encountered during our family reunions and get-togethers in Chinatown. His humble demeanor and soft-spoken nature commanded respect.

Uncle Edward's story of survival inspired me. He migrated to the United States in the 1950s and settled on Mott Street.

Like many Chinese immigrants, Uncle Edward's elders made a living in New York by doing odd jobs or working in sweatshops.

He enrolled at the City College of New York and excelled in his studies. After entering the ROTC program, he befriended a young man named Colin Powell, who later became the US Secretary of State. Uncle Edward studied from 1954 to 1958, first at the City College and then at New York University, and completed a bachelor of science in mechanical engineering.

After working for Boeing, he worked at the giant aeronautical company Northrop Grumman. It was the height of the space race between the United States and the former Union of Soviet Socialist Republics (USSR). Falling way behind Russian space milestones and pressured by the Kennedy administration, NASA partnered with Northrop Grumman to accelerate its technological development. Uncle Edward became part of the Northrop Grumman team that worked on NASA's space program, with the critical mission of landing a man on the moon ahead of the USSR.

Due to an employee confidentiality agreement with NASA, he never spoke about his involvement in developing the lunar module and other technologies crucial to the Apollo missions. On one occasion, his granddaughter gifted him a space blanket she bought while on a school trip to Washington, DC, excitedly telling him that the astronauts used this when they were in space. He accepted her present with a secret smile; he was one of the engineers who helped develop it.

In 1970, NASA launched Apollo 13 on another mission to land on the moon. However, the module failed due to an unexpected technical malfunction. This drama garnered worldwide attention on the fate of the three Apollo 13 astronauts: Jim Lovell, Jack Swigert, and Fred Haise.

As America and the rest of the world anxiously watched

the Apollo 13 mission unfold, Uncle Edward worked tirelessly with the NASA teams to ensure the astronauts' safe return to Earth. Through their dedication and hard work, they accomplished this mission under intense pressure. Hollywood turned this real-life drama into a movie in 1995.

Uncle Edward received the prestigious Apollo Achievement Award from NASA in recognition of his dedicated service to the nation as a member of a team that advanced the nation's capabilities in aeronautics and space. His contributions were instrumental in many of the outstanding accomplishments leading up to Apollo's successful landing on the moon on July 20, 1969.

My great-uncle, who narrowly escaped death at the hands of the Japanese, helped put a man on the moon.

Po Po may not have realized how her stories of using courage and wits to stay alive shaped my own tenacity. Her resilience, determination, and quiet strength imprinted on me, a boy eager for tales of war, as well as the attention of someone who dearly loved him.

Po Po worked as a seamstress in a Chinatown sweatshop. She woke early, preparing for the day in slow, measured movements and sipping tea until she had to leave. Because she worked twelve-hour days, she could come home midday to meet me when my parents dropped me off at her apartment after school. Then she'd take me to work with her because no one was home to care for me. In both the summer heat and winter chill, she and I walked to the sweatshop. Even illness didn't prevent her from working, exemplifying her generation's strong work ethic. Her determination and resilience infused my own work ethic, and perhaps also my sometimes stoic acceptance of difficult circumstances.

My earliest memories from around the age of four to nine

revolved around spending hours each workday in that sweatshop. Nestled in a narrow Chinatown alley, the dimly lit warehouse was a world of its own. Rows of sewing machines lined the cramped quarters, each manned by a grim-looking Asian woman working tirelessly in silence. From dawn until dusk, the rattle of machines echoed off the walls, creating a constant soundtrack.

The humid, stale air was laden with the scent of human effort. In summer, the sweltering heat turned the jam-packed room into a cauldron of sweat. In winter, despite the biting cold that chilled their bones, the women continued weaving and stitching with numb fingers.

In this secluded hive, time was marked by the needles' rhythmic dance and the silent determination of those laboring within. While the adults worked, I played with spools of thread as if they were Lego blocks, hopping from one fabric bin to another, building fortresses around *Po Po*'s sewing station.

I remember *Po Po* asking me for help threading a needle, which made me feel valuable and important. Looking back, she certainly could have done it faster on her own, but I think she wanted to involve me and give me a sense of accomplishment.

When boredom threatened, I turned my attention to the cats roaming beneath the shop's machines and tables. The sight of a cat with a mouse's tail dangling from its mouth became the highlight of my day, thrilling me with the spectacle of brutal nature. Sometimes, I put metal thimbles on each of my fingers, imagining they infused kung fu powers through my hands. That sweatshop became a sanctuary of my imagination, a place where I disappeared into my own world, weaving tales as intricate as the fabrics.

But watching *Po Po* in her daily grind, no joy on her face, sometimes sent me into darker ponderings. I didn't understand why she had to work so hard. I wanted her to spend more time with me at home. Unanswered questions weighed on my young mind, often making me drowsy. Sometimes I went behind *Po Po*'s seat, hugging her waist with my tiny arms, resting my head against her back, letting the sewing machines' symphonic cadence lull me to sleep.

As twilight neared, workers with faces etched by the day's toil sometimes praised my patience as I waited for *Po Po* to finish her workday. I prided myself on being good, never complaining or throwing tantrums.

Two near-fatal experiences that happened before I turned four remain vivid in my memory. Once, my naive curiosity led me to poke my finger into an empty light bulb socket in the bed's headboard, resulting in a loud crackle, an electric shock, and me collapsing on the bed.

In my second memory, I actually crossed the veil between life and death. When I was three, *Po Po* left me in our 1900s clawfoot-style porcelain bathtub to fetch my towel. I slipped, sinking beneath the water's surface, my hands too soapy to get a grip on the sides of the tub. As I inhaled to scream, water flooded my lungs. I couldn't breathe! My chest expanded with a stinging, unbearable heaviness, and my eyes bulged as I flailed helplessly. I couldn't get myself upright, and I quickly tired out and stopped struggling. The last thing I saw was the distorted ceiling through the water.

When my vision returned, I was floating above, watching myself drown. I saw the agony on my blurry face through the hazy water and came face-to-face with my dying self. I felt no pain or panic, only a quiet peace.

But then darkness blinded me, and I felt nothing.

Po Po wrenched me out of the water, and I opened my heavy eyes to see her face twisted in horror. After expelling water with my coughing, I wailed in her arms while wrapped in a towel and trembling.

Growing up, I sometimes pondered that near-death experience, especially in opposition to my mounting existential belief that nothing follows this human life. I told myself that when people die, they vanish, becoming nonexistent. However, briefly experiencing another realm raised questions for the rational person I thought myself to be.

When I was four, my parents enrolled me in the New York Chinese School at 62 Mott Street in Manhattan's Chinatown. I would continue to attend until I was about six.

I was overwhelmed at the first sight of the wide staircase at the school entrance, and later frightened each time I saw the bust of a Chinese figure in the lobby. The green color of the corridor walls gave me a curious sense of unease.

Later in 1973, we moved to Kensington, Brooklyn. We'd just settled in when a burglar broke into our house and stole my dad's cherished silver coin collection, which he'd saved from his days working in a laundromat as a boy in 1947. A few weeks later, my mom and I returned home from running errands and parked by the street curb. My mom exited and walked around to open the rear passenger door for me. From out of nowhere, a man charged at her, opened the front passenger door, and shoved her back onto the bench seat. He pinned her down with his body and pressed a knife to her neck.

I popped up in the back and saw what was happening. Opening my door, I stepped out into traffic. Seeing cars coming at me, I froze. A speeding car swerved to avoid hitting me, then screeched to an abrupt stop. Two men jumped out with guns drawn, and the assailant fled. Seeing my shock, they identified themselves as undercover policemen. Looking more like criminals than law enforcers, my mom looked frightened anew as they approached her, at least until they showed her their badges.

They escorted us to the station so she could view photos for suspect identification, but she couldn't identify the perpetrator. My dad later explained to my mom that the undercover cops needed to look like ruffians as part of their disguise.

This incident profoundly influenced me. I began to see the police as real-life heroes and became a fan of detective shows like *Baretta*, *Kojak*, and *Barney Miller*.

Following this harrowing incident, we moved back into *Po Po*'s apartment in Chinatown while my parents searched for a safer place to live. In 1974, just before my fifth birthday, my dad used his savings and borrowed money to purchase our first house in Brooklyn. That fall, I was to begin attending kindergarten at Public School 255 in Brooklyn, introducing me to the experience of commuting beyond Chinatown and going to a non-Chinese school. To prepare me, my parents taught me three key phrases in English: "Yes," "No," and "I need to go to the bathroom" so I wouldn't pee myself. I had to recite those words hundreds of times before starting school. These were the only English words I knew.

After the school day ended, my parents dropped my sister and me off at *Po Po*'s place on East Broadway in Chinatown, returning late at night to pick me up. On weekends, I continued my Cantonese studies at the New York Chinese School. I do not recall one weekend when my parents picked me up from the Chinese school. *Po Po* or my aunt always met me after I descended the staircase where other parents and guardians greeted their children.

I then spent the rest of the weekend at my *po po*'s because my parents worked extra days to pay their mortgage. Instead of owning the house, it seemed to me that the house owned them. A year after my brother, Jason, was born in 1977, my mom, like many Chinese women, found a way to work from home by buying a sewing machine and converting our basement into her own personal sweatshop. Now at least she could take breaks to care for her three children. I missed spending so much of my time with *Po Po*, though, being spoiled by her. We still didn't get much time with our mom since she worked as many hours as she always had.

Having immigrated here and experiencing struggle and poverty, my parents placed a high value on a secure life—a higher priority than spending time with their children and actually enjoying that life.

As we talked in preparation for writing this book, I learned aspects of my father's past that explained so much about who he was and why he hadn't spoken of it.

Born on February 14, 1940, in a Chinese village called Jung Wai in Taishan County, he was the eldest of five. He fondly recalled his village life to me, describing it as a time of freedom and happiness. He and the other children played all day in vast fields, creating their own world while their parents occupied themselves with farmwork. Despite their small house and few possessions, he never felt poor. At seven years old, with little parental oversight, he felt like a prince ruling his small kingdom. Sadly, this idyllic existence ended in 1947 when his father took him to a stranger's house and left him with new "parents" who would be taking him to America. That's how my dad became a "paper son."

The "paper sons and daughters" system evolved out of Chinese parents' desire to immigrate to America to make a better life for their family. At the time, immigration laws were extremely strict for the Chinese. To circumvent this discrimination, families in China would pay legal immigrants to adopt their child since immediate family members were allowed to come into the country. This practice was common until the mid-1900s. The families back in China also hoped that their child would eventually be able to send money to support their real family.

Though the man my dad was left with explained that his father had made the arrangement so that the boy could have a better life, my dad felt as if he'd been sold. In reality, his father had paid this couple to adopt him.

Leaving the fields and his lighthearted days with friends deeply saddened him. He was never able to find out more from his father because he never saw him again. A few years after they separated, his father passed away in China.

The man urged my dad to start calling him "Father" and pretend they were related. He falsified documents to start the process and returned to the US while awaiting the arrival of his and his wife's "paper son," who would be shipped by boat to San Francisco.

Despite his sadness at leaving everything he'd ever known, my dad embraced his solo journey across the ocean as an adventure. Upon docking, the Angel Island immigration authorities in San Francisco interviewed and medically screened him, a process that took two months because of the backlog, before releasing him to his pseudo-father. They then traveled over two thousand miles by train to New York.

"I was overjoyed when I got here," Dad recalled. "New York, with its towering buildings and fast-moving cars, was a world apart from my village. Everything about it thrilled me."

My dad, however, had to earn his keep, and his pseudo-parents put him to work in their laundromat in Brooklyn's Borough Park. There, standing on wooden boxes, he meticulously ironed clothes, never complaining. Over the years, he perfected this skill. No one could iron clothes better than my dad.

"My real parents had worked tirelessly to ensure we never went hungry," he told me. "Even as a child, I did my part to help. But with my new family, I had to earn my keep. I wasn't treated the same as their biological kids, so I never felt as though I fit in."

During his school years, my dad concentrated on learning English. He studied architecture and drafting at New York Community College, honing his skills in construction fundamentals.

He met my mom in 1966, the same year she came to America. My dad and his friend were in a car on East Broadway when they spotted four Hispanic men harassing a young Chinese woman. Without a second thought, they jumped from the car, wielding big sticks and boldly confronting the harassers. After a fierce fight, they chased away the troublemakers.

My dad and his friend walked over to the woman to make sure she was all right. My dad was so captivated by her beauty that he quickly forgot the recent altercation and invited her for coffee. She happily accepted. This encounter sparked a romance that quickly blossomed. In less than a year, they fell in love and got married. Should I be grateful then to the men who harassed my mom, as their actions inadvertently led to my parents meeting? But perhaps nothing in life is accidental, as evidenced by how my parents' paths crossed that night.

My mother, born on July 3, 1948, in Guangzhou, China, moved to New York in 1966 with *Po Po* and other family members. Upon her arrival at eighteen, she started working in a sweatshop, earning the same thirty cents per garment as *Po Po*. She continued working there after I was born, putting in those long hours that kept her away from me so much.

During those early years, I looked forward to *Kau Fu*'s return to *Po Po*'s apartment, excited for the midnight treats my uncle would bring from the restaurant where he worked as a waiter. For years, he also faithfully brought me the comics page from the *New York Daily News*. I would cut out the panels and create my own comic books, using kneaded rice grains as paste, a technique he taught me. He took me to see *Star Wars*, my first American movie in a theater, leaving me in total awe.

It was from him that I learned about gangs and Tong associations. During our walks in Chinatown, *Kau Fu* pointed out bullet holes in walls, narrating tales of wars between the Flying Dragons and the Ghost Shadows. Once, we saw a group of guys in a dimly lit parking lot on East Broadway. As we neared, *Kau Fu* squeezed my hand and cautioned me not to stare.

"Why?" I whispered.

"They are *fei jais*," he replied gravely.

Fei jai, meaning "gangster," was a common term in 1970s Chinatown. Whenever we passed gang members, *Kau Fu* would avoid eye contact, hasten his pace, and pull me closer. I knew they were something to fear.

On several occasions, I joined *Po Po* on visits to the On Leong Tong office on Mott Street to pay dues. Walking inside this mysterious den, we passed desks piled with cash. Stern-faced clerks counted the bills and wrapped them in neat bundles, the air thick with the scent of money and cigarettes.

"Why are we here again?" I asked her as we sat waiting in an office made dim by the smoke.

"To pay the Tong."

"But why?"

"They help us when we need it."

"Why do you keep paying? You work so hard for that money."

Po Po didn't answer, leaving me with my questions.

It took me until my teenage years to understand the Tongs and gangs. In Chinatown, Tongs started out as benevolent organizations, helping Chinese immigrants settle in America. They were organized by the ancestral provinces of members and served as vital sociocultural hubs. Racial inequality in the US made these Tongs even more crucial for the Chinese community. They provided essential services like employment, housing, loans, protection, and dispute resolution. Operating secretly and within a strict hierarchy, eventually their leaders turned to crime, including gambling, prostitution, and racketeering, which led to brutal turf wars in Chinatown. They used street gangs to enforce and expand their power, the two most powerful being the Flying Dragons and the Ghost Shadows. Instead of the Tongs unifying Chinatown, their turf battles now claimed many lives.

In Manhattan, Tung On dominated East Broadway, Division, and Catherine Streets, while the Ghost Shadows controlled Mott, Bayard, and Elizabeth Streets. Flying Dragons claimed Pell, Doyers, Bowery, and Grand Street. White Tigers operated in Queens. Each gang enforced their rule with terror.

Unfortunately, I experienced that firsthand. *Kau Fu* and I frequented theaters along East Broadway and nearby blocks on weekends. In these vermin-infested Chinatown theaters of the 1970s, moviegoers could often be heard screaming when rats brushed against their feet. I always sat on the armrest with my feet on the seat so that they didn't touch the sticky floor, leaning on *Kau Fu*. When the theater lights came on, we could see what looked like a slimy, moving *river* that was actually rats flooding the stage below the screen.

Even so, these theaters were often jam-packed, especially for new releases by Shaw Brothers. I was a huge fan of actors like Ti Lung, Fu Sheng, Chen Kuan-tai, David Chiang, Gordon Liu, and Bruce Lee. Through these films, the Chinese community in Chinatown connected with their heritage. These movie houses served as their primary entertainment, and they would brave rats, roaches, and even occasional shootings for a brief escape from the drudgery of their lives.

When I was eight, *Kau Fu* and I went to the Pagoda Theater to watch a movie. Arriving late, we took the last available seats near the emergency exit. Mid-movie, a loud *pop* triggered chaos. Fear paralyzed me. I'd never been that close to gunfire.

My uncle shoved me to the ground. I held still with my chest pressed against the cold, slimy floor amid the pandemonium, with people shouting "*Buk dai!*" in Cantonese ("Get down!"). Someone whom I assumed was the shooter leaped from the balcony, landing atop people before rushing out the nearby exit. When the commotion settled down, we dared to stand and check out the now-empty theater. It was over. I was alive. I patted myself, feeling the sticky substances on my clothes and skin. That and the stench almost made me vomit. Ever since, I've had an aversion to germs.

East Broadway was a jungle fraught with danger at every turn; any appearance of calm or peace was misleading. Thankfully, my family diligently shielded me from its worst dangers. Even so, some of it managed to get very close to us.

In 1979, two years after the movie theater shooting, Chinatown's gang warfare escalated. Two gang members, only eighteen and twenty years old, were captured by a competitive gang and brutally executed in a factory directly across from *Po Po*'s sixth-floor apartment.

On December 23, 1982, my family members and I witnessed the aftermath of gang-related violence across the street from our bedroom window. The NYPD established a perimeter in front of the Golden Star, a bar where a shooting occurred that resulted in the deaths of three people. Eight others were critically injured.

The violence reached a shocking peak on May 20, 1985. A fifteen-year-old gang member recklessly fired his gun into a crowd on the sidewalk near 30 East Broadway, close to where I lived.

His bullets hit a four-year-old boy in the head and a man in the chest. Police investigations later revealed he was targeting rival gang members, but his shots wrought indiscriminate devastation.

A gang's sinister influence tragically entangled two of my childhood playmates who lived one floor below me. One was killed in a barrage of gunfire, and the other ended up in prison. The three of us boys had once shared lighthearted moments on the fire escape, laughing as the sound of fireworks filled the air during Chinese New Year celebrations.

East Broadway, etched with tales of blood and shadows, serves as one of the eight veins feeding the heart of Chatham Square. At this junction, where Bowery, Doyers Street, St. James Place, Mott Street, Oliver Street, Worth Street, and Park Row meet, more than physical paths crossed. It was a battleground for gang rivalries and territorial disputes.

The street battles among factions transcended gang pride as they fought over economic interests. As sources of power and sustenance, gang territories were sacred. When a gang member spotted an unfamiliar face in their territory, he confronted the suspected foe with ominous questions like "*Bien lun doh?*" ("Where the fuck are you from?") or "*Ley gun bien gor?*" ("Who do you follow?").

Strangers from neutral gangs got an uneasy pass, a temporary truce in a world of coded behavior. But anyone marked as an enemy received no mercy. Rival gang members loitering outside their territory were often cornered, beaten, or shot. This was the law in Chinatown. Every step could be a trespass, every glance a challenge, in a relentless dance of survival.

Lin Zexu's statue towered over Chatham Square, a silent witness to chaos. A revered Chinese scholar and official, he stood for moral values during the Qing dynasty. Yet the gangs hanging out below ignored the irony, desecrating streets dedicated to Lin Zexu with their crimes.

East Broadway pulsated as Chinatown's artery, bustling with businesses. Stretching eastward from Chatham Square and extending under the Manhattan Bridge, it ended at Grand Street. It hosted a vibrant mix of shops, restaurants, theaters, bars, gambling parlors, and sleazy massage parlors.

But nightfall revealed the menacing side. Gangs mugged, robbed, and assaulted victims. They preyed on workers, taxi drivers, restaurant employees, and vendors, making East Broadway's high crime rates infamous.

Despite its violence nightlife, East Broadway was also a cultural refuge for Chinese immigrants. Unlike Mott Street, known for violent Chinese gangs, East Broadway thrived as a center of Chinese entertainment, culture, and art. The Sun Sing and Pagoda theaters, icons of Chinese opera and movies, stood as a testament to this. I watched Chinese opera at Sun Sing with *Po Po* and *Kau Fu*.

The Pagoda Theater opened in 1964 at the corner of East Broadway and Catherine Street and became a cultural beacon. Its neighbor, a modest store with a coffee bar, offered both American and Chinese snacks. As a child, the coffee bar offered a treasure trove of Chinese delights, such as chan pei mui and dried, shredded cuttlefish.

The East Broadway Mall, a bustling commerce center, was more than just a mall; it was the community's lifeblood, housing restaurants, employment agencies, grocery stores, hardware, jewelry shops, and financial services. It was a microcosm of the immigrant world, catering to diverse needs and wants.

As time passed, East Broadway's demographics evolved. The Chinese population, initially a minor part of the diverse community, surpassed the Jewish, African American, and Latino residents. This shift transformed the street into coveted territory for Asian gangsters who lurked at street corners and on building staircases.

The two iconic theaters and the bustling mall along East Broadway offered a perfect environment for racketeering.

Sadly, the vibrant cultural scene of my childhood on East Broadway faded away as gang warfare over turf took over. On East Broadway, Chinese immigrants were offered the essentials for carving out a shiny new life while its perils left some scarred, wounded, or dead.

East Broadway shaped me, and I inhaled its contrasting essences daily—a blend of tranquility and turmoil. The street's sights, sounds, scents, and textures influenced my perceptions and behaviors.

Despite my parents' flaws, I recognized their necessary sacrifices for our family. Their silent struggles formed an underlying narrative in our lives. All the time I spent with *Po Po* and *Kau Fu* gave me a comforting presence that supported me through those formative years. From their sixth-floor apartment window, I felt like a young monarch surveying his domain, untouchable above the dangers and chaos of Chinatown.

I was oblivious to the coming storm.

CHAPTER TWO

HOW BULLIES ARE MADE

Going to school when I was five began a long torturous nightmare. Throughout my school years, I was the only Chinese student in my class and one of the few in the entire school. My English wasn't good, and with a predominantly white student body—and only a few Black and Hispanic kids—my ethnicity starkly stood out.

Each time I walked onto the school premises, I was seized with terror. A small kid accustomed to the nurturing of *Po Po* and *Kau Fu*, I was tossed like a slab of raw, bloody meat into a pool swarming with sharks. That's how it felt anyway.

As I walked the school hallways, other students would blurt out nonsensical *Chinese*-sounding gibberish in unison, pulling at the corners of their eyes to mimic a slant. They'd call me "Bruce Lee" and "Ching Chong." They called me a communist; I didn't even know what that meant. I'm sure those kids didn't know what it meant either. While wearing smirks or grins that expressed their spite and rejection, my fellow students stared at me as I passed by, then snickered and whispered among themselves. They seemed to compete over how sharp their humiliating barbs could be.

Confused by their cruelty, my hands would sweat and my chest felt heavy. I found it hard to breathe until I finally reached my classroom. This torture happened sporadically throughout elementary school with varying levels of intensity.

Making the situation worse, my parents dressed me in purposefully oversized clothing to save money so that I could wear them longer before outgrowing them. Floppy shirts and saggy pants gave the bullies even more reasons to make fun of me. Mom would overdress me in layers of jackets to keep me warm in the winter, which distorted my appearance and led to more hurtful comments from my schoolmates.

One time my third-grade teacher, Mrs. Gilbert, wouldn't let me use the restroom after I raised my hand to ask. I fidgeted, shuffling my feet and crossing my legs in a futile attempt to ease the relentless urge to pee. My obvious discomfort provided entertainment for some of my classmates, which made it even worse.

I raised my hand again, but she insisted I stay put, saying that she was almost finished with the lesson. She didn't realize how urgent my request was. Eventually, the distressing ache in my lower abdomen made me lose control.

I felt a mix of embarrassment and physical relief. Urine soaked my lower body, seeping through to my socks and shoes. A puddle formed under my seat, inciting my classmates to burst into chuckles and jeers.

I spent the rest of the school day in that disgusting condition, and as I passed kids in the hallway, they pinched their noses and made gagging noises amid their laughter. I hated the squishy sensation inside my wet socks and the way the cloth clung to my skin. I wanted to cry, but tears would only draw more attention, giving them yet another reason to taunt me. I felt helpless.

Upon learning about the incident, my furious mother stormed to school the next day to confront my teacher in front of the principal. In full tigress mode, she demanded to know what possible excuse there could be for not allowing me to use the bathroom.

Her complaint was met with indifference, which further infuriated her. My well-being clearly didn't matter to them, nor did my humiliation merit their concern. The meeting ended with their cold, detached apologies, and we left the office disappointed and hurt.

As far as the bullying went, not once did a teacher or school authority ever ask me about my ill-treatment. Looking back, I suspect some school officials tolerated bullying due to their own racism. Even when it happened right before their eyes, they did little to stop it.

Those difficult years came with a few silver linings. In fourth grade, I befriended a chubby white kid named James Niefeld. After school we often wrestled and played at my house in Brooklyn. I vividly recall our laughter, tears streaming down our faces, as we engaged in pillow fights and rough play. Sometimes my carelessness had consequences: I accidentally broke part of our chandelier, leading to a scolding from my mom. Even so, any punishment was worth having fun with James.

Having a friend who accepted me for who I was, unconcerned about my accent, skin color, eye shape, or ethnic peculiarities, filled me with relief and comfort. James showed me a kindness I'd never seen outside my family and Chinese acquaintances.

But at school, the bullying worsened. In fifth grade, bigger bullies made me fight other kids for their amusement, treating me like a rooster in a cock-fighting ring. The first time this happened was the first time I'd ever been punched in the face—and the first time *I'd* ever hit someone else. In a way, it excited me. I liked hitting back for a change, but since we were only ten-year-olds, our punches didn't inflict a lot of damage.

I'd punch my opponent in the face and about the body and expect him to fall like how I saw in cartoons or TV shows. But it seemed like none of my punches had much power, and neither did my opponent's, maybe because of fear or adrenaline. My arms felt numb and heavy, and my punches seemed more like taps by the time they landed on his face. After only a few blows, a crowd gathered and caused a scene, but we would break it off before the teachers became aware.

Despite my skinny, small stature, I didn't back down if I was cornered. This forced fighting gave me practice for encounters with bullies.

But for the most part, the bullying sapped my spirit, even if it was a passive assault. Dropping into my classroom chair, I would jolt up from the sharp points of thumbtacks on my seat. Tacks piercing my butt would amuse the entire class, and they would burst into laughter at my pain and surprise.

This relentless heartlessness finally shattered my inner restraint, releasing a monster within. Fed by years of helplessness, pain, and desperation, my anger grew, emerging with a will for revenge. Bullying transformed me into a bully, and I took out my anger on weaker kids. In the sixth grade, I demanded lunch money from kids, thrashing them if they resisted. Being a victim had provided me with lessons on how to intimidate people.

Ian Einhorn was a frequent target of my extortion, and he spent many school days enduring gnawing hunger from the lack of lunch. Reaching his breaking point, Ian finally told his mother. Enraged, she accompanied him to the principal's office to report me, which led to my mom and me being summoned. Hearing Ian's story of my harassment filled my mom with shame and anger. To partly settle the dispute, she paid back the money I had stolen from Ian.

Back at our house, I received a terrible scolding from both of my parents, as it was indeed shameful and embarrassing to be called into the principal's office. Yet I did not reveal to them the reasons behind my stealing or the circumstances that had led me to become who I was. From an early age, I'd learned to keep my troubles to myself. It wouldn't have mattered: I doubted my parents could solve my predicament.

I was callous about the matter. My mom's harsh admonishments and directives to change fell like pebbles sinking to the river bottom without a ripple. It was clear to me that my bullies would never stop. Harassing me fed their egos and made them feel powerful. Now I knew what it was like to bend someone to *my* will using intimidation. While I sometimes felt bad for my victims, retribution was satisfying.

I resolved *not* to be at the bottom of the food chain. At school I turned into a menace, doing nasty things like regularly pissing on the radiator. This wasn't just a mere nuisance; it sent the stink throughout the entire school. I stole supplies from the stock room and took out my frustrations on whomever and whatever I could.

Middle school brought on a new level of bullying that made me long for the good old days of slanted eyes and gibberish.

In the seventh grade, the kids were released to the schoolyard after lunch in a chaotic rush of activity. Being the only Asian kid, I had no friends and would sit by myself on the steps leading out of the school. A tall, lanky white kid, adorned in heavy metal–style attire, unexpectedly sat beside me on the steps. His presence piqued my curiosity. Could this be a gesture of friendship?

His sinister grin suggested otherwise.

As he methodically began attaching open safety pins to the edges of his black leather boots, dread percolated within me. Those sharp points seemed out of place, like a weaponized fashion statement. His glances between me and his boots fueled my growing unease. Then, in a soft tone, he uttered a threat that sent chills down my spine: "You better start running."

Terror washed over me. I bolted before he even rose, my heart pounding in a frenzied rhythm. But I was trapped inside the fenced confines of the yard. No matter how swiftly I dashed this way and that, he was a persistent predator. His spiky kicks came fast and cruel, the shoes' sharp needles inflicting a barrage of fiery stabs through my flesh.

Panting and drenched in sweat, I darted through the crowd of kids, desperate for his sadistic amusement to end. The other kids, occupied by their own activities, remained unaware of my torment. His assault finally ceased, and he sauntered away, to my great relief. But alone and misunderstood, the pain cut far deeper than the visible marks of that day's cruelty.

I limped home with awkward steps, feeling the sting of tiny punctures on my thighs and legs. Once there, I acted like nothing had happened, trying my best not to wince whenever my wounds came into contact with something. My parents and other family members had their own problems, and I did not burden them with mine.

Alone in front of a mirror, I removed my pants to see what had become of my butt, legs, and thighs. I wanted to cry out in self-pity, but no tear fell at the sight of the red punctures all over my skin.

Silenced was the carefree, innocent, gleeful boy of East Broadway. I had heard stories about kids who snapped, and

I understood the agony and pent-up anger that many bullied children harbor while trapped in brutal environments. Being cornered can push a person to a mental breakdown in which they might explode in a vengeful fury, not caring about who they hurt. Bullying victims find their own ways to cope. Some victims drown their sorrows in alcohol, drugs, and other addictions. Others end their lives to escape the unrelenting pain. Then there are those who get revenge by killing their enemies.

I refused to give any bully the satisfaction of my breakdown. I would survive on my own terms. Focusing on my studies, I excelled academically throughout high school. Baseball card collecting also provided a refuge from constant bullying.

After being turned down many times due to my age and size, at fifteen I managed to get a job at a Chinese restaurant named King Ho on Avenue M and Ocean Avenue in Brooklyn. On Mondays, I answered takeout phone calls, and for the remainder of the week, I worked as a cashier at Waldbaum's supermarket. At sixteen, I worked at a Baskin-Robbins ice cream shop. When I had free time during the winter, I shoveled driveways to earn extra cash.

While I valued working, my jobs, my studies, and even building an impressive baseball card collection failed to ease my pain or subdue my anger. I wanted to do more than just mask my turmoil with a hobby. I needed a true refuge.

In high school, a big kid named Ralph Dols welcomed me to hang out with him in the gym during the phys ed class's peak bullying hours, when the rest of the class was playing hockey. Although he didn't know me, he seemed happy to talk. As a gentle giant, Ralph grasped my plight and his imposing presence at my side effortlessly warded off my bullies. I was deeply grateful.

But there were plenty of other instances where no refuge could be found. For instance, while we waited in front of the school for the doors to open, burly kids used my head as an ashtray. The ashes they flicked onto my hair were so light that I wasn't even aware of it until later. Even in class, kids were still making Chinese noises at me while the teachers ignored it. During hockey practice, bullies used their sticks to slap my fingers, making it look like part of normal play. Again, nobody noticed or tried to stop them.

At Triangle Billiards off Kings Highway and Coney Island Avenue, I regularly played video games with my study partner, Jordan Rini. Jordan, a tall, lanky white kid from my neighborhood, became my daily companion and a fellow target of local white gangs, especially the Kings Highway Boys and Avenue U Boys, who occasionally harassed us. Once, they jumped out of their car and chased us from a bus stop with a baseball bat, amusing themselves with our panicked run.

Despite the cruelty I endured over the years and the constant threat of harm on the streets, I refused to become a recluse, hidden away in my room. I grew resilient, determined to handle life's challenges head-on. Facing or fleeing threats didn't matter much to me; I would live my life without being cornered by anyone.

But I soon realized the futility of single-handedly fighting bullies and the impossibility of surviving the streets alone. This cycle of being hunted and preyed upon had to stop, but how? My persistent presence on the streets and frequent visits to hangout spots subconsciously hinted at my inevitable path: joining a gang.

I had been hanging out at Triangle Billiards not only for the arcade video games but to experience the life I wanted. The pool hall was a melting pot of kids from various backgrounds, a seedy haven for those who were happy to spend hours in a dimly lit, smoke-filled sanctuary of sorts. The sound of billiard balls rolling across the tables, the backdrop of techno beats from the arcade games, and the cacophony of engrossed gamers drew me in. Among the tables, patrons conducted deals in hushed whispers while keeping a wary eye on their surroundings. The hall was filled with tough-looking yet cool kids who seemed oblivious to any danger.

Could I be one of them?

That's where I was at age sixteen when I first saw Cambodian Peter, a lone figure amid the buzz of the pool hall. His sleek black hair, combed back with a splash of gold tint at the front, caught my eye. His tank top revealed a dragon tattoo snaking across his skin, and he had a beeper clipped to the pocket of his blue jeans. Unlike Jordan and me, often the subjects of torment and disdain, no one dared to bother Cambodian Peter.

He bore the unmistakable look of a gang member, his attire speaking volumes in the silent language of the Asian underworld. It was akin to the Roman legions and their exclusive uniforms, a badge of identity no outsider would dare mimic.

I could hear my *kau fu*'s warning label from the past: "*Fei jai.*"

But I didn't fear Cambodian Peter. I secretly admired him, intrigued by a persona that stood in stark contrast to my own. In a pool hall brimming with brash, trouble-ready kids, he moved with confidence and ease. Envying his commanding presence, I studied him, his choice of words and tone, and how he interacted with others.

One afternoon, I happened to cross paths with Cambodian Peter as he walked alone on Kings Highway toward the pool hall. I offered a nod in greeting. We'd seen each other numerous times at the Triangle but had never spoken, and he usually seemed content just watching others play pool.

"Goin' to the Triangle?" he asked, his words carrying a distinct Cambodian accent, spoken in a measured, deliberate tone.

This show of cordiality from a gang member surprised me. I was taken aback that he even deigned to speak to me. We walked together, making small talk. From that day on, our meetings at the Triangle became routine, and gradually we became friends. Over time I learned more about how, as Chinese immigrants moved from Manhattan to Brooklyn and Flushing, newly located Chinatowns attracted new gangs who were looking for recruits. Notable gangs there included Fuk Ching and the Green Dragons.

In Manhattan, Fuk Ching held sway over Allen, Chrystie, Eldridge, and Forsyth Streets. The Green Dragons extended their influence in Flushing, Jackson Heights, and Elmhurst in Queens.

I imagined the possibilities, with my small world as a bullied kid fading into insignificance. Now I knew where to find refuge and how to acquire the power possessed by Cambodian Peter. Yet even after several weeks of knowing him, he had not revealed his gang affiliation, nor had I asked, sensing it was not yet time.

After several months of cautious observation and growing familiarity at the Triangle, I finally mustered the courage to ask about his gang membership during a billiards game.

He didn't even pause as he took a shot. "Fuk Ching. I'm a *Dai Ma*, forming a new crew in Brooklyn." The ball swirled into the corner pocket.

"*Dai Ma*? A horse herder?" Then I nodded. Knowing that in Cantonese *Dai* meant "lead" and *Ma* means "horse," I understood that the pack of horses Cambodian Peter led was his crew—or soldiers.

"We're expanding our territory," he told me. "I'm recruiting people to follow me. My *Dai Lo* is Rooster, and Rooster's *Dai*

Lo is Ah Tai, the leader of Fuk Ching." He lined up his next shot. "He has several *Dai Los* under him, and in a way they are all our *Dai Los* as well, as that's what we call anyone above us in rank. But Rooster will oversee the Brooklyn crew." He paused, allowing me time to think about what he said.

I nodded, indicating that I understood.

He smiled with pride as he bent over to take his next shot. "We have each other's backs. No one dares mess with us. We're focused on making money, but if trouble comes our way, we hit back hard."

At those words, I felt my chest expand. If I were in the gang, I would have support. A posse. And over time, I'd develop the same confidence as Cambodian Peter.

Cambodian Peter deftly cleared the table while explaining that Fuk Ching was under the jurisdiction of the Fukien Association and had between twenty and thirty members. Inevitably disputes would break out among the various gangs, often turning violent. To increase membership and gain more influence, Fuk Ching had decided to recruit new members in Brooklyn and Queens.

The gang had several gambling spots that needed protection, one located next to the Rosemary Theater. Rooster also operated gambling spots on Eldridge Street and Chrystie Street, and one in a high-rise condo in Flushing, Queens. So far, Cambodian Peter had recruited just one kid, a guy called Big Chicken. Cambodian Peter assured me that he would eventually introduce me to Rooster and the other guys in Chinatown.

He dropped the eight ball into the side pocket, set the cue on the edge of the table, and looked at me. "You with us?" he asked in a solemn tone.

I set my stick on the side of the table across from him. "Yes."

He gave me a quick nod of confirmation.

In that moment, I became a Fuk Ching associate, at least informally. My body buzzed with excitement, anticipation, and maybe a little trepidation. I needed to belong to a crew for my safety and well-being, so my spontaneous decision didn't surprise me. "It will only be just the three of us in Brooklyn?" I asked.

Cambodian Peter picked up his cue stick, ready for another game. "Yeah. We just lost one of our *hing dai*. Our brother was arrested for shooting a rival at Golden Q Billiards. But we have the full backing of the crews in Manhattan and Queens." He gestured for me to rack the balls and slanted me a smile. "We're small but we're tough."

Weeks later, Cambodian Peter recruited Shorty, and I got my friend Carrot Head to join us. I'd met him through his sister, and we'd worked together at the Baskin-Robbins. Our founding core crew formed the Fuk Ching Brooklyn faction in 1986. Saying yes to Cambodian Peter bound me to the gang without a big announcement to the crew or the excitement I thought he might express. He was, after all, a very low-key kind of guy. I kept my enthusiasm to myself.

Carrot Head was a fifteen-year-old American-born Chinese. He stood out with his loud and brash personality, as well as his six-foot height and 150-pound frame. When he joined our gang, I dubbed him "Carrot Head" due to his spiked hair, which reminded me of a carrot's stem. Also, his American name was Robert, which in Cantonese sounds like "carrot."

A dedicated martial artist, he earned his black belt in Shotokan karate in his late teens. His spiky hair fit his boisterous nature and spontaneous approach to life, which complemented my more reserved, calculating demeanor.

It didn't take long to experience the inherent risks of gang life. Ah Tai was fatally shot, and Ah Kay assumed the role of our leader. Cambodian Peter cautioned us about police profiling at funerals, particularly an officer named Mike Lau, who gang members said used tactics like taking our photos to track us. Based on his advice, Rooster decreed that we should avoid attending our fallen brother's funeral. As Cambodian Peter predicted, newspapers captured photos of Fuk Ching members who attended the ceremony.

Though around my age, Cambodian Peter exhibited a maturity far surpassing his years. Well-known in the small Cambodian, Vietnamese, and Lao communities in New York, parents often warned their children about him, but as far as I saw, he never troubled anyone or pressured them into joining his crew. He didn't need to, as kids were flocking to gangs in the eighties.

Loyalty was a central theme in Cambodian Peter's stories about the gang's adventures. He relayed an incident at Golden Q Billiards in which loyalty had led to the imprisonment of a member named Insane. Cambodian Peter and Big Chicken had gone to secure the place for their *Dai Lo*, Rooster, playing at a back table while waiting for Rooster. Insane stayed near the entrance, using a pay phone. Rival gang members barged in, grabbed Insane, and started beating him. Insane managed to escape and ran outside, chased by his assailants.

Armed with cue sticks, Cambodian Peter and Big Chicken rushed to Insane's aid. To their surprise, the assailants who had beaten Insane ran back inside the pool hall, with Insane in pursuit, gun in hand. He opened fire, wounding two and killing one as the attackers hid under tables, before running out.

Cambodian Peter and Big Chicken then spotted Rooster arriving in his cherry-red Porsche 911, oblivious to the turmoil. They crammed into his car, and the three sped off to look for Insane. But in a grave error, Insane returned to the scene to check on his friends, which led to his arrest by the police.

Insane's story highlighted what the gang expected: fierce loyalty, brotherhood, and the will to fight when needed. While aware of the dangers awaiting me as a gang member, I was unafraid. I even found incidents like what had happened to Insane thrilling. I wondered when my mettle would be tested.

In those first weeks with Cambodian Peter and my gangmates, a newfound bravado and confidence grew within me. I was a new person, free from fear and the adherence to rules. With a gang backing me, I felt invincible. I left behind that helpless kid terrorized by bullies and emerged as a bold, daring street soldier.

I was content with my role as a soldier, loyally following Cambodian Peter. I made it a priority to bolster his image as our competent leader for new members, ensuring that they followed him as dutifully as my other gangmates did.

One of my earliest gang fight instigations occurred with the Kings Highway Boys. A kid in their crew called Moe intimidated me with nasty glances whenever we walked past their crew under the train overpass on Kings Highway and East Sixteenth Street. I suspected he was trying to provoke a conflict, as he often whispered to other kids while glaring at me and gesturing in my direction. We were always outnumbered; there were usually two or three of us and eight to ten of their crew.

But if he wanted trouble, I'd give it to him. I knew from the rules of the street that I had an obligation to shut down this kind of nonsense. I had to go beyond retaliatory intimidation; to send a strong message, I had to take him out.

I happened to encounter this guy while I was driving with a close associate. I kept pace alongside him as he walked down the sidewalk, one hand near the gun on my lap. A desolate area under the train tracks and devoid of witnesses offered the perfect place to kill him.

He kept an eye on me, maintaining his cool—until I started rolling down my window. He darted into someone's backyard before I could aim. I was furious with myself for not succeeding that day; the attempt only escalated tension between our gangs. It also hit me with a startling truth: I'd been ready to kill someone for a pretty flimsy reason. Just as Fuk Ching had readily adopted me, I had adopted the brutal gang mentality. I wondered what price I might pay for that down the line.

I'd already paid one price. My study partner, Jordan Rini, and I had drifted apart as I started skipping school and canceling our study sessions. I never told him I had joined a gang, but he'd noticed that my clothes, demeanor, manner of speaking, and overall disposition had changed.

Jordan grew distant. If only I had told him that life had come full circle and that I'd gotten back at one of the boys from the gang who'd once chased us with a baseball bat. Now I was the one doing the chasing. In the intervening years, we seldom interacted the way we used to, other than occasionally crossing paths on the streets. I felt the loss of his friendship but also thought I'd made the right choice. And likely he'd made the right choice, too, in distancing himself from me.

As our ranks swelled with new recruits, Cambodian Peter ushered the group to an Asian party inside a Brooklyn College building, where he introduced us to his *Dai Lo*, Rooster. I knew this was an important moment.

Cambodian Peter led us through the partygoers who spilled outside to where Rooster got out of his Porsche 911. At first glance, he appeared like a simple Chinese laborer you might encounter on the street and dismiss without a second thought, but his car and Rolex set him apart.

After Cambodian Peter identified his crew, the *Dai Lo*

silently assessed us, meeting our gazes and committing each new soldier's identity to memory. He then produced a thick wad of hundred-dollar bills, peeled off a stack, and handed it to Cambodian Peter. "Take care of your boys. After the party, take them to eat and shoot pool." He gave us each a nod and prepared to head inside with his crew, who positioned themselves in front of and behind him.

Rooster intrigued me. His charisma and charm drew young men to pledge their allegiance to him. Not only did he exude the vibe of a man to respect, despite his young age, he also seemed to respect his men.

A guy who didn't dress like a gang member sidled up to us, and Cambodian Peter introduced him as Ah Gum.

Ah Gum gave me a nod, but his gaze slid to Rooster for a second. "I'm assigned to safeguard the *Dai Lo* tonight." Ah Gum subtly opened his jacket to reveal a gun nestled at his waist. "If I have to start shooting, don't worry 'bout me, just get out. I'll slip away and make it back to the apartment."

He meant that we were to eschew the credo of looking out for each other and just get out; he could handle himself just fine. Ah Gum followed Rooster like a delayed shadow.

"Why is he dressed so different from us?" I asked Cambodian Peter, always inquisitive.

"He's the guy with the gun. He's gotta look unassuming, like an FOB." This meant "fresh off the boat," a disparaging term for recent immigrants. "He either trails behind or walks ahead of the *Dai Lo*, ready to take action when needed."

During the party, I completed a deal with a kid named Kenny Wong, who bought a gun from me after an introduction facilitated by Shorty. Kenny and I gradually became friends, and I tried recruiting him to Fuk Ching. But he revealed that being born into the Ghost Shadows already made him a lifelong member. Kenny's father was a businessman with ties to Kid Jai (pronounced kih-jie), whom Kenny regarded as his uncle. Kid Jai was the legendary *Dai Lo* of the Ghost Shadows, who all the young gangsters wanted to emulate.

Kenny's friendship and loyalty transcended gang boundaries. When a kid snatched my beeper while I waited for Carrot Head outside a school, Kenny gave chase. He caught the snatcher, gave him a harsh beating, and returned my beeper to me.

The first day of my senior year, I entered high school with a confident stride, my shoulders high. As a Fuk Ching member, I would not disgrace my gang by cowering or succumbing to bullies. When I entered my first-period class, I stunned my staring classmates into silence as they took in my new energy and look.

I took my usual seat in the first row to distance myself from the rowdy kids at the back and heard a kid mimicking Chinese sounds, drawing laughter as we awaited the teacher. Glancing back, I saw an athletic Black kid perched on his chair, feet on the seat, showing off to his new classmates. Months ago, I would have sat there silently, wishing for the day to end.

But today was different. *I* was different. I stood and casually wandered toward him.

He continued chatting, probably thinking I was heading to the clothes rack in back. As I reached him, I grabbed his shoulders and slammed him to the ground. He lay in shock as I mounted him and relentlessly punched him while the class watched in stunned silence. The teacher walked in just as my classmates finally pulled me off.

Standing up, I fixed a piercing gaze on him and whispered with deadly seriousness, "Mess with me again, and my boys will murder you."

After that, no one ever dared to bully me again.

Triangle Billiards marked a turning point, the place where my miserable, bullied life ended. It was there that I met the person who eventually changed the course of my life. Cambodian Peter turned me into a hero to myself and a villain to others. Without him I could have been eaten alive by the tyrants of the streets.

CHAPTER THREE

THE GANG OF FIVE

At sixteen, I was dividing my time between my parents' house, school, and one of the many safe houses that Fuk Ching maintained throughout the city. I adopted the look of my gang affiliation: spiked hair, skinny jeans, no socks, *Miami Vice*–style unstructured jackets. We carried brick-sized cell phones and never went anywhere without a beeper and a $500 Dupont lighter. I was now experiencing an exquisite kind of freedom I never could have imagined. Rooster provided us with not only money but the freedom to pursue side hustles. We could commit all the petty crimes we wanted and keep the booty for ourselves.

It was in committing those crimes that I learned more about each kid in our "gang of five." Shorty, Cambodian Peter, Big Chicken, Carrot Head, and I grew to be like brothers, and the camaraderie we shared compensated in part for all those years when I lacked real friends. With our immigrant family backgrounds, we bonded over shared experiences. Neglect, poverty, and violence threaded through our lives and family histories, building unity and strengths, making us both reckless and desperate to experience what we'd lacked growing up: security, family bonds, and material things. We developed perseverance, fortitude, courage, and blind faith that we'd come out of anything alive.

I came to clearly see the difference between third-world-country poor and first-world-country poor. My version of poverty paled in comparison to theirs. Having holes in my shoes was better than going without shoes. I might have worn oversized clothing, but I had new clothing, not third- or fourth-generation clothing that was threadbare.

Shorty, a tough, spunky, and energetic fourteen-year-old from Thailand, exemplified loyalty and friendship, qualities I'd rarely encountered in my early years. He spoke in a high-pitched, fast-paced tone but paused between nearly every word, giving his speech a unique cadence. Despite his difficulty pronouncing certain English words, listeners could still understand him. His storytelling talents captivated the kids he hustled at billiards.

Once, when two Ghost Shadows from Bayard Street confronted him at Triangle Billiards, Shorty—standing at just five feet five—managed to seize a gun from one of the kids and chased both of them out. He later claimed that, out of respect for the business owner, he had refrained from shooting the Ghost Shadows inside the pool hall. I commended Shorty's restraint, as he usually operated on a hair trigger, always read for action. But the elderly owner of Triangle was good to us, offering us free table time and a place to hang out even when we weren't spending money, and we repaid his kindness any way we could.

Shorty and I enjoyed each other's company in the safe houses while smoking weed, drinking, cooking ramen, and planning crimes. While play-fighting, he introduced me to

Thai kickboxing. He'd target my legs with painful kicks, and no matter how hard I tried, I couldn't land a hit on him.

Originally from Laos, Shorty's family had fled civil strife instigated by the North Vietnamese communists against the Laotian government, crossing the border into Thailand.

"We were refugees," he told me. "We came to the US in 1981 when I was nine. A sponsor helped us. Government paid church workers with vouchers to take care of us. Mother stayed behind in Thailand. Made us sad."

Shorty's family lived in Brooklyn in a first-floor apartment in a predominantly Black neighborhood right off Parkside Avenue and Parade Place. To support his nine children, his father worked in construction. They lived in a small cramped apartment, and meals often consisted of a bowl of rice and a single hot dog.

Shorty took to the streets, running small-time rackets for money.

"It was tough for an Asian kid growing up in New York," he said later. "At that time, Americans dunno the difference between Chinese from other Asians. It didn't matter if we from Laos, Vietnam, Burma, or Korea, dey called us *chinks*. Dey dunno know my country. Dey never heard of Laos."

"The Blacks beat me a lot, but I never back down from any fight. Yes, I'm small, but didn't matter. I fight anyone, no matter how big. I'm Asian, I relate wid other Asians, I take their side and fight wid them when needed."

Early on I recognized Shorty as someone who would never abandon a friend.

I was closest to Carrot Head; though we had been friends earlier, being in the gang brought us even closer together. He preferred speaking English because his Cantonese wasn't so good. He often seasoned his sentences with phrases like "to tell you the truth" and "believe it or not." Because of his booming voice—even his whispers were loud—outsiders often mistook us for enemies in a heated argument, ready to tear into each other. At the peak of our exchanges, he and I would call each other an idiot, only to break into chuckles.

Carrot Head and I spent hours swapping stories about our parents' lives after they migrated to America in the 1960s, as well as the circumstances that had turned them into overworked, exhausted parents with no time for us. After Carrot Head's parents took several odd jobs in New York, his father became a cook, and his mother sewed clothes in a sweatshop. Obsessed with owning a house, Carrot Head's parents—like most Chinese Americans—enslaved themselves to achieve this trophy of their hard work.

Mostly we vented about our parents' frugal practices, which became a warped kind of contest. I recounted how, despite my dad's financial success with his construction company, he remained excessively frugal. At home, my parents only prepared new meals after we had fully consumed the leftovers, usually chicken.

Carrot Head shared in a playful voice, "Believe it or not, my father assigned four to five sections of toilet paper each day to each family member! To save money on the water bill, no one flushed the toilet until everyone had used the bathroom! Can your father beat *that*, Mike?"

I'd try. I told him that we seldom spent time together bonding like other families, watching movies or dining out. The only outing I ever had with my father involved a trip to Lake George when I was around seven years old. To save on hotel expenses, we slept in the back of his construction van, where he stored water in a fifty-five-gallon drum for bathing. My sister and I ate food my father cooked on a portable grill.

"At least you *had* a vacation. Us, we go nowhere, do nothing. We usually kept our house dark like a bat cave because we could only turn on the lights when absolutely necessary. Whenever food fell off our dining table, my father would pick it up and declare, 'This isn't dirty since the floor is clean. You can still eat this.'"

Their family unable to afford a babysitter, Carrot Head and his siblings had to lock themselves in the house until their parents returned in the evening. At age nine, he started working at Di Fara Pizza in Brooklyn, one of New York's finest pizza joints. During summer mornings, he set up chairs and arranged tables in the pizzeria, earning two slices of pizza and a soda from Domenico DeMarco, the Italian owner.

His parents kept working and saving until they had enough money to buy a $50,000 house in Midwood, Brooklyn. It took a heroic effort to save the down payment, given that his mother earned just eight cents per garment and his father was a waiter in a Manhattan restaurant. Yet, less than fifteen years after migrating to the US, they bought a house while raising four kids.

Eventually Carrot Head's father got cancer. As he lay dying, he instructed Carrot Head to retrieve one of his shoes from the cabinet. Hidden inside the shoe, Carrot Head found bills amounting to $10,000 that his father had secretly saved over the years. When both his parents passed away, Carrot Head received several hundred thousand dollars as his share of the cash inheritance kept in the safe deposit of a local bank, plus a paid-off house.

Chinese elders often sacrifice their spending to leave a financial legacy for their children. Unlike Americans, who often encourage independence for their children at legal age, Chinese patriarchs and matriarchs try to ensure their children's future by saving for them.

I imagine how disappointed his parents would be if they knew he'd lost his entire cash inheritance on several gambling trips in Atlantic City before a single blade of grass could grow on his mother's freshly dug grave. At least he still had the house.

Despite his circumstances, Carrot Head remained an exuberant and carefree individual, living in the moment. At his heart, though, he placed righteousness high on his list of priorities. He once pulled a gun to defend a group of white kids from members of a vicious gang at the baseball park. Carrot Head stood up for the underdogs and protected people he barely knew.

He later realized and complained that his unique nickname was a disadvantage—if he made a mistake, the police could easily identify him as the only person known by that name. In contrast, he noted that they would have a hard time finding me since I didn't have a nickname and there were a lot of Mikes in Chinatown. Precisely why I chose not to have one, I explained. Members sometimes were given nicknames by their comrades, but because I was a senior member and one of the original crew, no one could stick me with any kind of moniker—something I was relieved about.

Carrot Head and I shared lots of laughs. His bold presence and endless wild questions and ideas never failed to draw me out of my quiet demeanor. Our complementary natures made us great partners in the criminal capers we pulled off together. He sought out risky action while I remained calm and quiet. I planned the details, and he jumped in 100 percent. As new gang members who were sixteen, we sought quick scores in the streets. We drove around at night looking for potential victims to rob, me driving my dad's Oldsmobile once I had my learner's permit.

Carrot Head jabbed his finger to the right, pointing to a Hasidic Jew dressed in traditional clothes walking out of synagogue.

"Look, a target! Quick, park your car around the corner. Jewish people are loaded."

"Yeah, you're right! They leave money in synagogues and yeshivas in their donation boxes, and I used to take it. They must have piles of money to just leave it unattended like that."

I shook my head.

"You won't see a single coin left unattended in a Chinese or Black store's boxes."

We slipped out of the car we'd parked out of the victim's view and sidled up to him. I pulled a gun. He froze, staring at the barrel as we demanded his wallet.

Being young, we were nervous, just wanting to get the cash and split.

But the man methodically lifted first the top layer of clothing, starting from his tallit, then the next layer, then unbuttoning the next in his multilayered suit. It felt like opening a set of those Matryoshka dolls, popping off the top of one only to find another doll nestled inside.

Finally, as we were about to scream in frustration, he reached a pocket in the innermost layer of his undergarment. We were ready to see a stack of cash, but he took out a small purse, unzipped it, and dropped some coins worth less than a dollar into Carrot Head's palm. At that moment, I realized the gravity of our risk for a few lousy coins.

As nerve-racking as that was in the moment, we had a good laugh about it later.

We never robbed a Jew again.

In another instance, we mugged a white kid, taking his money and jacket at gunpoint. We fled without incident, pleased with our smooth robbery.

I wanted the jacket, but it didn't fit me, so I gave it to Carrot Head. "Wait a few weeks before you wear it, though."

But Carrot Head proudly wore the jacket the next day to his job at Baskin-Robbins. Wouldn't you know it, the kid we'd robbed sauntered into the store for an ice cream. He blinked at the sight of his jacket, then studied Carrot Head with narrowed eyes.

My friend nonchalantly took his order and then his money for the ice cream. The kid kept glancing back as he left, and Carrot Head gave him an innocent smile each time like a model employee.

Carrot Head called me right after the guy left. "Do you think he recognized me and called the police?"

"Nah, we all look the same to them. But next time, maybe listen to me."

More misadventures followed, but we started to mostly target Chinese individuals entering gambling and prostitution houses, as they were less likely to report the crime. However, we avoided committing multiple robberies in the same area so as not to establish a pattern that could help opposing gangs track us. Carrot Head and I committed these robberies together in our early gang days to flex our criminal muscles, but we outgrew them when we turned seventeen.

Big Chicken, Cambodian Peter's right-hand man, always held the crew back when we wanted to fight, preferring compromise over war. That's how he'd earned his nickname. Deep down, we understood that it wasn't cowardice but concern for our well-being that motivated him. He actively balanced our impulsive drive for action with caution. Big Chicken often chose to be our getaway driver, distancing himself from the central action.

That's not to say he was passive. Like many of us, he came from a background of poverty. When he decided to engage in battle, Big Chicken tapped into the rage over his past and transformed into a formidable street soldier.

I took on the roles of planner and adviser to Cambodian Peter, developing an ability to think ahead and honing my skills in scenario planning. I could forecast possibilities and prepare for eventualities through rational thinking. Shorty and Carrot Head always took the front lines, eager to dive headfirst into battle. Big Chicken supported us as backup and as our getaway driver.

Big Chicken had a laid-back demeanor. He showed more interest in girls than gang politics, and his beeper chimed every few minutes with a different girl's number. According to the girls, he was the best-looking guy in our crew. His charm and killer smile always made ladies giggle. A skilled sweet-talker, he had a talent for making every female, conventionally attractive or not, feel beautiful. "Hey," he'd say with a wink, "ugly girls need love too."

I thought I knew who Cambodian Peter was, but I didn't get his life story until our conversation about my memoir prompted him to open up. How had I remained unaware for *three decades* of the horrific tragedies Peter endured before arriving in America?

He shared his story piece by painful piece, much like my *po po* had. He was just six in 1975 when the Pol Pot–led Khmer Rouge began ruling Cambodia, resulting in a genocide that claimed millions of lives through mass executions, forced labor, starvation, and disease. By then, his father had passed away from natural causes, leaving his mother in charge of the family's escape. But before they could act, revolutionaries captured his mother and her three sons. The soldiers commanded his aunt, uncle, grandparents, cousins, and others to dig their graves before shooting them.

"Pol Pot aimed to transform Cambodia into a purely agricultural country," Cambodian Peter explained. "The regime rounded up citizens and residents for labor camps. They made us work twelve hours straight at gunpoint, always threatening execution." To weaken the captives' resolve and discourage resistance, a soldier chose Peter to demonstrate their brutality. He was hog-tied and tortured with stinging insects.

"Sadly, the Khmer Rouge forced my thirteen-year-old brother to become a soldier," Cambodian Peter said. "Riding a horse with ammunition across his chest and an AK-47 in hand, he warned us to leave the camp before sundown because of an impending Vietnamese attack. Then he rode off. We never saw him again."

Explosions and gunshots in the distance confirming his brother's warning sent Peter, his mother, his brother Kit, and several other families into the jungle toward Thailand's border. Peter and his family trekked hungry and barefoot from village to village, finding nothing but death and destruction.

"Straying from our group was dangerous due to land mines. Every step felt like it could be our last."

They ate whatever they could find, including crickets, frogs, lizards, and various insects. "Mom had sewn some jewelry into her shirt, which she traded for food when we came into a village."

After nearly two grueling years, mother and sons reached a Red Cross camp at the Thailand border. They received food, shelter, and medicine but still faced hunger when supplies dwindled. His mother's supply of jewelry lasted throughout their ordeal.

Before the revolution, his mother's cousin had served as a Cambodian senator. When the hostilities began, he'd fled to America and worked with the US government.

"Mother implored the Red Cross staff to contact her cousin and inform him of our presence in the refugee camp," Cambodian Peter recounted.

After several months, the Red Cross located her cousin in New Jersey, and he arranged for the family's migration to America. Peter was nine when he arrived in the United States. The family initially lived with the cousin in New Jersey. But when he received a work assignment in Virginia, Peter's mother decided to move to Brooklyn, not wanting to impose further on her relatives.

Cambodian Peter smiled with pride. "My mother wanted to make it on her own."

Without knowing our stories, people label gang members like us as cold-hearted, ruthless, and brutal. Externally, our actions and deeds deserve condemnation; we caused harm to society and posed severe threats to individuals.

I share a bit of our backgrounds in hopes of changing how people view us. Many Asian immigrants and American-born Chinese from my generation have similar histories to those of our gang of five. Many of us buried so much pain and repressed rage in our hearts that we had to armor-plate ourselves just to survive. We didn't have the luxury of getting therapy or a proper education, nor did we gain any comfort from the abstract idea that we could make a better life. We worked with what we had, and indeed many emerged from those gang years learning from their mistakes and creating better lives for themselves.

But my gangmates and I still had a treacherous journey in front of us.

CHAPTER FOUR

TURF WARS

Being in Fuk Ching offered me brotherhood, money, and protection, but it also plunged me into a violent, hazardous world. In 1986, any gang dispute could easily escalate into a full-blown battle. A look, a challenge, a theft, and even something as innocuous as taking the wrong street home could incite a war. New York City and Brooklyn contained hot spots where rival gangs could bump into each other—even everyday places such as billiard halls, diners, roller-skating rinks, bowling alleys, streets, and parks. Before we entered any venue, Cambodian Peter sent a spotter ahead to scope out any rival gangs. A risk assessment had to be done before any drop-ins. Any place outside our turf was behind enemy lines.

We were young, brash, and proud, often disregarding the consequences of our actions. The teens were the most reckless, acting without thinking. But I didn't throw caution to the wind entirely. Even in our lawless world, I knew to follow certain rules, and the rational and wise on the streets avoided war whenever possible. But though disputes could sometimes be resolved through sit-downs, the lure of adrenaline and the power of ego could also entice those with guns or knives to resolve conflicts through physical confrontations.

Loyalty motivated many a conflict. We wouldn't remain indifferent when another gang targeted a member of our crew. I interpreted even a minor slight or a small bump with a rival gang member as a declaration of war. And especially, I would tolerate no hint of being bullied, threatened, or hurt as I had been in the past.

One day, as I walked down the street, three Black kids I passed purposely bumped into me. We exchanged words, and they lunged at me. Three against one—time to split. Fueled by an adrenaline rush, I evaded their grasp with skills I'd mastered as a kid.

I sprinted across the street, weaving through traffic and causing a cacophony of honking horns. The commotion drew the attention of onlookers in the predominantly white neighborhood, prompting the kids to back off. Surviving the streets required not just brawn but brains too.

I relayed the incident to Cambodian Peter. We decided to act after Crazy John, Shorty, and several new members rallied to the intention to hit back. Crazy John, one of those new members who was always eager for a confrontation, armed himself with brass knuckles.

I drove us to a park near the site of the earlier scuffle and identified the three guys who'd attacked me. Crazy John crept up behind one of them, tapped his shoulder, and then struck his face with the brass knuckles.

He fell like a tree cut at its roots.

The other two, taken aback by our sudden charge, froze.

One opted to escape, while the other stood his ground. Shorty and I moved in on him as he clumsily pulled a knife from his pocket. We tackled him to the ground, and the rest of our crew jumped in. The *whoop* of a police siren sent us scattering in every direction.

My heartbeat thudded from physical exertion. My feet pounded first asphalt and then earth as I raced into someone's yard. I shuffled garbage cans around me to create a makeshift barrier. As the police radio echoed in the distance, I hunkered down and remained silent for about an hour before feeling safe enough to emerge.

Cambodian Peter and Shorty weren't so fortunate. Police officers handcuffed them and hauled them off to the Sixty-First Precinct. They were subsequently released with a court date to appear later. Crazy John initially evaded capture, but the police soon arrested him for a robbery connected to several other heists.

To avoid justice, Crazy John pleaded insanity, thinking it could get him off the hook. Unfortunately, his defense strategy backfired. Not only was he sentenced to several years in prison, but he faced unforeseen consequences when he seemed to continue to feign mental illness in jail while awaiting his court date. The medicine they gave him to help his fake condition probably messed up his brain chemistry. When he rejoined us at our safe house in Queens after being released, he wasn't the same. He spoke loudly and followed us around while talking incoherently. My poor friend did not bathe, and warts popped up all over his hands. He danced in the street naked and ate from the garbage.

A new threat moved into our sphere in 1986. A Vietnamese gang called the Canal Boys, who had already marked their territory on Canal, Baxter, and Lafayette Streets in Chinatown, made their presence known in Brooklyn, overlapping our hangout spots. We had to remain ready to take them on if they caused any trouble, and from what we'd heard about this violent gang, we expected it.

Because of their ruthlessness, the cops referred to them as "Born to Kill." The Canal Boys liked that moniker and adopted it as their own. Over time, it was shortened to BTK, three letters for what became one of the most notorious gangs in Chinatown history.

Not all my encounters in the street were imbued with fear or terrible costs. We had a few comedic, unexpected outcomes.

I chanced upon a chubby Chinese teenager whose innocent appearance and lack of awareness of his surroundings made him an easy target. At my sudden, ominous appearance on his path, his expression turned from shock to fear.

The kid, who was about my age, looked at me with pleading eyes. "Please don't kill me. I'm s-still a . . . a v-virgin. It would be a shame to die without ever having pussy."

I stopped, thrown by a plea I'd never heard before. My lips twitched in a suppressed grin. *He don't want to die 'coz he never had pussy!*

The kid, oblivious to my suppressed laughter, continued stammering in Cantonese. "Please . . . have some pity . . . Don't hurt me. Let me go."

I tapped his flabby cheek twice and walked away without taking Virgin Boy's money. Maybe he ran off and got laid after encountering what he thought was a near-death experience. My amusement was tempered, though, as I pondered whether these small shakedowns could have a lifelong impact on some victims. I could justify my actions with my own past trauma, but my conscience reminded me of how my actions could hurt others. In that moment, I decided to use the power I now possessed not on the innocent but *against* bullies. I adopted the mindset of being a "bully killer."

This outlook included protection of the girls who hung out with our gang. Many had left abusive homes, only to join other gangs whose members beat and raped them. Seeing them as vulnerable in gang settings, I made it my mission to protect them whenever I could.

In another situation where I felt there was wrongdoing, a kid named Sam asked Kenny Wong from the Ghost Shadows to beat up a kid named Chan because he had been flirting with Sam's girl. Carrot Head and I joined Kenny and gave this unlucky kid a thrashing. We stole his jacket, and Kenny presented it to Sam like a trophy.

Some months later, Chan joined the Vietnamese gang that would be later known as BTK. After searching for Sam, Chan found him, beating him twice as severely and taking back his jacket. Was a beating and a stolen jacket enough to make this kid join one of Chinatown's most violent gangs? I'll never know.

Cocky new gang members commonly made mistakes like taking on more than they were ready for. An overeager recruit named Viet Jim displayed so much brashness upon joining our crew that we made him our shooter. He frequently boasted about always being the first to shoot, never fearing anyone or anything. One day, Cambodian Peter sent me and Viet Jim to scout a roller-skating rink in the Bronx.

As we walked down the sidewalk, five BTK members turned the corner and headed our way. Closing the distance, I expected Viet Jim to draw his gun. I readied the car key, preparing for our getaway. But Viet Jim did nothing until we came face-to-face with the BTKs.

"*Bien lun doh?*" one of them asked.

Viet Jim remained silent, his body stiff with fear.

I shot Viet Jim a sidelong glance, silently urging him to pull out the gun.

Instead, he just stood there gaping at them with wide eyes.

Probably sensing his weakness, two BTKs rummaged through his jacket and confiscated his gun.

Seeing his gun in the guy's hand shot Viet Jim into action. He took off, but his legs were so wobbly that he stumbled and fell to the pavement after about twenty feet. He sprang up, sprinted another twenty feet, and fell again. Once more, he picked himself up and ran until he turned a corner and disappeared.

I watched with shocked confusion, and once he was out of sight, I turned to find the gun pointed at me, inches from my chest.

"*Bien lun do?*" the guy asked.

I would not falter like Viet Jim. With confidence, I answered, "Fuk Ching."

No one moved or said anything. Right then I was thinking two things: They could probably hear my heart pounding, and the guy was going to pull the trigger.

I broke the silence, and the tension. "Fuk Ching is about making money, not trouble. I'll return to my car and leave."

Their gazes remained fixed on me, and I held my breath, waiting for a sign from any of them that would dictate my next move. When no response came, I cautiously stepped backward toward my car. I got in and drove off, wilting in relief as I turned the corner without being shot at. Fortunately, Fuk Ching was not at war with the BTK then.

The only casualty, per se, was that the embarrassed Viet Jim never returned to our safe house. Little did I know that Viet Jim would save my life one day.

The unpredictability of violence was one of the risks in the streets, and conflicts frequently arose from mistaken identities and bruised egos. It didn't matter whether we were in the wrong or right; all we wanted was to fight.

A gang of white kids started terrorizing a neighborhood in Brooklyn, harassing Black and Asian kids. Soon enough, a childish incident accelerated into a full-scale gang war.

As Chinese gang members watched a movie with their girlfriends at a theater on Kings Highway, white kids in the back seats started throwing popcorn at them and laughing. The Chinese kids sprang up, guns aimed at the instigators. As white kids fled the theater, the Chinese kids fired the weapons indiscriminately, though they missed their targets.

We heard about the incident but didn't know who the Chinese kids were. We assumed they were Green Dragons or White Tigers from Queens, as our friends in other gangs told us it hadn't been their people.

Shortly after the shooting, a group of Chinese kids returned to Kings Highway and did a drive-by. A white kid caught a bullet in the leg. Hungry for revenge, the white kids scoured our mutual territory and chanced upon Big Chicken, Cambodian Peter's right-hand man. Thinking he was part of the Chinese gang responsible for the drive-by, they brutally beat him.

Cambodian Peter, a man with few words but inspiring actions, once more showed us what an actual gang leader is like. He and Big Chicken chanced upon those same four white kids. Cambodian Peter asked Big Chicken, "Is that them?" When Big Chicken said "Yes," Cambodian Peter went straight for them, leaving Big Chicken no choice but to take action alongside him. Without warning, they rushed up, started throwing fists, and neutralized two of them, then chased the other two as they ran.

Had someone with a fraction less character chanced upon those four white kids, he could have easily backed out and mouthed excuses for avoiding conflict without losing face. After all, our two members were unprepared and outnumbered in this chance encounter. He would have said, "Let's get them another day when we have the numbers and are ready."

Cambodian Peter, with the instinct of a lion, had charged at the enemy with eyes ablaze and nothing but his knuckles. For those white kids, the sight of their outnumbered foes acting as if they had the upper hand signaled that our guys were prepared to do everything possible to defeat them and exact revenge.

Unbeknownst to Cambodian Peter, his decision served a higher purpose: It taught the gang, through his actions and not words, the true meaning of standing by each other. He demonstrated the essence of brotherhood and the extent to which we must be willing to sacrifice for each other. It did not matter to him whether he won or lost. It was more important to lead by example: This is what being a big brother means.

Still, the neighborhood white kids continued to harass Big Chicken and his younger brother, Little Chicken, each time they passed by their home near Kings Highway. One day they ganged up on Little Chicken, who was around sixteen, when he was alone in front of his house. The white kids knocked him down, dragged him across the pavement by his legs, and rained blows on him. Little Chicken broke free, raced into the house, and came out firing a gun.

The blast sent all but one scattering. That unlucky one fell to the street, shot dead.

The police arrested Little Chicken. Believing it was a clear case of self-defense, his lawyer advised him to turn down the plea bargain offer of a manslaughter charge. The judge, however, found Little Chicken guilty of murder and sentenced him to twenty years to life. He served twenty-two years in prison. There might be justice on the streets, but there wasn't in the court system.

While busy with gang activities and friendships, I also juggled my personal life and school. Before my gang affiliation, I'd maintained good grades and regular attendance at school, but after joining Fuk Ching, my attendance plummeted. By mid-year, I regularly missed classes and failed tests.

My parents suspected that I was mixed up with a gang or involved in illegality. No doubt my shady hours, gangster look, and expensive accessories incited their worries. I ignored their questions and went about my business, which only made them angrier, but I didn't care. *All those years they were too busy to bother with me*, I thought, *why should they care now? Why should I care what they think?*

Anger with my dad had begun long ago when he prioritized work over quality time with his children. Financial responsibilities took precedence, especially during those difficult times barely surviving as an immigrant. He worked over ten hours a day, seven days a week, to make ends meet. While I understood his sense of responsibility and appreciated his heroic efforts, I longed for even a little of his attention, a conversation, words of encouragement. This lack left a void within me as I longed for a father's guidance.

Instead, during my formative years, I had to learn on my own how to navigate my struggles. While the gang played a significant role in filling that void, it wasn't enough.

My relationship with my dad took a turn for the worse when I discovered he was spying on me. Rather than discussing it with me—the kind of deep father-son moment I longed for—he got hold of a lineman's test phone and listened to my calls from our basement phone switch box.

After I heard a strange clicking on my calls, I went looking for the cause. Sure enough, I found the test phone and destroyed it with a baseball bat right in front of my dad.

This didn't deter him. He started following me when I left the house. In addition to being on alert for gang violence, now I had to watch out for my spying parents. Feeling betrayed, I withdrew further from my father.

Our encounters with the BTKs accumulated like gunpowder packed into a keg. I worried the slightest spark would ignite it fatally.

While walking with a girl I was dating, I spotted three BTK members about fifty feet away, exiting Blossoms Diner. I recognized one of the guys as Uncle Sam, though he and I'd had no previous interactions. They stopped and waited for us to pass. Though apprehensive, I had no option but to continue walking and showing no fear.

As we were passing them, I heard their inevitable question: "*Bien lun doh?*"

My girlfriend stiffened, tightening her arm around me.

Three men blocked our path and stared into my eyes.

I stared back at the kid who'd asked the question. My gang affiliation could either be a free pass or my death warrant.

"Fuk Ching," I responded sternly.

All three kept eyeing me from head to toe, awaiting their leader's next move. My breath held in my chest. I knew they were considering how to handle me and what risk I posed to them. Of course, I was outnumbered, and I had my girlfriend's safety to consider as well.

One by one they stepped aside and made way for us.

My girlfriend and I walked past without incident. Fuk Ching was one of the few gangs that had no beef with BTK at the time. And while that wouldn't necessarily keep the ruleless gang members from attacking, that day it had helped.

After this incident, the girl left me, never to be seen again.

Another time I strolled through what I thought was an empty park, minding my own business.

Someone tapped my right shoulder.

Before I could turn to see who it was, a blow struck the right side of my face.

I collapsed, and the next thing I saw was the night sky above me.

"Get the fuck out of the park," the teen growled. He stepped into my view, a shadowy figure who lifted his jacket to show me a gun at his waist.

Calmly, I nodded my agreement, got to my feet, and left. Sometimes it's wiser to accept defeat and move on. I resolved to hone my awareness and tune in to my instincts, though, so I wouldn't be caught like that again.

Only later did I find out the guy who'd slugged me was a newly recruited BTK member.

While the Flying Dragons and Ghost Shadows battled it out in the streets of Chinatown with BTK, some of our crew, such as Cambodian Peter, had friends among the notorious Vietnamese gang. Cambodian Peter was a well-known figure in the Vietnamese neighborhood where he'd grown up.

Friendship didn't stop the BTK from testing us, though. One of the girls who went from gang to gang told us of a rumor that some BTKs planned to take Carrot Head's gold chain, part of his signature look. Rather than hiding it after hearing that, he flaunted it, as if daring the toughest kid to take it from him. The karate he practiced so diligently in his sensei's basement gave Carrot Head a sense of invincibility.

I always felt secure walking around with him—he had a black belt—but over our nearly four decades of friendship, I never actually saw him win a street fight. In fact, I often ended up visiting him in the hospital. Martial arts may benefit the mind and body, but I preferred guns and knives for self-defense.

Carrot Head decided he wanted to tackle the situation head-on, so he and I went to Blossoms Diner to confront the BTKs. We spotted Uncle Sam eating breakfast with a few girls. He was one of the three guys who'd stopped me and my girlfriend weeks earlier. They'd given me a pass, and now Uncle Sam could see that Carrot Head was with me, which meant he was Fuk Ching too. Maybe that alone would resolve this situation.

Carrot Head's temper, though, could ignite the powder keg, and before I could say anything, he stormed straight over to Uncle Sam.

"Heard you and your boys are looking for me." Carrot Head's voice dripped with defiance.

Uncle Sam flinched in surprise at the confrontation. "No, it's cool. We ain't got no problem wit' you," he said in his heavy Vietnamese accent.

That failed to assuage Carrot Head. "You and your boys want to take my chain." He looped his finger over the thick chain. "Well, I'm here. Try and take it!" Carrot Head loomed over the diminutive Vietnamese, who gaped from his seat.

Without his crew to back him up, Uncle Sam needed to defuse the situation. "I didn't know my boys be saying that. I go talk to 'em." Uncle Sam patted the table. "Come, sit and talk." He gestured for the girls to leave.

Once we joined him at the table, he said, "'Stead of being enemies, we can work together. Let's talk 'bout makin' money."

At that time, our Fuk Ching crew in Brooklyn had just formed, as had the BTK, and both were trying to forge their name and reputation. We were feeling our way through the streets, figuring out how to expand our rackets. Forming an alliance with Uncle Sam could prove advantageous, considering that our gangs had factions in both Brooklyn's and Manhattan's Chinatowns.

"What'cha got in mind?" I asked, happy to avoid bloodshed.

"We du wobberies." He told us about a store near Canal Street that regularly closed around eleven p.m., one of the last to shutter on that block.

"Closing time, not many people," Uncle Sam said in a hushed voice, leaning closer to us. "We can hit the people coming out of dat place ib you want."

"Let's do it tonight," said the ever-spontaneous Carrot Head.

This time I agreed with him. Hitting the store immediately meant less chance of a setup—as long as we kept our rivals in sight for the rest of the day. A joint venture would solidify our peace agreement and establish us as serious gangsters in their eyes.

Uncle Sam blinked. "Tonight?"

"Tonight," I said.

He asked if I had a gun, and I flashed the revolver.

"How 'bout car?" he asked.

"Got one, along with a guy named Big Chicken as our getaway driver. Come with us now. We'll get there early to case the store and plan the route back to Brooklyn."

Uncle Sam looked surprised, but backing down now would show weakness. "Okay, we go now."

Big Chicken drove to Manhattan, maintaining the speed limit since we had guns in the car. A furious driver came up right beside us on the rear passenger side where Uncle Sam sat, screaming unintelligibly at us. We didn't want trouble, nor did we want to bring attention to us. Uncle Sam asked for my gun, which I readily handed him. Unrolling the car window from the rear seat, he waved the gun, which shut down the angry motorist and his passengers. They sped off. That's the gangster mindset. Most of these guys have been through a lot—hardships, abandonment, abuse—and they're in survival mode. They just want to be left alone to do their business. But if someone threatens them, they react. It's instinct. And that day, Uncle Sam's instinct got rid of a man in full road rage.

Before we reached the store in Chinatown, we chanced upon a man wearing a leather jacket and blue jeans coming out of a gambling house on Bowery. He'd have money and be less likely to report the crime, given his illegal activity. That made him a perfect victim, so we averted our original plan and parked.

We rushed him from behind, but before the three of us could reach him, as if he knew our next move, the man slowly turned to face us. He maintained a confident, calm manner, even with Uncle Sam pointing my gun at him.

When we approached to search him, he said, *"Bei ley mah, bei ley oh. Lor hui ah."* He spoke it almost like a hushed command, prompting us to stop. He'd told us, "If you want it, you can have it. Take it." We stepped closer to frisk him, but he used his right hand to slowly reach over to his back pocket.

When it hit me that Uncle Sam had *my* gun, my heart jumped to my throat. I felt vulnerable without a weapon in this potentially life-and-death moment. For all I knew, this guy was about to shoot us. Then I took in his slight mustache: He was a Chinatown gangster.

I got nervous and gestured for him to pause. But the guy slowly pulled out his wallet, exuding a sense of control that kept us from moving quickly toward him. He opened his wallet with both hands, pulled out $780, and handed it to me. He took his time to defuse the tension and look at our faces. At that moment I felt like we were amateurs.

Cash in hand, we ran off around the corner to our waiting vehicle.

Sometime after the incident, I spotted a familiar face on the news: the mustached man in the leather jacket we'd robbed. He was a high-ranking Flying Dragon, which explained his calm and confident demeanor during our robbery. Knowing that teenagers new to the gang life were the most reckless, he likely didn't want to incite trigger-happy newbies into doing something that could get him killed.

That night we went on with our robbery spree and divided the spoils equally with Uncle Sam, solidifying peace between the two gangs . . . which I predicted would not last.

At seventeen, as I delved deeper into gang life, I became desensitized to the escalating violence around me. Driven by pride and the need to prove myself, my heart hardened with each passing day, becoming impervious to feelings of sympathy or empathy. Compassion and similar emotions were luxuries I couldn't afford on the streets. They could dull my survival instincts. A select few could occasionally draw out these guarded emotions, but only in dire situations.

Amid my everyday chaos, I had grown fond of reading newspapers—perhaps because of my curiosity and desire to stay abreast of what the media was reporting about my fellow gangmates and rivals. On the evening of July 12, 1986, while goofing around with my crew in our safe house, the TV blared with news of an NYPD officer named Steven McDonald being shot by a fifteen-year-old named Shavod Jones.

While patrolling Manhattan's Central Park, McDonald had noticed a suspicious bulge in Jones's socks. McDonald approached the teenager to investigate, but before he could ask any questions, Jones fired three shots at him, hitting him in the head, throat, and spine. He was taken to the hospital, and no one was sure he'd survive.

A cop getting shot? No big deal.

A police officer being attacked, shot, or killed was a common occurrence in New York. Yet something about McDonald's story piqued my interest. One of the three bullets ruptured his spine and resulted in his paralysis. At the time of the shooting, he had been on the force for just two years and had a twenty-three-year-old wife, who was three months pregnant.

I dismissed my interest in his story as a passing fancy, or perhaps saw it as a glimpse of my possible future. I could be the kid who shot a cop if I continued on my path.

In the following weeks, I found myself following McDonald's story. Despite the doctors' grim prognosis after the surgery, he eventually recovered but became a quadriplegic, reliant on a ventilator and a wheelchair.

Steven McDonald drew national attention and heartfelt sympathy due to his resilience and dedication to duty. The public empathized with his wife, Patricia McDonald, who showed grit and unwavering loyalty to her husband.

About eight months later, at the baptism of McDonald's son, he shocked the city with a public statement to the effect of, "I forgive the boy who shot me. He was just a product of his environment." The unexpected announcement generated intense public interest and media attention in the form of editorials, newspaper columns, and special TV reports. Later, he said that "the only thing worse than a bullet in my spine would have been to nurture revenge in my heart," which would have infused his tragic injury into his soul and hurt his wife, son, and everyone around him.[1]

The way Steven McDonald had reacted, completely different from how I would have, troubled and perplexed me. How could he forgive some punk kid for something so horrific? The Chinese movies I'd grown up watching were all about revenge. If Shavod had wronged me the way he did McDonald, I'd find ways to come back for him even if I *was* handicapped. Even if I had to wait decades for his release from imprisonment, someone would be waiting as he walked through that gate.

I also pondered the idea that Jones was "a product of his environment," which deeply resonated with me. I'd never heard of this concept. It made me consider myself as someone shaped by his surroundings: the bullying, racism, and threats from gangs. Yet it also dawned on me that I couldn't entirely blame my environment as I had made my life choices willingly. I could only absolve myself so far for my actions.

McDonald's attitude challenged my beliefs and convictions, though my dark side, ever craving things unlawful, overpowered the light of his virtue. Still, his story was like a seed buried deep in my subconscious, waiting to grow roots and break through when the time was right.

---

1. Steven McDonald, "Why I Forgave," *Plough*, January 8, 2017, https://www.plough.com/en/topics/life/forgiveness/new-york-police-department-steven-mcdonalds-story.

CHAPTER FIVE

HIGHER ED

In the spring of 1987, the New York City school system, being what it was, graduated me with my class despite my failing grades and sporadic attendance. I enrolled in St. John's University's pharmacy program, a path not of my choosing.

Despite my stubbornness and active resistance, I had given in to pressure from my parents and relatives to become a pharmacist. Chinese elders often decide their children's careers based on what they think is best, not what their children want.

I may have given in to their plan, but in no way did I leave gang life behind. To higher education I brought my proficiency in picking combination locks and gaining access to students' lockers to steal pricey textbooks and other valuables—my way of rebelling against my forced schooling.

Armed with a five-shot .38 Saturday Night Special, Shorty and I entered Mike's Tattoo Parlor, ever vigilant for potential rivals. Tattoo Mike, known for his tattoo artistry, attracted Chinatown gangsters to his establishment, so you never knew who might be inside. But it was clear, and on September 23, 1987, I got my first dragon tattoo a mere two blocks from the Sixty-Sixth Precinct.

For most gang members, getting a tattoo marked an official transition into the underworld. At that time, no Chinese person would have a tattoo unless they were a gang member.

Not long after, Cambodian Peter's *Dai Lo* told Carrot Head and me to come to his apartment without explaining why. Having been with Fuk Ching for a year, I understood that such a summons usually signaled serious matters.

We speculated on our way over. Gambling was one of the driving factors in the Chinatown economy. Would our *Dai Lo* instruct us to execute a hit or collect an unpaid debt related to the gambling houses he operated? In Chinatown there were people like Sister Ping, the infamous human smuggler, whose brother would often lose six-figure sums in one session but would invariably return again and again to his usual haunts.

Our *Dai Lo* led us to a room with an altar dedicated to Guan Yu, the revered Chinese god of war known for bravery and loyalty. Many Chinese grew up honoring this red-faced warrior, a symbol of protection. The altar displayed a cooked chicken, oranges, burning incense, and a bottle of rice wine. I relaxed. Our visit wasn't about a task; it marked our initiation into Fuk Ching.

This signified that our *Dai Lo* trusted me and saw my potential. Beyond that, I believe he saw my contentment as a street soldier without a hunger to rival or supersede my *Dai Lo*. My loyalty to Cambodian Peter over the last year had proven my loyalty to the gang as a whole.

Gangs typically interpret Guan Yu's image as a warlord when he's depicted with black shoes and his battle-ax pointing downward. In contrast, his image in red shoes with his battle-ax raised signifies him as the protector of a business. Commercial establishment owners position his image facing the door to greet people as they enter.

The ceremony at our *Dai Lo*'s quietly commenced with our gang's creed recitation, highlighting brotherhood and loyalty. Amid the rising incense smoke, we pricked our middle fingers, allowing a few drops of blood to fall into a cup of rice wine. The choice of the middle finger, the name for which sounds like "loyalty" in Cantonese, symbolizes the ritual's significance.

Gangs, often viewed as bad or immoral by mainstream society, have their own unique values and principles. These rituals show adherence to a set of ideals. Our commitment wasn't to a life of crime but to a brotherhood. Like fraternities and similar associations, gangs use the concept of brotherhood to pursue various causes, good or bad.

After the ritual, I felt a subtle sense of security and contentment, and a deeper feeling of belonging. The gang had trusted me enough to include me as one of their own. In the same way, I fully committed to them that day, and it felt right.

As I balanced college life and gang life, Chinatown's streets ran red with blood as gangs battled for power and control. The possibility of sudden violence erupting at any time cast a shadow of fear and uncertainty over the entire community.

Beneath the unassuming facade of 81 Catherine Street, a powerful Tong operated an illegal gambling den. In the early morning of November 5, 1987, seven men targeted the den to send a bloody message and eliminate rivals. The shooters' targets included Frankie Wong, an influential leader and president of the Fukien Association. Despite successfully navigating Chinatown's violent landscape and amassing power, Wong met a grim end that day. Gunshots tore through the cramped basement, and one fatally pierced his chest.

Up to this point, through the early seventies and probably into the eighties, law enforcement had ignored crimes related to Asian gangs, perhaps happy to let minorities eliminate each other through gang wars. The indifference of the New York City government fueled the Chinatown gang phenomenon.

In fact, Ghost Shadow founder Nicky Louie told me, "If the police don't care about us, we'll police ourselves."

But the police couldn't ignore the seriousness of this latest shooting spree. This was no random act of violence but instead a calculated execution, a statement by one Tong against a rival Tong encroaching upon their territory.

As the aggression escalated, and innocent bystanders were increasingly caught in the cross fire, the police couldn't ignore the problem anymore. Making matters worse, during panicked moments the neighborhood's narrow streets and crowded venues often created a logjam. People found it difficult to escape to safety.

These battles spared no one. The daily news recounted killing sprees and crimes by infamous gang members, yet kids in Chinatown *still* aspired to join gangs, attracted by the security and confidence they offered. A lure I well understood.

Gangs were just as eager to bring those kids on board because there is strength in numbers. Gang members, in pairs or small groups, approached potential recruits, ingratiating themselves into these kids' lives before persuading them to join. By the mid-1980s, the gang phenomenon had grown to alarming proportions.

Society tended to categorize us as mere thugs, but it's a misconception to view gang members as aimless kids on the streets. Given the chance, many of these kids could have succeeded in mainstream society. Asian gang members thrived because they honed skills such as negotiation, strategy, planning, and communication. Running a gang requires CEO-level expertise and abilities. The success of Chinatown gangs depended on this more than brute force and violence.

Asian gangsters took pride in flaunting their beepers and early-generation mobile phones, symbols of their status and connections. They enjoyed playing with expensive Dupont lighters, just as I had, savoring the distinct sound of flipping them open. These gadgets and accessories were more than mere possessions; they were social statements essential to gang culture, subtly broadcasting their presence and dominance.

Tattoos and hair dye, now fashionable trends, once had deep ties to gang culture. Non–gang members who imitated this style, with spiked, colored hair, jackets, and sunglasses, unwittingly drew the attention of real gangsters. Those having the wrong style in the wrong place would face scrutiny and pressure to disclose their gang affiliation. The wrong perceived gang association could trigger irreversible consequences.

In 1987, the Brooklyn Fuk Ching crew started taking on bigger tasks for our *Dai Lo*. Only four gangs had Tong associations backing them: Flying Dragons, Ghost Shadows, Tung On, and Fuk Ching. We collected protection money from Asian-owned businesses in the Fukien Tong's territory all over Brooklyn and Manhattan, applying pressure to owners who were late with extortion payments and gambling debts. We also drove away rival crews, protecting the Tong's territory. We were under our own pressure, having to constantly prove our worth to the Tongs or they'd look elsewhere for support.

It helped that word on the street attributed several violent crimes covered in the newspaper to our crew. These included when three BTK members were killed, when Shorty killed the Hispanic guy, Little Chicken killing the white kid, Danny Boy's robbery and shooting, the Golden Q homicide, the killing of a Tung On member on East Broadway, and more. Our aggressiveness fueled Ah Kay's fierce reputation. In that way, our Brooklyn faction benefited Ah Kay and thus made us valuable to him.

Extorting money took finesse. It couldn't be too obvious. When we went to businesses to pick up extortion money, we'd place three or eight tangerines (always a lucky number) or a kumquat tree (considered lucky itself) on the store's counter, wishing the owner a happy New Year (or whatever). Then we'd leave with a red envelope stuffed with cash tucked in one of our jackets. We never checked the amount or argued with the owner. For the most part, the owners happily paid us so that we took care of them. Though it *was* extortion, we did protect the businesses from other forces on the streets. Another gang might demand even more money from them.

The only businesses who gave the gangs trouble were those with connections to the police. Generally, gangs knew which businesses had ties to cops and avoided them.

One of the easier ways we earned money was during holidays like Chinese New Year or the Mid-Autumn Moon Festival. We capitalized on the festive atmosphere by selling overpriced mandarin orange plants and moon cakes to business owners who eagerly purchased from us to create goodwill. Some also hired students from martial arts schools connected to the Tong association as performers for lion dances at their stores to attract good fortune, rewarding the performers with red envelopes filled with cash.

Asian gangs operated differently from Italian mobs, which followed a pyramid structure with money flowing upward. In our gangs, money moved from the top down, allowing the *Dai Lo* to maintain his gang's membership. We were more flexible than the Mafia, and the Tongs permitted the street gangs to earn independently, provided their activities didn't conflict with their interests.

The Tongs naturally aligned with the strongest gangs, as there was no tolerance for any sign of weakness. The Tongs depended on their gangs to defend and expand their territories.

The gangs' rackets expanded horizontally, often without higher echelons' approval. When Chinese gambling machines arrived in New York, for instance, anyone with a connection to the gang or a gang member could operate them independently. Placed in hidden dens or in the back room of a legitimate business, these illegal devices became a lucrative revenue source. The operators kept the profits, generously sharing with those involved. It was a fluid ecosystem. Everyone knew their place and what they needed to do and who to pay off to continue making money.

Then there were the darker ways of earning a living. Being involved in the drug trade was considered a shortcut to a cash windfall. In those days, a gang member acting as a drug mule could earn up to $10,000 for a single flight from Asia. Smuggled heroin from Hong Kong cost around HK$80,000 per kilo, translating to just over US$10,000. By the time it reached the US, its value was $65,000 per kilo for the gangs. With the high demand for cocaine in Hong Kong, drug mules frequently smuggled cocaine from the United States to Hong Kong, then returned to America with heroin.

While some gangs engaged in this racket, others avoided it, as it put them on the FBI's radar, with the risk of facing federal charges. Rooster wouldn't let our gang go into the harder drugs because, on top of bigger consequences to us, they caused the deaths of innocent people. Besides, he didn't need to; he made plenty of money on gambling.

Members of my Fuk Ching gang honored his thinking. We also made sufficient money pursuing our own rackets. For some, these included regular robberies and home invasions in affluent New Jersey neighborhoods or targeting wealthy Asians. We took a cut of their earnings only if they voluntarily shared.

Though I had once robbed the civilian population, I continued to abstain after my shift to the bully-killer way of thinking. Once I understood the gangs' inner workings, I felt compelled to subtly warn potential victims who were just trying to make an honest living by giving them *general* safety advice—without revealing that I was a member of the gang.

For instance, my mom's friend operated a hair salon inside her apartment in my Brooklyn neighborhood. Like most kids, I got my hair styled by her. She skillfully recreated the signature haircuts popular among various gangs. Gang members would queue up outside her house, awaiting their turn in her styling chair. Her business thrived, and she eventually saved enough money to buy a house. She moved her salon to her new home's basement for a more professional setup.

She'd inadvertently put herself in a potentially precarious situation: a budding cash business without the visibility of a commercial storefront. As I sat in her chair, I saw the unlocked cash box in which she put her proceeds. She had no protection and was naive in the ways of the street. I advised her to be cautious and to accept customers by appointment only, thereby vetting them. I warned her about the BTK gang and their reputation for targeting homes.

Unfortunately, she disregarded my warning and continued to allow walk-ins off the street. BTK members later invaded her house, tied up her family, and stole her cash and jewelry. No doubt they netted a lot of cash, as she would have kept it in the house since this would have been unreported income.

Gangs were often formed to protect neighborhoods. That's why business owners in Chinatown paid protection money. We took our role seriously and did everything necessary to keep trouble away from the owners we'd pledged to protect. Gangs that failed to fulfill their promises lost credibility. Protecting neighborhoods and businesses fit into my sense of right and wrong, as well as my warped sense of justice.

On a sweltering summer night, Manhattan's Chinatown pulsed with life. A stocky Black guy swaggered into a noodle restaurant on Bowery. With tinted hair, a thick gold necklace, and a muscular frame, he radiated arrogance and entitlement.

From our corner table, my two gangmates and I observed him order takeout.

As he waited, he scanned the room with obvious disdain, then snatched the bag and headed to the door. He paused to check the bag and, with a scowl, stalked back to the counter and held up the opaque container as though it were a dead rat. "This ain't wonton soup! You messed up my order!"

The Chinese clerk, taken aback, tried to reason with him. "That is wonton soup."

"No, it's not! Wontons don't look like this! Gimme my money back!" His voice echoed through the restaurant, and spittle flew from his lips.

"But it is," the clerk said in a quiet voice. When he tried to show him the menu, the man pounded the counter, grabbed a stack of menus, and flung them at him.

The Chinese customers averted their eyes, murmuring among themselves.

One of my gangmates shook his head in disgust. "That fool is looking for ghetto wonton soup in Chinatown."

I said, "He's the kind of guy who won't listen to reason."

My friends' faces stiffened with anger as the man continued to demand his money back, his aggression mounting. The clerk, visibly shaken, headed to the register to refund the money.

We'd been watching, waiting to see what would happen next, ready to act. An outsider bullying one of our own on our turf? Unacceptable. Inaction would stain our reputation in Chinatown, exposing our racket as a sham.

I picked up a teacup, quietly approached the agitated man from behind, and smashed it against his skull. He staggered, shocked, blood trickling down his face as he tried to comprehend being hit by a wiry 120-pound kid.

My gangmates and I lunged at him. He fought back, his fist connecting with my chest, knocking me to the floor. I jumped back up, my punches ineffective against his hulking frame. As he got me in a headlock, my friends pounded his face until he released me and stumbled out and then into another restaurant across the street.

We followed, and the brawl continued.

He defended himself against our attacks amid the frantic shouts of customers. We armed ourselves with teacups, teapots, and chairs, relentlessly striking him. A solid hit to the head with another teacup finally slowed him down.

Dazed and confused, he wobbled out to the sidewalk and collapsed. We left him on the pavement, bleeding and motionless, his gold chain still around his neck as a message to him—if he survived. This wasn't a robbery but a lesson not to disrespect us in Chinatown. I had learned early on that fairness was a myth. A fair fight didn't exist in my world.

In my experience, there was no such thing as a small mistake in Chinatown, for one slight error could put your life and your gangmates' lives at risk. Being brave and brash meant nothing if not accompanied by discretion and level-mindedness.

I brought a childhood friend into our gang, someone I'd known since we were toddlers. We called him "Banana"—a guy who seemed more at home with white guys than with fellow Asians. Introducing him to Fuk Ching was like throwing him into the deep end on many levels. While I balanced my double life of college, girlfriend, and gang activities, Banana plunged headfirst into the underworld. He even flew to Hong Kong with Rooster, our *Dai Lo*, immersing himself so deeply that he returned with a dragon tattoo as his badge of honor.

Cambodian Peter tasked Banana and Dog with overseeing our gambling den on Canal Street, a place next to the Rosemary Theater that buzzed with gamblers all night long. During one shift, Banana made the rookie mistake of venturing alone across Pell Street to get food. Stepping into the Flying Dragons' territory at night was like entering a mythical dragon's den, and he was viciously attacked. Battered and bleeding, he stumbled back to our gambling den.

When Dog saw Banana's state, fury overtook him. Armed and alone, Dog stormed into the Flying Dragons' territory and opened fire on any rival gang member in sight. But unseen in the chaos, a cop shot him from behind, shattering his vertebrae and leaving him paralyzed.

Months later at a party, Banana landed in hot water again by flirting with a rival gang member's girlfriend. The boyfriend slammed a beer bottle against Banana's head, leaving a nasty scar along the side of his face. These harrowing incidents clarified the brutal reality of gang life, and Banana disappeared, never to be seen again. There were many guys like Banana, who thought gang life was fun with its money, power, and girls until they got a harsh taste of reality and realized it wasn't for them.

Tragedies like Dog's shooting may have troubled us, but we quickly returned to our usual gang life. These incidents didn't bother me much if they hadn't happened to one of the few people with whom I felt close. I viewed them as learning experiences for all of us. Perhaps I'd created this mindset because I knew that gang life was hazardous, and I couldn't let every tragedy suck out my soul. Depression and grief led to distractions, which could prove deadly on the street. Maybe I'd learned to shut down empathetic feelings as a child, dealing with bullies and a lack of affection from my parents. Either way, we continued on, goofing around, watching TV, and fitting in intimate moments with our girlfriends. Our safe house often became crowded, yet we managed to play cards and drink. We lived our lives and relished our freedom.

A few days after Dog's shooting, Rooster stopped by. Like a drill sergeant, he offered tips on handling—and avoiding—situations like Dog's and Banana's and answered our questions. I clearly remember his advice on street self-defense. He stressed the importance of never letting anyone take my gun and instructed that if someone invaded my safety zone, I should shoot without hesitation. If I were caught off guard and surrounded, he advised backing against a wall, using one arm to fend off attackers, and quickly drawing a gun and firing with the other hand. To drive his point home, he demonstrated, pushing me with one arm while pretending to draw a weapon with the other. His forceful push, momentarily stunning me, effectively illustrated the lesson.

Those lessons would come in handy. The brewing bad blood between our gang and BTK would not simmer down anytime soon. Momentary truces or partnerships never lasted long, bound only by a tenuous thread. Each gang naturally disliked the other, and beneath our calm facades lurked a desire to obliterate the other.

We had a chance to make a connection when my gang and BTK ended up at the same Asian party in 1987. We were always on the lookout for parties that high school and college fraternal organizations put on. Here, they had appropriated the high school gymnasium to set up a disco ball and a monster sound system. Alongside Cambodian Peter, Carrot Head, Shorty, Big Chicken, Shadow, Cambo Dan, Peter Wang, and Richard Chan, I entered a place alive with music and flashing lights. We left our guns in our cars due to a security checkpoint at the entrance. Inside, we saw the dichotomy of clusters of kids breaking into dance and gang members warily eyeing each other from across the room.

I scanned the room and recognized familiar faces, including Uncle Sam's and those of around fifteen BTK members. Carrot Head stepped away to use the bathroom. There, he found himself beside a Vietnamese member of BTK at the urinals and snickered at his manhood. Furious, the gang member rushed out, returning with his crew just as Carrot Head emerged from the bathroom.

He pointed at Carrot Head. "Dat's him!"

The BTKs converged on Carrot Head and attacked. Our crew rushed to his aid, plunging into the brawl. In the melee, a BTK member stabbed Carrot Head in the side. Blood gushed out as he cried out in pain and collapsed to the floor.

While the rest of our crew chased the fleeing BTK members, I stayed in the chaotic hall with Carrot Head. Squatting beside him, I put a hand on his forehead and slid a jacket under his head, offering words of reassurance. Blood pooled into a red mass on the floor.

Minutes later, reporters swarmed the scene, trying to piece the story together while EMTs worked frantically to save Carrot Head. I ignored the reporters' questions about gang involvement and focused on comforting my friend.

Later, at the hospital, doctors informed us that Carrot Head's robust health might have been his saving grace. Still, I realized that my friend had brought this misfortune on himself with his childish antics. This could have so easily been avoided.

The following night was fraught with anger and anxiety, fused with our intense determination to retaliate against the BTK. Cambodian Peter handed out weapons at the safe house. With guns loaded, we split into two groups. Cambodian Peter, Big Chicken, and I headed to our usual spot at the Parade Grounds of Prospect Park in Brooklyn. Meanwhile, Shorty and two others targeted the pool hall on Nostrand Avenue near Avenue H, another BTK hangout.

Inside my shiny black IROC-Z, it was silent except for the hum of tires on asphalt. As we approached the final turn at Parade Place and Prospect Avenue, Viet Jim sprung from the shadows, signaling us to stop.

He leaned into our open window and whispered with restrained intensity, "It's a trap! I saw them from my apartment window. The BTKs are waiting for you. Dey all inside a parked van armed with Uzis. You make that turn, you all ain't gettin' out alive!"

We exchanged glances, understanding the danger. We had Lorcin 380s, but Uzis stacked the odds against us. BTK had gained their vicious reputation by using much more powerful weapons than most gangs.

"Mike," Cambodian Peter said calmly, "turn the car around. We'll get our revenge later."

Though he'd had no problem running at four men when

he was only one of two, Cambodian Peter knew better than to drive into an ambush with BTKs waiting. These guys had lived through and been displaced by the Vietnam War. They were like no other gang at the time. They'd lost everything, even family, and had nothing to lose. Their rage transformed them into killing machines who took out anyone in their path.

I stomped on the accelerator and sped away from the ambush waiting just around the corner. Viet Jim had been victimized by BTK in the past, so he'd been happy to help us.

Meanwhile, Shorty and the other two found no BTK members at the Nostrand Avenue pool hall. Unfazed, Shorty played it cool, shooting pool while keeping an eye on the place. Unbeknownst to him, a BTK member had stabbed a Hispanic kid there a week earlier.

Shorty heard, "There's the guy who stabbed one of us!" and turned to see a Hispanic guy pointing at him from across the crowded room.

Caught off guard, Shorty shouted out in a squeaky voice, "You got the wrong guy. I hab no idea what you're talkin' about!"

The Hispanic wasn't convinced. "We'll be back for you," he warned, jabbing a finger at Shorty as he left.

"I'll be right here," Shorty responded defiantly, in his usual feisty way.

Soon enough, the guy returned with a posse of about eight guys. The lively atmosphere of the pool hall, usually filled with the clatter of balls and casual chatter, simmered with quiet tension.

The accuser tipped his chin to the door. "Let's settle this outside."

They all moved to the street. The Hispanic reached under his jacket. Reacting instinctively, Shorty pulled out his gun and shot him. The Hispanic fell to the asphalt, convulsing in a growing pool of blood. Witnesses screamed and scattered.

News of the killing spread quickly through our ranks. Shorty evaded the police by going off the grid, not telling anyone where he went.

In the turbulent days following Carrot Head's stabbing, several BTK members in the Bronx confronted our crew member Cambo Dan, a man more accustomed to quiet conversations than violent encounters. With his lean, muscular build and military precision, Cambo Dan was a calming presence in our crew.

One BTK member pointed a .22-caliber pistol at Cambo Dan. "*Bien lun do?*" he challenged venomously.

Cambo Dan, not one to back down, wrestled the gun away in a fierce struggle, a dangerous dance ending with the gun discharging and the stray bullet hitting his leg. Undeterred, he spun and fired back, forcing the BTK members to flee.

Tension between us and the BTKs was escalating.

Carrot Head survived his surgery. Shorty's absence, though, cast a long shadow over us. Then he surprised us by returning to New York soon after his escape.

Worried for his safety, I warned him, "You're taking a big chance showing your face here."

He waved off my concern. "Nah, it's fine. I bolted to Virginia, but it was boring. I'd rather be in prison than be there all alone."

Barely a week after returning to New York, the police arrested Shorty outside his sister's house following a tip-off. My gut twisted at the mental image of my friend being hauled away in cuffs. At just sixteen, Shorty went to prison on Rikers Island.

Rikers is mainly a temporary holding facility for perpetrators awaiting court sentences. In the face of uncertainty, most detainees become restless and ruthless, turning the facility into an "animal house." Being unable to post bail meant spending time in a dangerous, unforgiving environment. Yet Shorty, true to his nature, transformed his drawback into an opportunity by befriending a Black kid. Together, they controlled phone access and privileges.

Shorty was later overjoyed to reunite with my Ghost Shadow friend Kenny Wong at Rikers. They embraced, finding rare comfort in a place filled with strangers and desolation. Shorty made life easier for Kenny, giving him hard-to-find amenities like a toothbrush and toothpaste.

The court convicted Shorty of homicide and sentenced him to fifteen years.

"I should have been charged as a juvenile, not as an adult," he reflected in a recent interview. "It was unfair. I acted in self-defense. The system is messed up. My lawyer was useless. He just took my money.

"After a year and a half in Rikers, they transferred me to a bunch of different prisons during my term: Elmira, Coxsackie, Green Haven, and Cape Vincent [near] Canada. Authorities transfer prisoners around to prevent them from getting comfortable. But man, there ain't nothing comfortable about being in a maximum-security prison, looking at walls every day."

Interestingly, life behind bars united Asians regardless of gang affiliations. Outside they might be sworn enemies, but inside they bonded for survival.

Shorty served fourteen years, seven months, and two weeks in prison from 1989 to 2003.

Carrot Head recovered enough to return to the streets. Surviving a vicious stabbing had, it seemed, made him even more attractive to girls, proving his toughness. His biggest challenge now was choosing which one to date.

Soon after his recovery, he was in another fight where someone hit him in the head with a bat, putting him into a coma. The doctor doubted his survival, but once again Carrot Head pulled through, waking up days later. He told me he'd heard everything I said by his bedside while unconscious.

I chuckled. "So, you know I joked about your karate skills always landing you in the hospital?"

I was heartened to hear him laugh, but he soon grew pensive. "Imagine, Mike, all those people in comas for years, hearing everything but unable to act. Honestly, I'd rather be dead than trapped in my body, unable to do anything but think and dream."

Looking back—and considering Carrot Head's experience—my life in the gang feels like a long coma. Absorbed in criminal activities and entrenched in underworld culture, I was trapped in a world I wrongly believed would free me. After Carrot Head's stabbing and Shorty's imprisonment, our crew began to unravel. The stark realities of gang life led some members to drift away.

One of those realities was Officer Mike Lau.

He was a familiar name to most Chinatown gang members in the 1980s. A character to be reckoned with, this paternal figure strived to maintain order in the streets, ensuring that we didn't cause trouble for others or ourselves. As a vigilant Chinese American law enforcer, he patrolled Chinatown, letting nothing slide by, not even minor infractions. He could blend into the crowd, yet he'd miraculously appear to apprehend law-breaking kids. Despite our disdain for him, we respected him.

Cambodian Peter had an unfortunate encounter with Lau when he and two crew members tried to shake down a deli owner at Chrystie Street and Bowery. They stormed the store, creating chaos when the owner refused to pay. One of the guys kept watch outside.

They had no idea that the business owner and the cops had set a trap, with plainclothes police positioned nearby. The undercover cops rushed in, arresting the two inside the store; the lookout managed to escape.

I visited Cambodian Peter at Rikers. Stepping inside, I smelled the heavy human odor of the place and felt its hopelessness. Gray walls with peeling paint, long stark hallways echoing with distant voices, and cold steel bars dominated this 413-acre prison built in 1932. The gloomy expressions of the guards added to the grim atmosphere.

When he entered the visiting area, Cambodian Peter tried to appear strong, but his facade wilted as he sat close to me at the table. His eyes had lost their sparkle, and his head hung over his stooped shoulders. The sight made me sad for him, but I also knew I could easily end up here too.

"How are you doing?" I asked.

Cambodian Peter just shook his head, clearly unable to even voice his struggle.

"How many guys are in your cell block?"

"About forty to fifty," he answered.

"Do you know any of them?"

He slumped over the table. "I only saw two other Chinese guys, probably Flying Dragons, but they're not in the same cell block as me. Besides, most Asians are doing federal time, so they don't stay in Rikers."

Shorty had already been moved to a state prison by this time.

"You look tired," I said sympathetically.

He rubbed his hands over his haggard face. "I am. I haven't slept well."

"Why not?"

"This Hispanic guy keeps bothering me."

I fell silent, trying to figure out how I could help him—and coming up empty. This was a whole different world than the one I lived in.

"First, he shoved me," Shorty went on. "I threatened him, and the guards heard. They said they'd leave us to fight."

"The guards *left*?"

"Yeah. They watched us fight through the window."

I shook my head in disbelief. "Did you win?"

"Our fight ended on the floor when a supervisor broke us up."

I looked around at the other guys with their visitors. Big mean-looking guys. "You're not safe here; he has friends, and you're alone."

"That's why I don't sleep much."

"Let me know if you need anything from outside. Hopefully, you won't be here long."

The gang took it hard when Cambodian Peter was incarcerated, but we were more concerned about his mother. Whenever I took her to Rikers, I saw how hard it was to see her son behind bars. Honestly, it was hard for me to see him there, so I couldn't imagine her pain. Fortunately, he was only there for four months before being released.

Shortly after, Cambodian Peter wanted to satisfy his craving for Chinese food at the Wo Hop restaurant on Mott Street. His brother Kit, who avoided gangs and focused on computer engineering studies, usually declined our invitations. It surprised Cambodian Peter when Kit, Big Chicken, and a friend named Annie joined him for a late-night dinner in Chinatown. Afterward, Big Chicken drove them home on the Brooklyn-Queens Expressway.

A sudden downpour slickened the roadway. When a speeding vehicle cut them off, Big Chicken yanked the wheel to swerve away but lost control and crashed into the guardrail. The impact killed Kit and Annie instantly. It left Big Chicken with a concussion and memory loss and plunged Cambodian Peter into a coma. A doctor assessed his condition as unlikely to survive. He spent a month in intensive care before emerging from his coma.

For the next two months, I accompanied his mother to the hospital for their weekly visits in the ICU. These visits were even harder on her than the prison ones. As difficult as it was to see her son in such bad shape, she just couldn't cope with his brother Kit's death. She'd done everything possible so long ago to keep them alive during their grueling two-year-long escape through the jungle. She'd learned how her family members left behind had been ordered to build their own graves, into which they were ordered to jump before being executed. She'd seen one of her sons sent off to fight, never to return. She'd watched Peter tortured as an example to the other labor camp residents. She'd suffered so much already, so it was no surprise that she fell into a deep depression, which sent her to a psychiatric ward for months.

The hospital staff was so sure that Cambodian Peter wouldn't survive that they screamed when he opened his eyes and spoke. Once he was well enough to go home, Shadow—our burly, dark-skinned enforcer—carried him up three flights of stairs to his apartment. He performed this task for several months whenever Cambodian Peter needed to leave his apartment.

The death of his brother, his mother's breakdown, and his months away from the gang weighed heavily on Cambodian Peter. It may also have messed with his head, as he began to suspect that Shadow wanted to replace him as our *Dai Lo*. I knew Shadow had no such intention.

A few of us, including Shorty's younger brother, Monkey, were hanging out at Cambodian Peter's apartment one day, and he got jealous at seeing other gang members laughing with Shadow.

"You looking to take my place, Shadow?" Cambodian Peter spat out.

Shadow flinched. "Why would you say that?"

Cambodian Peter flexed his arms and attempted to stand by himself but failed. "You got all the guys following you, ignoring me. Are you trying to take my spot? Remember, they follow me!"

"You're imagining things. Let it go."

But he wouldn't. Their argument escalated until Cambodian Peter pulled out his gun and fired several shots at Shadow as he ran out the front door. Monkey scrambled out the window to the fire escape.

I worked to defuse the situation, finally convincing Cambodian Peter that Shadow knew his place and didn't even want to lead. I reminded him that although Shadow had a following, he was loyal and always directed others to obey Cambodian Peter.

"Plus, he carried you up and down the stairs for *months*."

During dinner with Shadow later, I explained that Cambodian Peter's trauma and losses had contributed to his losing grip on his followers. He was obviously feeling insecure and out of sorts.

Shadow huffed, crossing his arms over his chest. "Peter wanted to kill me! The bullet missed by *inches*."

Months later, Shadow returned to meet with Cambodian Peter, who was finding ways to recover calmly and composedly. His resilience demonstrated the fortitude of the Cambodian people.

With Richard Chan, I suffered a double loss. I'd met him soon after I joined the gang while recruiting for Cambodian Peter. Richard made many long trips via public transportation to hang out with me and my crew. He hung around with me a lot, and we shared deep conversations that I valued. He'd patiently wait in my car for hours while I attended classes at St. John's University. It seemed that he valued his time with me as much as I valued my time with him. Although he tried to emulate the intimidating demeanor demanded by our gang, I could see that it wasn't him. Deep down, Richard remained a soft-spoken, amiable guy whom any girl would be proud to introduce to her mother.

After a year of lukewarm commitment to our gang, he started questioning what he wanted to do. "Fuk Ching isn't taking me anywhere," he confided, his voice heavy with disappointment. "I'm thinking about switching to Tung On."

Richard harbored a desire for our lifestyle's rewards. Despite his aversion to violence, the allure of easy money had drawn him into Fuk Ching. Raised amid poverty like many of us, he saw hustling as his escape route.

He was right about one thing: Tung On was flush with cash. Known as "the money gang," they were heavily involved in prostitution, drugs, gambling, and the entertainment industry. In contrast, Fuk Ching was still establishing its network and was committed to staying away from the edgier crimes.

"Brother," I said earnestly, "you're not made for that life. Tung On is into heroin and other high-risk ventures. With that kind of money involved, you have to be ready for anything—even to kill or be killed."

Richard shook his head. "Ah, it'll be fine. Better than fine."

"You might look and talk like a gangster, but deep down that's not who you are."

But he stood firm in his decision.

I sighed in resignation. "I understand. Just be careful. Tung On has formidable enemies, like the Flying Dragons and BTK."

Still, he left Fuk Ching to pursue his fortune.

About a year later, I bumped into him on East Broadway.

I nodded at his thick twenty-four-karat gold chains. "Tung On seems to be treating you well."

"Yeah, I'm doing great." Richard grinned. "Told you, this is where the money is." He tapped his chains. "You should join us."

"Nah, I'm good." I wasn't the least bit tempted. I was satisfied with Fuk Ching, I valued my friendships, and I honored my sense of loyalty. We hugged and went our separate ways.

A few years later, on November 19, 1992, I learned on the news that Richard Chan had been killed by Flying Dragons, sparked by an altercation for being in their territory. With his docile demeanor and caring nature, he shouldn't have been in that life. I felt the sting, thinking about what his family was going through, and reflecting on all those deep conversations we'd had when we were alone.

Amid the chaos of the streets, I continued my double life as a college student and gang member. I went from stealing textbooks to starting rackets. Senior students interning at pharmacies supplied me with controlled substances like Valium and Xanax, which I then sold. I craved excitement beyond the monotony of classrooms, reading doctors' illegible prescriptions and dealing with pills all day.

Although I enjoyed the benefits and power of the streets, the fates of Shorty and Cambodian Peter stood as stark reminders that my turn to face the consequences could come at any time. *Would come.*

If a gun or knife didn't take me out, the stress might. Every time I stepped onto the streets, I had to be on alert. Was I being followed by either my enemies or the cops? I had to be aware of my surroundings, mindful of paths or streets I dared not tread upon. I had to scan every place I entered for rival gang members who might take me out simply because I was a Fuk Ching member. While I'd escaped many dangers, I couldn't indefinitely evade the karmic repercussions of my choices. The tug of morals, stress of the gang lifestyle, and knowing that death or imprisonment lurked around every corner weighed heavily on my soul.

CHAPTER SIX

CONFLICTED

One perk of boring pharmacy school was meeting my first serious girlfriend, Eileen, in late 1988. I was a year ahead of her in our studies, and though we often crossed paths in the hallway, I hadn't introduced myself. Finally, mutual friends arranged a group lunch where Eileen and I got to know each other. We quickly went from friendship to dating.

Having a common major and immigrant parents brought us closer together. Eileen had arrived in the United States when she was nine years old, and her parents, like most migrant Chinese in New York, had to grind through numerous odd jobs to make ends meet.

We established a routine of eating dinner after school; then I'd take her home. Sometimes, when her schoolwork allowed, we'd watch a movie or hang out at the mall. I loved that she was caring and family oriented. She even helped me to better my family relationships. I also liked her innocence and propensity to view life through a rosy filter. This, and her lack of exposure to New York City's gang life, helped to conceal my underworld affiliation from her. Through that filter, she saw me as a typical Chinese guy destined for a steady job behind a pharmacy counter.

I worked hard to hide my double life, dressing in decent, clean clothes and shirts with long sleeves to cover my tattoos. I kept Eileen apart from my friends in the gang, other than a couple of times when I needed to pay them a visit for one reason or another. She met Cambodian Peter and Carrot Head. Later, she mentioned to me that they looked like gang members because of their spiked hair, attire, and demeanor, but I downplayed it by saying that maybe they did, but I'd known them since we were kids, which was why we kept in touch. She accepted that. Although she enjoyed their company—especially Carrot Head, who was loud and funny—she jokingly remarked that they were not exactly the type of guys a girl would introduce to her mother. Unlike me, ironically enough.

I never lied outright to her, though, just concealed the truth to protect her from what I considered the dark part of my life.

I felt bad when she told me that, before we'd met, her locker had been broken into and her books and other items had been stolen. Of course, I couldn't admit that I'd done it, but I tried to make it up to her. I took her out for expensive dinners; bought her jewelry, her first cell phone, and a car; and helped her family out—also in ways I couldn't reveal. For instance, once she vented to me about a schoolmate who owed her a substantial amount of money from before we started dating. This guy refused to pay her back and now studiously avoided her. One day I handed her the money.

She blinked in surprise at the cash in her hand. "What's this for?"

"That's from the guy who owed you money."

"What? How did *you* get it?"

I gave her a coy smile. "I have my ways."

While she likely had her suspicions when she found out the guy had unenrolled from the pharmacy program and never attended school again, she didn't ask me about it.

Another time, she told me about a guy spreading rumors about having had sex with her best friend. Although it was not my business, spreading false rumors, especially about a woman, went against my principles. Several days later, Eileen was shocked to see this guy, troubled and bewildered, in the university's parking lot, replacing all four tires on his car. After that, he seemed wise enough to avoid speaking the girl's name. Again, Eileen did not link me to the incident.

It surprised me that she didn't pry more into this next one: I was called to an emergency meeting with my *Dai Lo*, Cambodian Peter, when Eileen was with me. Without time to drop her off, I reluctantly took her to the illegal gambling house in Chinatown, and she marveled at the sight. Eileen was unaware that only select people were allowed in such a place and that she'd been allowed access only because of me.

She told me later, "The gambling den looked exactly how they portray it in the movies: dimly lit, smoke everywhere, and gamblers hunched over their racks of mahjong pieces at the tables."

She never even asked why I, of all people, had been summoned there.

In 1989, after three years straddling two worlds, I began gravitating toward a career in law enforcement. I had never forgotten police officer Steven McDonald's story. Far from it, his moral code haunted me. That seed planted by his humanity began to germinate.

Just as I was contemplating which path to choose, I chanced

upon an NYPD newspaper advertisement. The department was recruiting, and the ad gave details about the application process and the entrance exam schedule. Convinced this was a sign, I called the number and submitted my application.

In January of 1990, on the eve of the NYPD entrance exam, though, I hung out with several female friends at an upscale restaurant, talking and listening to the band. I wanted to head home, knowing I shouldn't have gone out at all, but I felt obligated to remain. I didn't prepare for the test, perhaps subconsciously sabotaging my aspirations to become a police officer. Dreaming about it was one thing; taking the first step was quite another. This seemed a much bigger transition than saying yes to Cambodian Peter. Joining Fuk Ching had been a sure thing, with someone by my side to prepare me for what was ahead. Becoming a cop was a long shot requiring many steps with no one to guide or prepare me.

I got home at three a.m., and by seven, I was at a Brooklyn high school taking the written test. I had low expectations for the results and carried on with my days afterward, indifferent about the outcome.

A few months later, I received a letter from the NYPD. To my surprise, I had passed the entrance examination with a score of 90 percent. Rumor had it that out of sixty thousand applicants, only two thousand would get hired. I waited for further notification from the department regarding next steps, which could arrive in months or even years. As a qualified recruit, I could be called to report at any time.

Throughout the previous few years, I'd never even hinted to any of my gangmates, relatives, or Eileen about my desire to join the NYPD. This secrecy added to my anxiety, as the gang would view my plan as a betrayal. I kept my aspirations to myself, knowing that my future was at stake and not everyone would understand my motivation. I was evolving, realizing there was more to life than underworld activities. A lot of the guys in the gang didn't seem to think they'd ever leave.

I struggled with losing the perks of gang membership: Its protection reached beyond its members to our families. Imagine having a 24-7 support group, always ready to assist you when needed, even in personal matters. I'd solved quite a few problems with the active support of my gangmates.

For instance, when my younger sister, who'd just got her driver's license, pulled her car into our driveway, an impatient Italian kid cut her off, causing a collision. Both cars had minor damage, so they exchanged numbers and agreed to repair their own vehicles. However, the Italian kid, realizing my sister was a new driver, started harassing her with calls for money and even threatened to visit our house. She was shaken and in tears as she explained what had happened.

"Don't worry," I assured her. "I'll handle it."

It felt good to be able to tell her that, especially at her grateful, relieved smile. I called a contact of mine who worked as a phone technician, asking him to give me the address linked to the Italian's phone number. Armed with this information and accompanied by Shadow, I went to his house off Avenue U.

I rang the doorbell, and when the kid answered, he found himself face-to-face with me. Shadow stood just behind, his arms crossed over his chest.

"That girl you had the accident with, leave her the fuck alone, or I'll be the last person you'll ever see," I told him, my voice deadly calm, my gaze fixed on his.

The streetwise guy turned pale. Stuttering, he finally asked, "H-how did you know where I l-live?"

Without a word, Shadow and I casually walked away. The

Italian kid never bothered my sister again. I chose not to tell her how I'd resolved the situation.

My phone company contact came in handy again when I got scammed with a devalued baseball card. I'd purchased a 1967 Topps Tom Seaver rookie card for around $600 at a baseball card show. Initially, it seemed in mint condition with sharp corners and perfect centering—a rare find that justified the above-book value I paid. However, back home, I noticed the card was slightly smaller than my other cards, leading me to conclude it had been trimmed at the edges to look mint.

The venue's host only had the seller's phone number. I called the seller, demanding a refund since the card was worthless. He denied knowing anything about the card being trimmed.

Thanks to my AT&T contact, I had already obtained the seller's address: an apartment in Coney Island, Brooklyn. After his continued refusal to rectify the situation, I finally demanded, "Meet me tomorrow at Burger King on Coney Island Avenue off Avenue U at seven p.m. Give me back the six hundred dollars, or I'll come and get it from you."

"You don't know where I live," he taunted.

I stated his exact address, including his apartment number. After a dead silence, he stammered, "How do you know that?"

"Be there," I said firmly. "Or you better have eyes in the back of your head while you're moving merchandise to your car for the next show."

"Where should I meet you again?" he asked in a squeaky voice.

In an ordinary world, I wouldn't have been able to solve my sister's issue with the bullish Italian kid or get my money back from the collectible scammer. People with bad intent look out only for themselves and take advantage of others, stepping on the weak and throwing their weight around to get what they want. As a gang member I had at my disposal a quiet, compelling power enabling me to make things happen by instilling the fear of death, a potent motivator.

Giving up that power was not easy.

In 1990, I dropped out of college and gave up the pharmacy course. Why work and study hard to do a job I knew I would hate? Eileen was sad and disappointed. She was looking forward to a simple nine-to-five life with me, but I was not a nine-to-five type of guy. I was more like a *nine-p.m.-to-five-a.m.* type of guy. But in all fairness, she didn't know that.

I celebrated my bolting out of college in a peculiar way: I stole a car.

One of our gang's hustles was stealing cars and stripping them for parts. I didn't participate in these crimes, but that night in Brooklyn I spotted a BMW 5 Series in which its owner had left the keys. Seizing the opportunity, I drove it away with Rooster's cousin Tommy in the passenger seat. We joyrode through a heavy layer of recently fallen snow. Reveling in the car's handling, I revved the engine and tested its ABS, a new braking technology at the time. I repeatedly pushed the speed and slammed the brakes, impressed by the BMW's stability.

After we'd had our fun, I took the car to a body shop, but the owner, who knew Tommy, refused to change the VIN on it. Probably because he didn't know me. So, I drove home and parked it in my garage. That night, I was startled to discover two cops checking out the area and the house, their radio chatter blaring and lights flashing across the yard and through my windows. I hoped they wouldn't ring the bell and wake my parents. Hidden in the shadows, I peered around the curtain's edge, watching the cops until they left, thankfully without ringing the bell.

I wondered who'd betrayed me. I ruled out Tommy, his

loyalty proven during numerous past rackets. Who else knew about the stolen car? I tried to think about everyone I'd seen in the last couple days, but no one came to mind.

First thing in the morning, I slipped through the interior entrance to the garage and wiped down all the fingerprints. I walked the neighborhood to make sure there were no cops waiting for me to leave. Seeing nothing suspicious, I drove the car a good distance away, parked it, and took the bus home.

This incident taught me valuable lessons about discretion and trust. I learned not to flaunt or be flashy and to confide only in a few trusted individuals. I'd recklessly pursued the thrill of the moment by showing off my new BMW. But the biggest lesson was that stealing cars was not for me.

For years I'd watched people making money by wheeling and dealing, operating gambling houses and selling guns. I'd had a taste of that selling pills during my years in college. On the legal side, I'd dealt in card collectibles. Now I felt a growing desire to be an entrepreneur. Shaking down business owners and committing small street crimes carried high risks with little reward. That insight and a natural inclination toward sound enterprise management inherent in my Chinese heritage propelled me to venture into business. Whether or not I became a police officer, I had a fallback plan after my gang life.

A childhood friend's boyfriend, Dean, informed me that the two Italian brothers who owned the Brooklyn car service company where he worked were looking to sell their business. Dean was a Burmese guy a few years my senior, and he'd been working as a dispatcher there for quite some time.

"Mike," he told me, "the brothers have lost interest in the business, and we're down to just two cars. It's kinda limping along right now, but we could build it back up again."

The idea interested me, both the business opportunity and the challenge to revive it. We talked to the brothers, but before I finalized the purchase of the business, I needed to learn as much as I could about how it worked. For a month I put in twelve-hour shifts, driving and dispatching, learning the daily operation of the business. I quickly grasped the trade, recognizing the need to rebuild its reputation and expand the fleet to make it once again one of the most established car services in Brooklyn.

During this time, I got to know Uncle Louie, an older Italian guy with slicked-back dark-brown hair who hung around the office quite a bit. He exuded a retired mob boss aura and had been a fixture on the company premises since day one. Though I wasn't clear exactly what his connection was to the previous owners, he obviously looked out for the business. In fact, he was the one who'd proposed the idea of selling it to Dean, perhaps wanting it to succeed with new blood running it.

Uncle Louie became my mentor, and I learned so much from him. He was as fascinated with my life as I was with his. We took regular "walk talks," during which I shared stories of the creative ways the Chinese underworld made money, including counterfeit goods, credit card fraud, and casino scams. From him I discovered how similar the Italian and Chinese mobs were in conducting their operations, along with how they were different.

Uncle Louie was a character. He'd say things like, "Mike, whoever thought of selling bottled water was a *genius*. We grew up drinking tap water from the faucet, and now people are *paying* to drink water!" He laughed. "We should muscle into that business, put our own label on it, and push it to the restaurants."

He knew a lot about business and had known some Mafia legends like Bugsy Siegel, Meyer Lansky, and Lucky Luciano. But it didn't seem as though he was still actively involved, and I was grateful that he spent his days hanging out at the car service with me. He really became like an uncle to me. I loved talking to a seasoned man for advice in the criminal industry. Once, he said, "Mike, be mindful that law enforcement has lip readers. Watch what you say, even if you're not actually speaking aloud."

During that time I had longer, deeper conversations with Uncle Louie than I had with my father over my whole life. Our friendship meant a lot to me, as it does even to this day.

The car service business had its downsides. Being a driver in New York and Brooklyn could be dangerous, especially during the crack epidemic and the proliferation of illegal guns. On Time Car Service had a history of notable incidents involving their drivers, some of which made the news. For instance, one of its Russian drivers was robbed and killed. Another was shot dead by an off-duty NYPD cop in a road rage incident after the driver exited the vehicle with a metal rod and approached the cop.

I experienced this danger as well when an enraged driver pulled up alongside my car and started screaming at me. Since he was clearly high on drugs, I ignored him and pulled away, but he continued to ram my car's bumper, chasing me for more than a dozen blocks. I radioed other drivers, who converged at a nearby gas station to meet me. The mad driver drove away when I pulled into the station where the others were parked.

Another harrowing experience occurred around two a.m. My car stopped at a red light on Ocean Avenue and Avenue T, and a scruffy-looking Caucasian male in his late twenties jumped into the front passenger seat, his hand concealed under his jacket. Before he could speak or make a move, a police car slowly passed in front of us.

Time stood still, and I held my breath. We both watched the car as the officers stared directly through my windshield. The man hastily exited my vehicle. I knew that I might have been stabbed or shot if that police car hadn't appeared; at the least, I would have been robbed. I could tell by the look in his eyes that he was willing to do whatever it took to score his next hit.

I'd let my guard down, not ensuring that my doors were locked and not paying attention to my surroundings. Though even the most street-smart among us occasionally slipped up, I resolved never to be lax again.

Obviously, the risks were substantial, but with my eye on the potential payoff, I decided to invest in the Brooklyn business. Dean and I agreed to buy in fifty-fifty. Since Dean was ten thousand bucks short, he borrowed the rest from Uncle Louie's friend, Vinny.

In his forties, this suave Italian man always donned tailored suits and shiny shoes. Vinny drove a brand-new Jaguar, which he regularly entrusted to Dean for weekly detailing, even when it already gleamed.

Uncle Louie remained with us after we bought the business. While he clearly enjoyed our company, he also seemed to be Vinny's eyes on his "investment" in Dean's part of the business. On top of that, Dean became Vinny's gopher. Every month, Dean would tour Bay Ridge to collect envelopes filled with cash from upscale bars, restaurants, and clubs for him. I joined Dean on these runs a few times and always marveled at the size of those envelopes. I speculated that Vinny was involved in loan-sharking or extortion. Vinny, it seemed, ran quite a lucrative operation.

Just before Vinny's daughter's wedding, Dean and I visited his Staten Island home to transport cases of vintage red wine from his cellar to the hall. He told us he'd saved this wine specifically for the occasion. On the wall of Vinny's home hung a picture of him on his yellow speedboat with Donald Trump.

Vinny surprised us by inviting us to his daughter's wedding.

He jokingly said, "You two are my Asian connection." At the ceremony, we stood out as the only Asians among the guests. Eileen came too, and we were blown away by the grandeur of this wedding, with high-end luxury cars lined up for valet service, intricate ice sculptures, and the largest wedding cake I'd ever seen—as tall as me! Vinny had spared no expense for this waterfront event.

After a couple of months, we moved the car service to a new location in a large residential area and renovated the space. We then needed a certificate of occupancy from the building department so we could get our base license approved. After several unsuccessful attempts at the government office, Uncle Louie went with us. We spoke with a supervisor this time, but still, the man barely acknowledged us until Uncle Louie said something in a stern tone. The man blinked as he took in Louie, a man about his age, who carried himself like a Mafia guy—this was during the height of the Mafia days.

Uncle Louie told the man, "These guys are with me," making it look like he was the behind-the-scenes power.

As the little Jewish man and Uncle Louie talked, I admired how every sentence Uncle Louie uttered conveyed hidden meaning, subtly shifting the balance of power. Whether it was his mob confidence or the way he leaned a little closer and asked, "Is there anything I can do for you?" in his Italian accent, the man approved our CO right then. He clearly didn't want to go *that* route. It was impressive how smoothly things ran when Uncle Louie got involved.

Dean and I built that faltering business into a profitable twelve-car, twenty-four-hour operation. He managed car maintenance while I handled the books. We agreed that after paying our salaries, the profits would be reinvested into the business.

While I was flush, Dean's frustration increased as he saw *his* profits going to Vinny in the form of "vigorish" (interest) to pay off his loan. Dean felt he was working for nothing, and his lack of financial savvy and penchant for alcohol only worsened his troubles.

Speaking of faltering, being a workaholic and learning a new business meant that I didn't see Eileen much. We drifted apart. I gave in to my drive to succeed, which took most of my time and energy.

When no one else was around, our office occasionally became a meeting spot for the gang to plan crimes. About two years into the business, when Rooster told me that his cousins Tommy and Jackie needed jobs, I hired them both.

Tommy, always seeking quick moneymaking schemes, proposed that I join him in a robbery/home invasion. He claimed to know a businessman who kept a lot of cash on hand. We arranged a meeting and recruited two others from Rooster's crew, but I opted out. Tommy's plan involved crossing state lines; splitting the loot four ways didn't seem worth the risk, and I was doing just fine with my business.

Part of that business was my side hustle of selling guns, and I'd acquired Italian, Black, and Asian contacts to facilitate that. Once, after I'd received a new gun shipment, I showed Uncle Louie a few items. He picked up a small black .22-caliber handgun and closely examined it. Laughing, he remarked in his heavy Brooklyn Italian accent, "This is cute! It's a *gurl's* gun! My daughter would love this." Uncle Louie, accustomed to bigger guns from the days of Meyer Lansky and Bugsy Siegel, saw the handgun as a novelty.

I offered the gun to Uncle Louie as a gift. He looked surprised but pleased with my generosity. I was happy to give it to him. His presence was crucial for our business's smooth operation. I used his Italian connections for car maintenance, even though that could be a bit hair raising. In one garage I took a car to, I saw a huge custom-made tank holding a small alligator and a crocodile the size of a door! I'd learned on the streets not to ask questions, but I thought that indeed this could be a clever way to dispose of bodies. That they'd shown it to me meant they trusted me.

Uncle Louie served as our anchor, and without him, it would have been impossible for two twentysomething Asians to succeed in this business. He also lent us an air of credibility with our team of old racist drivers. Earning the respect of men more than twice my age was challenging. These men, mostly low-income Irish guys from Gerritsen Beach, were hard to win over.

Finding good drivers was problematic, so I had to take whomever I could get. I hired a former kitchen worker, an ex-corrections officer, a security guard, potheads, and a Vietnam War veteran who'd turned into a drug addict to deal with his PTSD. These were men who'd gotten fired from their jobs and needed to get back on their feet. They were from all walks of life but mostly from the bottom of the barrel. These unreliable men were not easy to deal with, especially for a guy like me, who at that time held in my frustration until I snapped. This taught me how to deal with different personalities while trying to get them to do what I wanted.

But Uncle Louie's mere presence compelled them to fall in line with the company's rules and regulations. At the height of the Italian mob's dominance, with people disappearing on a regular basis, he didn't have to take any action. The drivers wondered what the relationship was between me and Uncle Louie. It was an oddity to see a young Chinese guy hanging out with an older Italian guy all the time.

Soon after masterminding the home invasion, Tommy asked me about buying the car service business. He and his brother had come in to some money playing baccarat in Atlantic City—or so they claimed. Money was money; I didn't need to verify where it came from. Dean urged me to accept the deal, as it would help him escape his debt. So we quoted a price.

The next day, Tommy arrived with a black suitcase full of cash. We shook hands on the deal. We gave Uncle Louie $30,000 as a token of gratitude. Dean paid off his loan to Vinny, having paid more in interest than the original loan amount. I often chided Dean that his vigorish had probably funded Vinny's new Jaguar.

With my pockets full of cash, I had the means to embark on a new adventure.

As a lifelong New York Yankees fan, I'd started collecting baseball trading cards around the age of eight, when some still referred to them as "bubblegum cards." Since elementary school, I had a knack for flipping cards with other kids to win the ones I wanted. This game caused many bent corners and banged-up edges, making it harder to find older cards in mint condition to this day.

Cards and comics had been a way for my mind to escape the bullying I endured. By high school, I had progressed from buying individual packs at candy stores to purchasing entire card collections at local card shows and conventions, places like flea markets and garage sales, as well as from private sellers—often from people who didn't know the value of their collection. As I grew older, I attended and participated in various New York card shows and amassed a sizable collection. In the back of my mind, I always had the idea of opening a retail store dedicated to trading cards.

In the summer of 1992 on East Flatbush, in the commercial area infamously known as "the Junction," I opened Collectibles, a baseball card collectible shop with a Korean business partner, Henry. We had been introduced by a mutual friend who recognized our shared interest.

Henry specialized in selling comic books, so we divided the store and shared rental costs. In my half, I sold and traded baseball cards and other merchandise appealing to sports enthusiasts.

Barely a month after opening, a thirtysomething white man walked in with a bag of baseball cards and laid it on the counter in front of me. His sunken eyes and fidgets indicated his need for a hit of drugs.

He pulled out two rubber-banded decks of cards and set them on the glass counter. "You buy cards?"

It was a treasure trove of rookie cards—Nolan Ryan, Willie Mays, Reggie Jackson, Pete Rose, and Tom Seaver, among others—most in near-mint condition to mint condition. A quick glance told me they were worth at least twenty thousand dollars.

"Sure, where'd you get them?"

"Had 'em since I was a kid."

"How much?"

"Seven," he said.

Seven thousand sounded reasonable. Most cards had sharp corners, were centered, and looked fresh out of the pack, but I aimed to get him down to five thousand.

"How about a better price?" I asked. "Seven is a bit high."

"I can't get seventy dollars for these?"

His question shocked me. Did I hear right? Seventy dollars?

I tried not to show any surprise or emotion, but I was thinking, *What luck! This guy's selling his prized collection for seventy dollars! He has no clue about the value of these cards.*

"Just give me your rock-bottom price," I said casually.

"Okay. Make it sixty."

I nodded, feigning a bit of reluctance, and handed him three twenties.

Years ago, the guy had taken pride in his baseball cards, but drugs had turned him into a walking score. If I didn't buy these cards at an undervalued price, someone else would. If I gave him close to their wholesale value, the money would be gone soon anyway. The guy left happy, with enough cash for another hit.

I paid $750 to a "fixer" with NYPD connections to secure a gun license for me, thinking the store might encounter trouble at some point given the high-crime area it was in. A fixer is a middleman who can get things done within the police department.

My investment bore out. Several months into the business, a group of young gang members from "the Veer," a run-down, crime-ridden housing complex near the shop, stormed in and grabbed whatever they could.

We jumped into action, but Henry and I were outnumbered, each handling four thieves. As we threw punches and shelves got overturned, I steered the fight outside the store. One of the kids knocked me to the pavement with his relentless punches and kicks.

An adrenaline rush numbed the pain from a pulled leg muscle and a fractured bone. I couldn't stand, but I mustered enough strength to whip out my licensed .38 Smith & Wesson revolver. The flash of silver sent our assailants running before I could even aim.

They had bested me, but I had landed a few good hits. That thought comforted me as I nursed my wounds

I was splitting my time between my parents' house and a small one-bedroom apartment I was renting close to my business. With the extent of my injuries, I needed my mom's help for a while. My parents didn't ask any questions when they saw me; they were used to me keeping my life to myself, and they also knew I wouldn't answer their questions anyway.

Because of our age difference, my brother, Jason, and I never attended school together, and my gang activities had also kept me out of the house a lot, so we didn't spend a lot of time together.

I tried to shield my brother from my lifestyle as much as possible, but it was inevitable that he'd see the benefits I gleaned from being in a gang. As his big brother, though, I forbade him from joining any gang, including my own, and he acquiesced. Then, a group of non-Asian teens stole his brand-new Mongoose BMX bike. Poor kid hadn't even got to warm the seat!

Jason didn't like feeling and looking vulnerable. But at the time, if you dressed like a tough guy, gang members would assume you were in a gang and check you. While riding that fine line, he started hanging out with some of the new Fuk Ching crew who were his age, including Danny Boy and Chinatown Jack. Many of our early crew had been arrested, and new members filled the gaps. It was inevitable that Jason and Danny would hang out. Danny's family had rented the second floor of my dad's first house when I was growing up, and the two already knew each other.

I remained strongly opposed to Jason joining the gang, but how effective could my opposition be to a young, rebellious kid? I determined to do my best to limit his gang affiliation to just that: hanging out with gang members and not becoming one.

I meticulously spliced and edited scenes from kung fu and Chinese action movies to play on a television set inside my shop window to attract passersby and those waiting at the nearby bus stop.

The first time I saw Diamond, he stood engrossed in watching the martial arts clips. Stocky, the guy bore a striking resemblance to Mike Tyson. His strut suggested he'd spent time in prison.

From then on, I noticed him almost daily, watching my two-hour kung fu tape from start to finish. I decided to go out and meet him.

I stepped up beside him at the window. "So, you like kung fu movies?"

Diamond's steely face lit up, revealing a sparkle from his gold tooth with a blue diamond embedded in it. "Yeah, mon," he answered with a Guyanese accent. He launched into detailed discussions about martial arts movies: titles, characters, release dates, actors, and plots. This guy was a walking encyclopedia of the kung fu genre. Not only that, he had excellent taste. He loved Chow Yun-fat flicks like *A Better Tomorrow*, *The Killer*, and *Hard Boiled*. We tossed titles back and forth, but then he schooled me on John Woo.

"If I could fight like that, I wouldn't need a gun," he said with a grin as feet and fists flew on the tape running behind us.

After many intelligent, passionate discussions about kung fu movies, I came up with an enterprising idea he would be perfectly suited for. "Diamond, how about starting your own business selling pirated videos of newly released kung fu movies? I'll supply you with everything you need to set up, and you'll pay me back for my expenses over time, plus eight hundred dollars a month to offset my rent. It's a win-win for both of us."

Diamond accepted my offer.

Using stolen credit cards obtained through a contact at the post office, I bought a few hundred blank VCR tapes, half a dozen video copying machines, some shelves, a color printer, and a register. Diamond's contact in the RadioShack in the Junction arranged for the equipment and supplies. Diamond was in business. Back then, pirated Hong Kong tapes were hard to find. Movie buffs in our area had to travel an hour to Times Square to buy them. West Indians bought these films in a big way.

Diamond had found his passion and took his responsibilities seriously. He rarely missed a day of work, and even women who came in to flirt didn't distract him when he was deep in a conversation with customers who enjoyed these movies as much as he did.

The kung fu videotape venture was profitable. Producing a pirated tape cost less than two dollars, and Diamond sold them for ten dollars each. The movies sold faster than he could copy them, and he quickly repaid my outlay of expenses.

Despite his windfall, he almost always wore blue jeans, a simple shirt, and Timberland boots. The only flashy thing about him was that gold cap on his front tooth with its diamond. He valued money differently than anyone I'd known. Instead of spending it on himself, he often gave away what he earned.

At first I found Diamond's generosity peculiar, especially the way he freely doled out cash. I strove to attain a balance of generosity and frugality, as I had learned through my street experiences that anything done in extremes wouldn't yield good results. I advised him to save money for other ventures and reinvest the profits, but my advice never sank in. For Diamond, life was a day-to-day affair. His pockets would be empty by the week's end, then refilled once again.

Diamond and I occasionally ventured to Chinatown in Manhattan to get videotapes, eat, or catch a movie. As Diamond and I crossed Bowery one night, I noticed two police officers observing us from their car.

The police often found reasons to stop, question, and frisk individuals, and with a Black guy at my side late at night, I was sure we'd be subjected to this treatment. As expected, the young officers sprang from their vehicle, pressed us against a wall, and conducted a pat-down search. They found my firearm, along with approximately ten thousand dollars in cash and the corresponding business receipts.

These cops were obviously rookies, given their excitement at finding a firearm and cash. I advised them to check my wallet for my gun license and to review the receipts. After doing so, one called their sergeant from a nearby pay phone and, upon hanging up, appeared displeased. "You guys are lucky. My boss said to let you go."

I didn't point out that it wasn't luck but the fact that we weren't doing anything wrong. Once they left, I turned to Diamond with a wry smile. "You know, I only get stopped by the police when I'm with you."

He just laughed. "You're right about that, Mikey! You are right about that."

When I gifted him a 10-millimeter handgun, it was a happy moment for both of us, a symbol of our friendship. But he refused the holster I offered, saying it slowed him down when he needed to draw. He carried his 10-millimeter in his back pocket like a wallet for quick access. If police chased him, he would shoot skyward, causing cops to take cover and radio for backup. By the time they resumed the chase, Diamond was gone.

"Works every time, Mikey!"

CHAPTER SEVEN

GAMBLING WITH MY FUTURE

Spurred by the success of my first Collectibles store, I opened a second on Avenue U in Chinatown eight months later. I added a third, smaller store in Brooklyn on Eighth Avenue, off-loading excess items from the original Collectibles to the two new ones. I hired a chubby nineteen-year-old Korean named Keith to manage the Flatbush branch. A walking sports encyclopedia, Keith became my "Diamond" in the collectible card business. With two stores in Chinatown, I was able to spend more time with my gangmates.

When I first went down to the large basement below my Avenue U store, I saw it as the perfect space to create a gambling den for high rollers. After years of protecting these kinds of establishments, and participating in them myself, I knew how to do it. It didn't take long to make it happen.

By operating four mahjong tables, one poker table, and Joker Poker machines, I earned five hundred to a thousand dollars daily. Unfortunately, I frittered away a lot of my proceeds at

Atlantic City gaming tables, my addiction to playing the odds getting progressively worse over the years.

How did I fall into my gambling addiction? Most people might assume it was because of my Chinese heritage. There's some truth to that: Gambling is deeply rooted in our culture. Looking at history books, you'll find that Chinese people placed bets hundreds of years ago. They even had games like keno, an early form of lottery. They used these games to fund major state projects, including the construction of the Great Wall.

Over the centuries, gambling became woven into the fabric of Chinese life. It wasn't just a pastime; it became a part of festivals and celebrations. Traditional Chinese culture emphasizes luck, fate, and fortune. For many, gambling is a way to improve and maybe even test one's luck. It's like a cultural experiment in fortune.

During my boyhood and up until I joined the gang in my early teens, I had come to see how gambling was tied to poverty. Poor Chinese migrants working several odd jobs to make ends meet saw gambling as a quick way out of their hardships. The idea of winning a one-time big jackpot as their ticket out of misery was almost irresistible.

But in my family, gambling was just a pastime for entertainment. We played poker, blackjack, and mahjong. To my knowledge, no immediate family member of mine fell into a gambling addiction. I played betting games with my dad, uncles, and relatives, but our bets were limited to nickels and dimes. Instead of gambling away their hard-earned money, my dad and uncles saved and safeguarded their fortunes.

For them, it was more of a vice. Vices are actions people can control, sporadic and less severe. Addiction, on the other hand, involves a compulsive and uncontrollable dependence on a substance or action that goes beyond enjoyment. For me, gambling was a vice turned addiction.

Being in the gang accelerated my downward spiral into addiction with the mindset of *easy come, easy go*. Two people fed the idea of the pleasurable torture in putting myself at the risk of losing or gaining everything. Carrot Head's obsession with gambling rubbed off on me after all those moments of feeling the adrenaline rush when the dice were thrown or the cards revealed. I'd also accompany my *Dai Lo* when he gambled in Atlantic City casinos. When he lost all of his money in card games, he'd send me back to the safe house or his illegal gambling house, to fetch money-filled bags so he could gamble again.

I wasn't the only addict in my community, so my operation flourished. Gamblers entered the basement using a side entrance, and a runner catered to any needs outside the store, like feeding their meters or buying snacks. This way, the traffic in my shop didn't arouse police suspicion.

Gambling wasn't my only way of earning money. Diamond facilitated our connections with the Black community, enabling us to purchase large quantities of weed from Jamaicans and firearms from African Americans. Chinese customers had priority, paying top dollar for their purchases. They preferred .38-caliber, five-shot revolvers and Smith & Wesson 9mm pistols akin to those used by Chow Yun-fat in the movie *The Killer*. Italians also purchased firearms, from 9mm pistols to shotguns to MAC-10s.

In 1993, a man with long dreadlocks entered my office in the backroom of the Collectibles store at the Junction and approached my desk, his gold chain swaying. He placed a black duffel bag on the desk.

"Rasta," I greeted him. "Good to see you."

"Yah, mon, same here."

I nodded to the bag. "Is it good stuff?"

"You know it is." The Jamaican gentleman unveiled several pounds of tightly packed weed from the bag.

I gave him a substantial amount of cash from my drawer. "Do you want to count it?"

"Nah, I'm sure it's all there. I'll be in touch soon."

Shortly after, another knock came at the door, and I instructed Shadow to let the visitor in. A lean African American man entered with another duffel bag.

"What do you have, Slim?" I asked.

"Everything on your list."

He opened the bag on the desk, revealing a MAC-10, .380s, .25-calibers, 9-millimeters, .38 revolvers, and even a sawed-off shotgun.

"Where are the bullets?" I inquired.

"Come on, Mike, I never carry bullets during a deal."

That made sense. I handed him a stack of cash and ushered him out. I smiled at the array of weaponry on the table. I had fulfilled all my contacts' requests. Business was thriving: three Collectibles shops, gambling operations, firearms, marijuana, and bootleg movies, among other ventures.

My smile faltered when I considered that I'd become a real criminal enterprise. Part of me didn't feel good about that. I'd intended for my shop to be a way for me to go legit, inspired by Steven McDonald, but my attachment to a life of crime kept pulling me back.

I met an Israeli named Ari through an Avenue U Italian contact, and he became a regular poker player at my gambling den. He was tall and about my age, with a stunning wife from a wealthy background. He never worked a regular job, but he was my connection for the brick cell phones that were in demand at the time.

My hacked phone provided me unlimited calls anywhere in the world for a flat one hundred dollars a month, a remarkable deal considering that local calls cost one dollar or more per minute. I supplied those to the hustlers in Chinatown who constantly had to make calls to Hong Kong and China.

I could have used him as a connection for cocaine, as he had access through his wife's contacts, but I was determined to avoid drawing attention from the Feds and the risk of draconian prison sentences. I was, however, open to other types of business opportunities.

One time, after a weekend of skiing in the Poconos, Ari returned to my establishment and placed a brown paper bag on my table. Inside were neatly bundled counterfeit bills. He handed me a stack, and I examined one of the bills against the light.

I shook my head in disbelief. "Impressive!"

He grinned. "Yup."

"What's the rate?"

"Thirty cents on the dollar."

I hesitated. "They look too perfect."

"You need to prep them. Soak, dry, crumple, and sprinkle with baby powder for the right texture. That's it."

"Are you sure?"

"Of course, I'm sure. I'll show you how to do it."

After buying the bills, I contacted Rooster and asked if he also wanted some. But he showed me a higher-quality batch with blue and red threads. "I charge fifty cents on the dollar for these, and there's no prepping needed." I purchased some of his and mixed them with my lower-quality stash.

Between the two sources, I acquired $25,000 worth of counterfeit bills. I spent hours pondering how to circulate the money without drawing suspicion. If I spent too much in the neighborhood, a pattern might point back to me.

An idea struck me. I called an old Korean contact who dealt in counterfeit goods. I told him that someone had stolen my shipment of counterfeit items from China, and I needed a quick resupply for customers eagerly awaiting orders. I offered to pay him a little more than his asking price.

"See you at the warehouse tomorrow!" he happily chirped.

Shadow and I spent hours preparing the fake money. Then we drove a van to meet the Koreans and pick up the counterfeit items, including hats and T-shirts with Gucci, Nike, Calvin Klein, and Versace logos. I handed the money to the Korean and worried about him closely scrutinizing the bills. Did he have a counterfeit detection marker? They were less common in those days.

As he counted the money, he occasionally paused to separate some of the new bills that stuck together, which made me nervous. Meanwhile, I had Shadow load the van as quickly as possible.

Fortunately, the Korean and his crew kept getting distracted with calls and orders from customers, as I had purposely chosen a busy Monday for the transaction. Every passing second felt like an eternity, and I hoped the texture felt right so the Korean wouldn't look too closely. He finished counting the bills, shook my hand, and bid us farewell as Shadow loaded the final boxes into the van.

We sped away, relieved.

The bulk of the counterfeit money was no longer my concern. In the days ahead, we sold the fake goods to Asian discount stores up and down Flatbush Avenue, converting the merchandise into real currency.

Later that night, while enjoying drinks with my gangmates, I pulled out a counterfeit bill and used it to light a cigarette, just like Chow Yun-fat had done in *A Better Tomorrow*. We laughed.

But even while celebrating my score, I felt a lingering sense of unease. One day my luck would run out.

Collectibles opened the door to other unexpected acquaintances for me: police officers. My youthful, innocent appearance probably made them think I was a typical lad running a legit business. Officers from the NYPD's Community Patrol Officer Program (CPOP) started visiting my shop to buy and trade cards. New York is a mecca of baseball, and Collectibles was the perfect place to find valuable items related to the sport.

I became friends with a few officers who came in several times a week to look at merchandise. They'd invite me to gamble with them in Atlantic City. That made me comfortable enough to suggest they come into the back room of my shop to play poker and blackjack for fun and money. I remember thinking, *Wow, it wasn't bad being a cop and getting to hang out for hours in a store playing cards.* I commented on how great their jobs were, allowing them to serve the community and play cards at the same time. I mentioned that I had taken the entrance exam for the police academy, and they encouraged me to pursue a law enforcement career.

One time I had gotten really high just before they came in. Seeing me in that condition, they turned around and left before any other customers could come in. They protected me by leaving.

My newfound cop acquaintances proved fortunate, especially when Diamond started facing trouble in the streets. Knowing the Guyanese man worked for me, my police pals would tip me off and drag their feet searching for him whenever he became a suspect in wrongdoing.

Secretive and cautious, Diamond trusted few. As our friendship and trust deepened, I learned more of his story—and how he'd become his tough, over-the-top self. Though we came from starkly different places and cultures, our lives shared a few common themes. He was born in 1966 in Guyana, on the northern coast of South America, and grew up in the slums of Agricola, a high-crime area in the capital of Georgetown. Diamond's family struggled daily to survive; he had five brothers, three sisters, and two half siblings. They lived in an encampment for families, where fifteen to twenty residents bunked in each run-down house and where they might share one pot of fish stew.

"My mom was a tough woman, the only person I was afraid of. If we came home with a black eye, she'd send us back to the streets so we could beat up the kid who messed with us. She wouldn't let us return until we got even. She told us, 'You'll get your ass whipped if you run.'"

His parents eventually sought work in the United States. Eleven-year-old Diamond and his siblings arrived in Brooklyn in November 1977, living in a cramped apartment on Ocean Avenue.

Diamond concluded that the violence in Flatbush and Brooklyn was even worse than in Agricola. Each block had its own small gang. As Diamond and his siblings walked the streets, they regularly witnessed shootings. In junior high, he was bullied and called a refugee.

Life was tough at home too. At fourteen, when he talked back to his father, his mother shot him in the leg. He dropped out of Franklin Delano Roosevelt High School and joined a crew of West Indian kids who were terrorizing East Flatbush.

"Maybe seeing my dad's success with running a weed shop put the taste of crime in my mouth," Diamond said. He began his own crime trajectory. "In 1980 or 1981, someone dared me to take a cop's gun. I smashed a cop's head with his radio and grabbed his .38 service revolver."

Fat Tony, the head of his own growing crew, often asserted his dominance in the Veer, a housing complex plagued by gangs. The American-born Jamaican viewed Diamond as a rival and threat. Diamond and Fat Tony eventually settled their beef when they both spent time in Spofford, a juvenile detention center. After their release, Fat Tony built his reputation as a street fighter who could beat anyone *except* Diamond—they agreed that their only fight ended up being a draw. The pair formed a friendship based on mutual respect.

Diamond progressed from snatching chains, mugging pedestrians, and holding up storefronts that sold marijuana—known as "weed gates," like the one his father operated—to gutsier endeavors.

He puffed up his shoulders. "Anyone with a gun can rob a store, but only a true gangster can stick up drug dealers."

I understood this calculated risk, as dealers couldn't report such losses to the police. For similar reasons, Chinese gangs robbed gambling and massage parlors and the Chinese businesspeople who frequented them.

"It was never my ambition or my style to be a drug dealer on a street corner," he told me. "In the eighties, we were the best robbers New York ever saw. Best as in getting away with it. All we did was rob drug dealers from different states up and down the I-95.

"We used to terrorize Far Rockaway, Queens. We made a name for ourselves as *those fucking robbers from Brooklyn*. When dealers knew we were in town, they hid their gold jewelry by tucking them under their shirt collar and sleeves. It was funny how street drug dealers got scared when real gangsters were in the area —sort of like how a great white shark is the apex predator but then becomes food when the orcas come around."

In 1984, Diamond learned from a friend working at a Miami hotel that a group of Colombians were discussing a large cocaine shipment. Assuming the staff member didn't understand Spanish, they spoke openly around her. Diamond assembled a team, including a guy he knew named Donovan, and headed to Miami to intercept the shipment.

As planned, Diamond, Donavan, and the team robbed the Colombians of their cocaine. They returned to Brooklyn separately to minimize the risk of getting caught. Dealing exclusively with marijuana, they were unfamiliar with cocaine's street value when they gave it all to Donovan to transport back to Brooklyn.

Donovan discovered the cocaine's value and took advantage of his partners' ignorance. He sold the cocaine and gave them a small share of the proceeds. He might have gotten away with it, but rumors began circulating that Donovan was flaunting his wealth. Diamond realized he'd been betrayed and aimed to get revenge.

He stalked Donovan to a club where he was partying. Once inside, he changed into a dress, put on a blond wig, and wound his way toward Donovan on the dance floor. As he got closer, obscured by the blinding lights and noisy, dancing crowd, Diamond tightened his grip on the gun. He stopped inches away and confronted Donovan. At first Donovan didn't recognize him, but then his eyes widened, shifting from glee to fear.

Diamond shot Donovan multiple times at close range. Escaping from the scene was easy amid the commotion. Back home, Diamond learned from the news that Donovan had survived. Maybe it was because of the rumor among criminals and drug users that a large amount of cocaine in someone's system could paradoxically save their life when under stress.

Diamond wasn't about to let it go.

On October 31, 1984, he approached Donovan's front door

holding a bouquet of flowers and a get-well card. Accompanied by his boys Bee, Steve, and Fly, who were hidden out of sight, Diamond rang the bell. Donovan's sister answered the door.

"I heard what happened to Donovan and that he's in the hospital," Diamond said, holding the offerings.

When she opened the screen door to accept the flowers, Diamond pushed his way inside, along with his crew. They swiftly tied up her and another woman they found inside and confined them in a bedroom, with Steve pointing a pistol at them as the others searched the house.

"We stayed there for five or six hours looking for drugs and cash," Diamond said. "We opened up speakers, couches, furniture, and walls . . . everything."

Donovan's two brothers returned home separately, interrupting their search. "We stuck up the first brother as soon as he walked through the door and tied him up. The other brother tried to run out when he opened the door and saw us, but we caught him. Steve kept them at gunpoint in the bedroom while we continued ransacking the house."

Diamond and Fly eventually descended to a basement through a separate entrance and found yet another woman, whom they also tied up. There, Diamond finally discovered the stash of drugs and cash inside two speakers. As they prepared to leave with their loot, a car pulled into the driveway. They heard footsteps pounding down the basement stairs and glass shattering upstairs, which ended up being one of Donovan's brothers, who had crashed through the bedroom window in a desperate bid to escape. By the time he landed outside, the car's driver was already at the basement door, heading straight for Diamond.

"The guy's about six seven, three hundred twenty pounds—he's a giant with Jheri curls," Diamond described. "And it hits me: My gun was upstairs." Thinking fast, Diamond grabbed a microphone, held it to his hip like a gun, and pointed the tapered end at the guy.

"Back the fuck up!" Diamond yelled.

The man—actually known on the streets as Jheri Curl—turned and ran.

With the loot secured, Diamond's crew scattered. Diamond and Fly leaped from one garage roof to another while a TV news helicopter whirred overhead. The chopper radioed their position to the police, leading to their arrest.

Diamond shook his head with his trademark grin. "By the time we made it to Rikers Island, we were superstars because we were all over the news. The inmates had been watching us live on TV all day—the chase and everything. They applauded when we got there. They called us the Bouquet Robbers."

Their victims faced a dilemma. They couldn't admit that Diamond and his crew had stolen cocaine without implicating themselves in a crime. To ensure their captors remained behind bars, Donovan's sister and the other women falsely claimed that Diamond had sexually assaulted one of them.

Diamond kept his cards hidden, even from his attorney. He had received treatment for gonorrhea and decided to use his prison medical record as evidence in his defense against the rape charges. He planned to argue that if the rape allegations were true, his accusers would also show signs of gonorrhea. Besides, Diamond firmly believed that real gangsters don't rape.

The court dropped the rape allegations, but Diamond still faced robbery charges. He first spent time at Rikers Island in 1984. When I heard the date, I asked him about a martial arts legend known as Grasshopper. Stories with variable and questionable details had been circulating among Asian gangs for years about how he and another guy fought numerous inmates and correctional officers at Rikers. It sounded like the kung fu movies we loved.

When Diamond nodded in recognition, I asked, "You actually *met* him?"

"I gave him cigarettes. When you first come in, you can't get cigarettes right away. It takes two weeks to get an account approved by the commissary."

I chuckled. "That sounds like a very Diamond thing to do. But why give cigarettes to some Asian guy?"

"He was an underdog. Lions and tigers, they're my opponents. Coming from underdog status, I'd tell them, 'I take pleasure in bringing your big ass down.' I like the underdogs, people who have it hard. Rikers is terrible if you don't have an aggressive attitude. Only two types in there: predators and prey."

The guards first put Grasshopper into a large cell with around thirty other inmates, where he spent the next four and a half hours. From the cell across the way, Diamond witnessed what happened.

"Those inmates immediately started bullying Grasshopper. When he'd had enough, he started fighting everyone. I wouldn't have believed it if I hadn't seen it myself." Diamond chuckled. "At first, they were coming at him, and a couple minutes later everybody was climbing on top of each other trying to get away. That dude thrashed them, just like in those kung fu movies, man. He fought and kicked their fucking asses. He really was a legend."

I shook my head in awe. "Ten years later, and those stories are *still* circulating among the Asian gangs. We just figured they were urban legends."

"Nah, it's true." He leaned forward, clearly enjoying telling me the stories. "Another time, Grasshopper and his friend fought the corrections officers. They attacked the officers and fucked them up. It sounded like elephants running past my cell when they sent in more COs. They locked Grasshopper and his friend between two gates to negotiate with them. Afterward, the two had to wear these yellow jackets in the yard and couldn't go within ninety feet of any fence."

I couldn't wait to tell my gangmates Diamond's stories, the closest to the truth that we'd probably ever get.

While at Rikers, Diamond visited the law library, where friends stashed cigarettes for him. Once, a corrections officer got suspicious and followed him in. Already having it in for Diamond, he sent everyone else out of the room except for Diamond.

Diamond squared off in front of the officer. "What you think is going to happen is not going to happen."

The man started searching him anyway, and Diamond clocked him.

As the officer went down, he managed to press an emergency call button. The riot squad rushed in and, seeing their colleague face down on the floor, started beating Diamond with their batons.

Diamond pointed to his mouth. "That's why I have no front teeth."

Within five years, he was transferred to Elmira, then to Coxsackie, and finally to Attica. Diamond's assault on the correctional officer and his other altercations shadowed him throughout his journey in the penitentiary system. "With that kind of record, you can't be placed in a minimum-security facility," he explained. "I was sent to Attica as a penalty for my conduct."

Diamond's sentence was cut short due to prison decongestion following violent riots. Upon his release on parole, he was more intelligent and savvier when robbing drug dealers. And he had a jeweler set a blue diamond in a gold tooth to replace an incisor the corrections officers had knocked out. He shed his old nicknames, and "Diamond" was born.

That distinctive tooth became a liability though. Detectives looking for him stopped men in the street and asked to see their teeth, searching for that diamond identified by witnesses. Diamond even saw a police sketch of himself on interstate news. He complimented the police sketch artist's skill.

Despite growing up in vastly different cultures, Diamond and I shared many interests: kung fu flicks, seafood, girls, and weed. But more profoundly, we both came from immigrant families that hustled daily to put food on the table. We saw life for what it was. Diamond was the only person I'd come across who was not Asian but still like me in many ways.

The people we knew often died young, but he and I defied the odds to survive. We protected ourselves by maintaining small circles of trusted friends. Getting to know him, I learned that the nature of crime is the same whether in China, New York, or Guyana. Most people turn to crime not out of an evil nature but because of evil done to them. Sometimes it is merely to survive or out of a strict code of honor that binds them to their brotherhood. While nothing justifies crime, I began to understand its perpetrators better.

Diamond and I both loved underdog stories and considered snitching unthinkable. We each had a handful of trusted friends who valued loyalty, respect, and brotherhood. For us, there were two families: one at home and the other in the streets.

CHAPTER EIGHT

NIGHTS AT DIAMOND BILLIARDS

In 1993, while running my thriving businesses, both legal and illegal, I received a package from the NYPD inviting me to the academy to start training, as they were now accepting recruits who had passed the entrance examination. Confronted with a life-changing decision four years after I took the test, I felt a thud in my chest.

I finally disclosed my NYPD application to Eileen, unsure how she'd react. It was high time I was transparent with her. After processing it, she told me that if I became a cop, we were done. She didn't want to worry about my safety every day. Little did she know that had always been the case! She reiterated that she wanted a steady nine-to-five life.

I told her I wasn't going to sign on to the police department at that time, not ready to lose her or my current lifestyle. Money flowed in, and more importantly, I felt fulfilled running my enterprises. But I had to be honest with her: I'd probably accept the next NYPD invitation. She told me to throw away the package, which meant throwing away a chance for another invitation.

Two things hit me. First, the mere thought of being that nine-to-fiver tightened my throat like a collar holding me back in life. Second, loyalty was one of my highest codes of honor. The woman I loved should be able to weather all the changes that would inevitably occur in our lives, and if she wasn't willing to allow me to pursue what I felt driven to do, how could we handle the unexpected trials that would surely come our way?

I took a deep breath and told her I would not toss aside this job possibility. She took this to mean I was choosing a police career over her, and she broke up with me. It was amicable. Though we had started as two people with (presumably) similar goals in life, I had diverted from that ideal, one I'd never wanted. In truth I hadn't given Eileen the real me. I gave her a version of me I thought she wanted, while deceiving her with my double life.

Still, I was devastated. I put all my focus on my businesses, determined not to date for a while. When I did resume dating, I didn't take any relationship seriously. I no longer trusted that any woman I loved would stick with me. The women I dated felt this lack of commitment and understandably didn't stick around long: They wanted marriage and kids.

I distracted myself with a new vision: opening a pool hall. By establishing such a place, I would position myself at the center of an underworld hub, using it as a facade for my rackets. It would bring my life full circle, as a pool hall had marked the beginning of my sojourn. Triangle Billiards, always etched in my memory, was where I first glimpsed the gang world and met Cambodian Peter. I wanted my place to be one of belonging and solace for kids like me at that time, disenfranchised and hopeless.

To prepare for my new venture, I put Keith in charge of all three Collectibles branches. I invested around $175,000 in

Diamond Billiards, a lively pool hall and snack bar in the heart of the Junction.

I splurged on a magnificent $50,000 fifty-foot neon sign that proudly displayed DIAMOND BILLIARDS, brightly illuminating the vicinity at night. I ordered nineteen top-of-the-line Brunswick pool tables and invested $18,000 in a cutting-edge security camera system. I installed a jukebox connected to a booming sound system, transforming the pool hall into a dance hall on busy nights. Diamond Billiards became a shining jewel in a rough area, a true oasis.

When I told Diamond I was naming the pool hall after him, he smiled bigger than I'd ever seen him smile. It made him feel special and important, and people in the community would think he owned it. I told him to go ahead and tell people he did own it, and to run it like it was his. We were in it together. He took that seriously. Years later he told me that event was the pinnacle of his life.

I wanted to keep the pool hall crime-free as much as possible, storing most of the illegal contraband at the Collectibles store across the street. I imposed an outright ban on coke and crack. Not long after the grand opening, I noticed a young African American teen playing pool with his buddies at a corner table. People seemed to gravitate toward him, and it became clear he was using his table time to conduct drug deals.

I called Diamond, who was at home, asking him to come over to see if this was a guy he knew before we acted. Once Diamond confirmed that he didn't know him, he made a beeline toward his table. Diamond was armed, and I hoped the kid didn't give him the wrong response because the situation would not end well.

Diamond leaned close to the table. "You sling drugs in here, you'll pay a much bigger price than going to jail. Ask somebody, if you don't know."

The young man left but returned a few days later with his supplier. I discreetly reached for my trusty .38 revolver and positioned myself nearby while they looked around the place for Diamond. With my body angled and finger on the trigger, no one noticed me shadowing them.

When the young man spotted Diamond and pointed him out, I saw recognition light up the supplier's face. He turned to the young dealer. "Oh man, you'll end up in a trunk if you pull that shit in here. You think *I'm* crazy? He's really crazy!"

The supplier walked up to Diamond with his arms open to give him a hug. Only then did Diamond's stone face break into a smile. The men exchanged a quick hug, and I figured out the man must be Fat Tony, once a fierce rival at the Veer until they settled their differences. He'd known Diamond by his previous nickname, Ranks. Apologetic, Fat Tony instructed his dealers to conduct their business elsewhere.

Diamond noticed Fat Tony was having difficulty breathing and asked if he was recovering from yet another gunshot wound. Fat Tony confirmed this by lifting his shirt and revealing not only a recent bullet wound but scars from many others. He pointed to one of them on his chest. "I lost a lung because of this one."

Not long before the grand opening of Diamond Billiards, Fat Tony needed a crew for a robbery in Miami and reached out to Diamond, but he turned down the offer. Fat Tony moved on and assembled a crew who successfully executed the Miami heist. However, the man who returned with the stolen merchandise was killed in the public parking lot next to the pool hall.

Speaking of not being involved, I continued to try to shield my brother, Jason, from the gangster lifestyle and kept on him about not joining the gang. But I couldn't stop him from going to the pool hall—it was open to the public, after all. Even if I forbade him, I knew he'd still come in his rebelliousness, which would create tension between us, or he'd go to another establishment where I couldn't keep an eye on him. I also didn't want to alienate him with my hard-line rules. So I looked after him and gave him advice.

Like many other kids, he was fascinated by the lifestyle and sense of freedom the crew had, only seeing the exciting side of gang life. But he started to see the risks and the risky behavior of his so-called friends.

When he was seventeen, Jason was riding in a car with three Fuk Ching members when one of them ordered the driver to stop and said he saw a kid he recognized. He told Jason to come with him as he approached the kid. At the way the guy stalked toward the kid, and the kid's look of fear at seeing their approach, Jason realized this was a robbery. He told the gang member to stop what he was doing. The other two guys in the car called Jason to get in the car, that they'd take care of the situation. Jason made it clear that he wanted nothing to do with this as they walked over to the kid. Finally, the gang members returned to the car, and they left. Jason then understood that seeing "someone they recognized" meant spotting a target, an early lesson in gang culture.

While I ran the pool hall, I also maintained my other businesses and gang operations. I converted the back room of Collectibles into a covert meeting spot for conducting criminal activities, making my legitimate business the perfect cover for storing and hiding our contraband.

I assigned Diamond to oversee the weed racket, and although it was not his forte, he recruited a few kids from the

Veer to sell our products. Selling drugs, particularly marijuana, was easy money. We would buy weed by the pound from Jamaicans, break it up into smaller quantities, and sell it to street dealers. I continued to stay away from dealing coke or heroin. I was under the radar and determined to stay there. We kept our racket even safer by mostly selling weed.

One kid made the mistake of storing his stash in a fridge, leading to rumors that our marijuana was moldy. Diamond summoned the kid to the pool hall, where he also learned that the teen had laced our weed with something to kill the mold.

The kid loudly denied any wrongdoing. Feeling disrespected, Diamond pulled out his 10mm and pistol-whipped the kid, cracking his skull. A shot rang out as a bullet pierced the staircase wall, just missing my brother, Jason. The kid leaped down a dozen steps in two bounds, trailing blood. My customers resumed playing pool as if nothing had happened—that was Flatbush in the 1990s.

The teenager told his older brother what Diamond had done to him. The next night, as an ex-convict himself, the brother brought another former inmate to the pool hall to confront the guy who'd pistol-whipped his sibling. They menacingly searched the pool hall, asking for Diamond, creating a tense atmosphere.

Jean, a Black Haitian thug with a scarred and burned face, served as our lookout, and he discreetly alerted Diamond by phone about the two guys looking for him. When Jean went into the restroom, our unwelcome guests followed.

After Jean leaned his cue stick against the wall and unzipped his pants, the two ex-convicts pinned him against the wall, seized his cue stick, and began beating him. Though Jean was tough, he could only stagger under the sudden, relentless onslaught.

The elder brother brandished a .25-caliber handgun. "*Where's Diamond?*"

"I don't know!" Jean yelled back, his voice tight with pain. Unseen, Diamond had slipped into the restroom.

"Where the hell is Diamond?" they demanded once more.

Jean spotted Diamond and blurted out, "He's right there!"

Diamond leaned casually against the door, his finger on the trigger of his 10mm gun aimed at the two intruders.

Silence descended as they realized the danger they were in.

Jean pulled away from them and broke the silence. "You motherfuckers come in here like killers, and now you're shitting your pants!" He grabbed his cue stick, stalking past Diamond and out the door.

The two men hadn't moved or spoken, their eyes wide and mouths agape.

"*Archie? You're* Diamond?" the brother asked. "I didn't know it was you!"

"Yeah, motherfucker, I'm Diamond now!"

Both men had previously served time in Attica and knew Diamond as Lil' Archie. Remembering his reputation, the brother turned pale and swayed out of the trajectory as Diamond slowly moved the gun barrel from left to right.

"You looking for me, motherfuckers?" Diamond continued.

"Fuck," the older brother stammered. "Archie, I didn't know it was you! But man, you pistol-whipped my kid brother. What did he do to you?"

"The same shit you guys are doing now, coming to my place and acting up!"

He held up his hands. "We're leaving. I'm going to take care of my brother and set things straight."

"You go do that," said Diamond.

Diamond's changing nicknames threw people off. He'd been "Ranks" as a teen. When he went to the same prison as his older brother Archie, they called Diamond "Lil' Archie" (though there was nothing lil' about Diamond, who was as big as Mike Tyson!). Now he was Diamond.

Had they not recognized Diamond from prison, the night could have ended with two dead bodies in our restroom.

Any business encounters unique challenges. Pool halls attract a particular crowd, especially at night. *Especially* when they're in a rough neighborhood. Diamond, as usual, often wanted to resolve issues on the spot with his gun.

Once, a kid broke into one of our video game cabinets and stole several hundred dollars in quarters. After viewing this on our security camera, we identified him as an eighteen-year-old street thug. He returned the next night, and Diamond watched and waited for the right time to approach him. When the thug headed to the restroom, Diamond cranked up the jukebox and followed him, gun in hand.

Diamond confronted him. Shaken, he admitted to stealing from us and apologized. I followed him into the restroom because I knew Diamond would kill him. I found Diamond pistol-whipping the kid and told Diamond I didn't want to deal with another body in my trunk. I advised him to let the kid go, possibly saving his life. Diamond warned the fleeing kid to never step foot in the pool hall again.

Though Diamond had direct and effective ways to eliminate a threat, I talked to him about using alternate ways to deal with situations.

A few months later, the kid sought me out at the pool hall and apologized again. He asked to be allowed to hang out in the pool hall, explaining that his friends frequented the pool hall and he felt left out.

Before I could say anything, Diamond saw him. Taking his mere presence as an affront to Diamond's authority, he pulled out his gun and shot at the fleeing kid. Bullet holes peppered the walls, but customers continued playing pool as if nothing had happened. I guess Diamond needed more time to assimilate my advice.

Incidents like the above gave our restroom a notorious reputation. Word on the street was that once you went in, you might not come out. It was the only place in the six-thousand-square-foot hall without security cameras. Some local dealers and neighborhood kids would go downstairs to urinate in the street to avoid using our restroom.

Unfamiliar people coming into the pool hall always warranted our suspicion. Just like on the streets, I was on constant alert. And not only for gangsters.

Several Black guys in their mid-twenties arrived to play pool, looking like gangsters. Watching on the security monitors, we observed that they focused more on looking around the place than shooting pool. We knew almost all the players in the area but had never seen these guys before. While it looked like they were casing the place, we figured no one would be stupid enough to rob us.

They shot pool without spending much money and left. The aura they presented pegged them as cops. A dead giveaway: Cops are cheap. The drug dealers dropped lots of money at our food counter and kept feeding the jukebox for music as they played pool all night. These guys just came in, paid for table time, and observed. It hadn't occurred to them how much they stood out, especially when I was monitoring their every move on the camera. Another dead giveaway that they were not there to shoot pool was the way they played. They took shots without rhyme or reason. Yeah, they were on a mission.

I couldn't blame the authorities for their suspicion. A pool hall in any high-crime neighborhood was a magnet for criminal activities. Despite precautions to remain inconspicuous, it was inevitable that my pool hall, frequented by individuals from diverse backgrounds, would attract the attention of authorities. Many whispered conversations, negotiated deals, and forged alliances occurred in our dimly lit corners. We hatched our plans amid the sounds of bouncing billiard balls and tipsy laughter.

I suspected the local cops were trying to penetrate our illicit operations, which made me extra alert to anything suspicious. Including people I knew.

Jean approached Diamond about purchasing a 9mm gun. This was odd because Jean usually had little money. He was always bumming pool table time from others. Diamond had known him for a long time, so I gave him the gun to sell to him.

A week later Jean came in, wanting four more guns. These guns went for $800 to $1000 apiece, so I found this request even more suspect. Where was Jean getting the money? Had he used the first gun to commit a robbery? But why would he want *more* guns? It raised a lot of red flags.

When Diamond and I discussed Jean's request, I said, "Can't you see that it's unusual for a Black kid in the neighborhood to buy multiple guns at once? He must be an informant."

Diamond agreed and turned Jean down.

Done deal, or so I thought.

Jean then had the nerve to come directly to me and ask for the guns. I never dealt with any of the Black kids; they went through Diamond. That was the ultimate red flag. I told the kid I had no idea what he was talking about.

Even though I anticipated police action at some point, when a team of NYPD officers in flak jackets stormed into the pool hall one night, it was still a shock. In the back, Diamond tossed his 10mm handgun behind the Joker Poker machine in a dark corner by the jukebox, making a distinct clunking sound. Fortunately, the officers did not associate the noise with a firearm hitting the ground.

Also fortunate was that their arrival coincided with reggae singer Major Mackerel being interviewed in the pool hall for a local news piece. My pool hall had started attracting a lot of Black celebrities, and many of them brought not only an entourage but press. With TV cameras around, the police behaved themselves. After giving the place a quick inspection, they left.

I knew they'd be back.

And a few days later they were, even more determined to pin us down with something. I allowed them to search my office, where I never kept anything incriminating. They saw the safe. Since they lacked a search warrant, and I told them I didn't have the combination, the best they could do was shake it to see if any guns rattled around inside. Three cops trying to shake down a seventy-five-pound safe was fun to watch.

They weren't going to find the guns because of our ingenious method of hiding our guns in the pool hall. A hole under the counter opened into the sealed upper ceiling space above the first-floor commercial establishment, The Salvation Army. We lowered our firearms with a string on an s-hook, the other end tied to the wooden cover with a barely visible knot. We could quickly pull up a gun if needed. On the several occasions the police raided the place to search for guns and drugs, they left empty-handed.

Because of that I became even more suspicious about Jean. We hadn't sold him those additional guns, but that might not stop the police from trying to bust us anyway.

Admittedly, we brought on a few visits ourselves by indulging in some target practice after hours. We'd crank up the jukebox volume, stack up thick books, and shoot at them to compare our firearms. One of Diamond's friends proudly showed off his Calico M950A, a submachine gun our gang had never seen before. Diamond pointed out that the weapon had been featured in John Woo's *Hard Boiled*, a movie his friend had watched countless times to observe the gun in action.

I enjoyed watching one of our regulars, a well-dressed, preppy African American young man in his mid-twenties, shooting pool in the hall. He conducted himself with respect, refrained from showing off, and exhibited true professionalism. He was widely known in the circle of pool hustlers and gamblers as a hustler, amassing bets in various New York pool halls. Watching him set up his marks intrigued me, but what I found hilarious was how he took large sums of money from my arrogant, stubborn associates who repeatedly underestimated his skills.

The sixteen-year-old gang recruit named Chinatown Jack, who hung out with my brother, for instance, couldn't resist challenging the hustler to a game. As expected, he initially held his own but gradually started losing on a consistent basis. Bruised pride and an empty wallet compelled him to seek more funds for another try. He couldn't accept defeat.

"Can one of your boys lend me a bike?" he asked Diamond. "I'll be back in a few."

Diamond instructed a Black teen to loan Chinatown Jack his bicycle. Chinatown Jack rode off, then returned within minutes, placing a thousand dollars on the pool table for another go.

"What'd you do to get that money so fast?" Diamond asked, tempering his question with a chuckle so it didn't come off as invasive. He was genuinely curious about how the Asian gangs worked.

Chinatown Jack was happy to tell him. "I rode over to the house of this kid from the high school. I told the kid's mom

I was with Fuk Ching, and if she wanted to see her son come home safe tomorrow, she had to give me a thousand dollars. Us Chinese don't need to put on a mask and go out and rob the way you Blacks do it."

Diamond and his friends had a good chuckle over that. I was glad to see that no one took offense over the remark. In fact, the mood was light, with an air of mutual respect between the gangs.

Chinatown Jack played another round of pool with the African American hustler. Once again, he lost.

Restlessness defined Chinatown Jack, which made predicting his actions impossible. A few months prior, he had committed a robbery against a Chinese businessman, yielding a haul of $15,000. He then spent his ill-gotten gains liberally at my pool hall, with a fondness for Joker Poker. As the machine slowly devoured his money, he turned to lottery tickets. Fortune favored him with a $10,000 windfall from a scratch-off card. He compulsively continued feeding my gambling machines until he found himself penniless once more.

Recognizing the penchant for gambling within our circles, we installed gambling machines from the Italians within the pool hall and other locations. Sharing the proceeds fifty-fifty, this initiative proved highly lucrative.

Remarkably, Chinatown Jack discerned a winning pattern on a specific electronic slot machine. Whenever it displayed three yellow bells, he knew placing a particular bet next always triggered a winning combination. This discovery cost him a lot of time and initial losses but ultimately proved worthwhile. He divulged his secret to his close friend Danny Boy, and together they exploited this anomaly on similar slot machines across Queens and Brooklyn.

Their greed eventually aroused suspicion among the Italian mob, which had suffered significant losses by this time. Once the mobsters figured it out, they located Danny Boy after staking out slot machine locations. With manhandling and intense interrogation, they coerced a confession from him, releasing him under the condition that neither he nor Chinatown Jack ever repeat their actions. Both boys upheld this promise by refraining from playing any electronic slot machines. Danny Boy told me that the Italians seemed more amused, curious, and even impressed, than angry at how two seventeen-year-olds had found a way to beat their machines. The manhandling had been a warning, much less than they could have done. I don't think they wanted a war with us, but they definitely wanted the scam to stop.

As Diamond and I had been putting deals together for a while, I contemplated forging a casual alliance between his crew and Fuk Ching. They could rob Chinatown's gambling and prostitution houses and other illicit cash businesses for us while we could offer them connections to our rackets. Gangs were typically neighborhood-based and ethnically homogeneous, so an alliance would open new markets. Also, since our gangs worked in different ways, I thought we could learn from each other.

I was unsure how my brothers in Fuk Ching would react to my proposal. Unlike some West Coast Asian gangs that had adopted elements of hip-hop culture, the tight-knit Chinatown gangs were *very Asian*, adhering to our traditions and beliefs and closed to outsiders. But in straddling two gang cultures, I saw the potential of aligning our crews, multiplying our pathways to money, and consolidating our power in the streets. Our pool hall was the perfect way to bring the two gangs under one roof to test the waters.

Initially, I was the only one who saw the promise of this union, as my Fuk Ching brethren struggled to comprehend the nuances of the Black gang culture and their unconventional methods. Diamond introduced his associates to my gang, and despite the awkwardness, they mingled, shared food, and played pool. My crew was taken aback by their brazen ways, particularly their open displays of firearms. Diamond's penchant for firing his weapon inside the pool hall and his crew's Wild West–style demeanor unsettled my gangmates.

Likewise, my Guyanese friend told his crew about the Chinese gangs: the unique lifestyle, the food, the gambling houses, and Chinatown. They couldn't fully grasp the intricacies, no matter how hard he tried to explain them. It was an entirely different gang culture than what they were familiar with: its hierarchy, illegal activities, and how things were done in general. Still, as weeks passed, both sides grew more comfortable with each other, fostering conversations and laughter.

Cambodian Peter respected my counsel on various matters. Knowing that I trusted only a select few and would never jeopardize our safety or divulge our secrets, he understood that my introduction of Diamond and his crew was rooted in logic.

I explained to Diamond that Cambodian Peter wasn't just my *Dai Lo* but also my *hing dai*—an esteemed term within Chinese gangs meaning "my brother." Eventually, they developed mutual respect, and Diamond became even more intrigued by the inner workings of Asian gang operations.

Rooster, our *Dai Lo*, treated Diamond differently. Rooster and I met at the pool hall often, exchanging moneymaking ideas and contacts. As a gambler who enjoyed sports betting, Rooster placed his bets with the Italians from Avenue U. He gambled in Atlantic City and made money from his multiple gambling establishments all over Chinatowns in Queens, Manhattan, and Brooklyn. He had other rackets too, like importing counterfeit casino chips from China, credit card fraud, counterfeit money, weapons, and loan-sharking. Rooster had a contact for almost anything I needed from the underworld.

But when he visited the pool hall for business, I had to escort Diamond out. This bothered me more than it did Diamond. Rooster adhered to traditional ways, maintaining distance, upholding hierarchy, and avoiding overfamiliarity—especially with outsiders.

As my pool hall became a sanctuary for my Fuk Ching brethren, who frequently bunked in my office, we spent less time in Fuk Ching safe houses. On one occasion, our *Dai Lo*, Ah Mun, planned a heist with Danny Boy, Chinatown Jack, and Ah Gow. They honed their marksmanship skills at my pool hall the night before this ill-fated attempt, which later made the Channel 9 evening news.

Given my long history with Danny Boy, I worried about his involvement in the planned robbery. Despite his quiet demeanor, he wouldn't hesitate to retaliate when provoked. His reputation within the gang was that of a capable fighter. It made sense that Ah Mun had enlisted him for their heist, which aimed to rob a diamond dealer who made deliveries around Chinatown.

Fortunately, Jason wasn't part of this plan, as he wasn't a member of the gang. The night before the robbery, though, he was in the pool hall with Diamond and the guys who were target practicing in preparation for the robbery. Jason thought it was fun, but for the crew, it was "job" training.

I was satisfied with my earnings in my gambling house and had no need to participate in a robbery like this. Unlike other gambling house owners who resorted to cheating techniques like loaded dice, marked cards, or even hiring professional cheats as dealers, I relied on commissions from my esteemed clientele of mahjong high rollers as a fee for using my place. The game has four rounds, and on each hand played—or each round played—we charged a commission based on the amount won. That was enough for me.

On August 23, 1994, the three trailed the jeweler and his bodyguard, a retired cop, through Chinatown, waiting for the right opportunity. They moved in as their target reached the corner of Hester and Chrystie Streets. Danny Boy and Ah Gow were to disable the guard and take his gun while the other two grabbed the bag of diamonds. As Danny Boy began his assault, the security guard managed to pull out his gun. He shot Ah Gow while Ah Mun and Danny Boy narrowly escaped.

Danny Boy and Ah Mun sought refuge in the salon on the second floor of a building on Ludlow Street. After about twenty minutes, believing it was safe, they emerged onto the street. A yellow taxi screeched to a halt, and two plainclothes police officers jumped out with guns drawn, apprehending them. Eventually, the authorities deported Ah Mun.

On top of paying a $50,000 bail, Danny Boy incurred over $100,000 in attorney fees as his trial dragged on. He received a prison sentence and was incarcerated in the Greene Correctional Facility in Coxsackie, where he crossed paths with Shorty, our feisty member of Fuk Ching.

1969 Live feed of the moon landing, Ed Lee in the front.

1969 Live feed of the moon landing, Ed Lee to the right.

1969 Live feed of the moon landing.

1986 Kenny Wong.

1988 Mike Moy and Carrot Head.

1989 Mike Moy standing next to his IROC-Z.

1990 Mike Moy and Tommy.

1990 Mike Moy, Cambodian Peter, and Big Chicken.

1992 Collectibles Store

1992 Collectibles Store.

1993 Diamond.

1993 Mike Moy and Diamond.

1994 Mike Moy

1995 Mike Moy as a probationary police officer.

1996 66 PCT locke room.

1996 Mike Moy.

1996 March NYPD Graduation.

2002 Police Officer Mike Moy.

2019 Mike Moy and Tommy.

Diamond Billiards outside.

Diamond Billiards

Diamond Billiards at Night.

Mike Moy inside Diamond Billiards

Mike Moy with Lian insode Diamond Billiards.

Mike Moy 16 years old.

Artist illustration of Mike Moy with his Grandma working.
Drawn by Pitroick Hanson

Grandma, Mom, Dad, Mike Moy, and Little Sister.

Mike Moy and Aunt standing in front of 26 East Broadway.

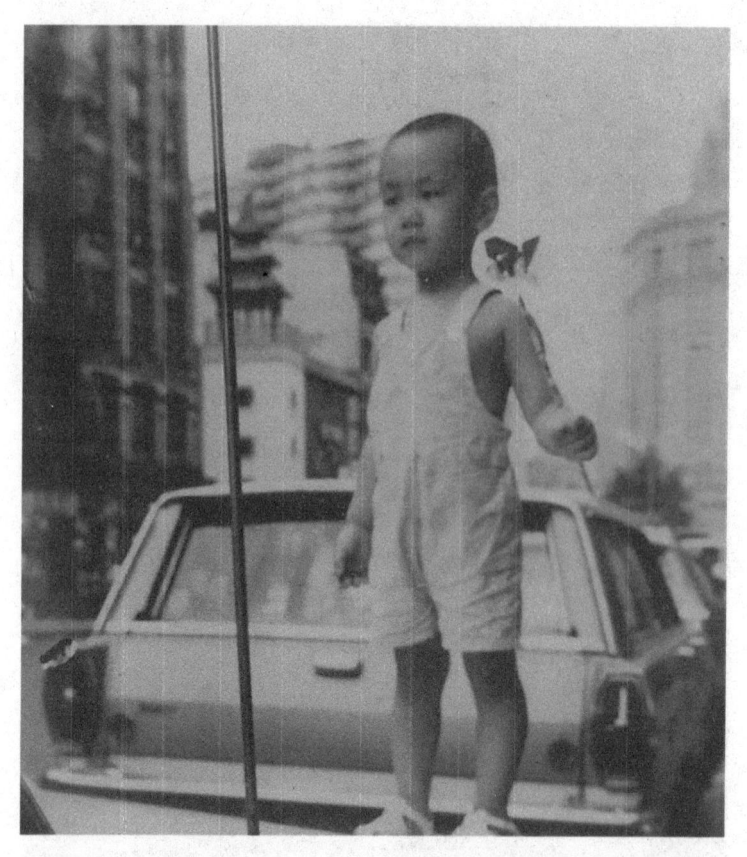

Mike Moy in front of 26 East Broadway, Pagoda Theater in background

Mike Moy Visits Shorty in prison.

Mike Moy with Eileen in front of OnTime Car Service.

Mike Moy 16 years old.

Mike Moy with Carrot Head.

Mike Moy with Philip Lam in front of 66 PCT.

Mike Moy with Uncle Louie.

Promotion to Detective with Police Commissoner Ray Kelly, and Mayor Mike Bloomberg.

Mike Moy working inside the 66 PCT Detective Office

Mike Moy with Diamond present day.

Mike Moy with Cambodian Peter, and Big Chicken present day.

Mike Moy with Shorty present day.

CHAPTER NINE

GUNS IN THE TRUNK

On the outside I remained the same old Mike: stoic and cold. No one suspected that a part of me had died when Eileen and I broke up. Over time, I understood that my relationship with her had been doomed from the start. I unfairly labeled her as naive, but in reality, she was simply trusting. I never allowed her to know all the parts of me because I assumed she couldn't adapt to or accept my lifestyle.

True, Eileen would have been shocked had I told her about my other life, but that didn't mean she was incapable of listening, accepting me, or finding a middle ground. Did I love her? Yes, but not enough to blindly trust her.

Had Eileen accepted me after I told her about my underworld life, maybe we could have grown to understand each other's worlds. Yes, it might have been rocky after that admission, and we could have ended up separating anyway. But at least I would have given her a chance to accept and love me for who I truly was rather than ruling it out. If our relationship had worked out, my decision to leave the gang and become a cop could have been a moment of celebration instead of conflict.

But I was now walking this path without her, and I threw myself into other endeavors to distract myself from my thoughts of her. With my pool hall occupying my time, I sold the Collectibles branch on Avenue U.

When a salon took over that space, I started getting my hair cut there. The first time Lian washed my hair, she accidentally got water all over my face, but I didn't say a word. I knew she was doing the best she could. In fact, I made all my future appointments with her. She and I grew closer, and my admiration for her grew as I learned more about her character and attitude toward life.

Lian had come to America from China when she was twelve without knowing a word of English. Her family had started their lives in the United States with almost nothing, and her parents struggled with poverty while raising four children. As a middle child, she was no one's favorite, but that didn't deter her from supporting her family. At thirteen, Lian used a fake ID to acquire a job in a nail salon, along with a fake nail technician license. Her employer suggested she wear a lot of makeup to appear more mature because customers viewed her as too young to be a good tech.

This salon was located in a crime-ridden section of Harlem. Nail techs often worked twelve-hour shifts, and the salon remained open late, sometimes until two or three a.m., to cater to clients in the nearby public housing projects. The small strip of commercial establishments became a popular gathering place for people to hang out with friends, smoke weed, and score drugs. Some of the singers, artists, and rappers who hung out there later became big stars.

Robbers targeted the salon so frequently that the owner

devised a way to keep everyone safe and mitigate losses. She assigned Lian the station closest to the door because she was one of the few in the salon who could speak a little English. Lian's job was to hand a paper bag filled with loose one- and five-dollar bills to the robbers when they entered. Often a robber would barge into the salon and point a gun at Lian, demanding money. This young girl stared down the barrel of a gun so many times that she got used to it. She'd calmly grab the bag of money and hand it to him.

Hearing this made me reflect on the difference between Black gangs and Chinese gangs. The former resorted to violence and risked severe charges, while we mainly acquired money through extortion. No woman would ever face a gun from one of our members.

Despite its location and frequent robberies, the salon made a significant amount of money. The salon's ten stations each earned at least $200 daily. Half of that net went to the nail technician or beautician, plus tips. After deducting the monthly rent of around $1,000, the owner still earned about $30,000 a month. It didn't surprise me when I learned that the owner had invested in other salons and beauty parlors and, after a few years, had even bought several buildings. Nail salons were pulling in this type of cash during the eighties—which is why, decades later, many former gang members muscled in on this business area after getting out of prison.

One time, the police chased after Black gang members for dealing drugs in the area. The suspects managed to outrun the officers and took refuge in the salon, hiding in one of the back rooms. Eventually, the police entered the salon and asked the owner and employees if they had seen the guys they were looking for. The employees didn't betray the hiding criminals and allowed them to escape safely after the officers left. After this incident, the robberies in the salon stopped, leading the owner to assume that the drug dealers they'd protected had instructed street criminals to leave them alone.

Over time Lian befriended the drug dealers, ingratiating herself by complimenting their expensive fur coats and fancy cars. She was a strong, fearless woman who could deal with anyone from any background with an open mind, and these traits impressed me. As we spent more time together, our friendship grew romantic. She was the ideal girlfriend for a gangster like me, who needed discretion when necessary and silence in critical situations.

Lian knew about my involvement in the gang but not the extent of it. She wasn't oblivious or naive. Growing up in Brooklyn, she'd seen a number of Asian gangs recruiting in her high school. She had friends in a gang. She never asked me outright, though, and I did not share that aspect of my life with her. A silent pact between us left certain things unsaid. Those outside this kind of life may not understand, but it made sense for us.

She respected my space without becoming overly attached, and she showed me affection without being clingy. She could sit next to me while I played mahjong for sixteen hours, enduring my vice without a word. Other times she'd sit on my office couch, waiting. Sometimes I'd get so engrossed in my daily operations that I'd forget she was quietly and patiently waiting.

Typically, a girlfriend would cause a scene, yell at me in public, or embarrass me, but not Lian. Right after we left, though, she'd scold me in private for being so engrossed with my gambling, daily business activities, and dealing with my friends that I'd forgotten she was there. In front of my friends, she played an obedient role, but when we were alone, I did whatever made her happy. I appreciated that she was someone I could talk to and ask advice of. I would have given her my kidney, even my heart, if she needed it. Most importantly, she knew I'd keep every promise I made to her.

She cared about me but maintained a distance from my gang life. She trusted me enough to let me be, and gangsters appreciate partners who are comfortable with not being in the know on everything. That's not to say she was submissive—far from it. She chose her battles wisely and knew when and how to argue for the right reasons. She may not have had a high school diploma, but Lian was smart—street-smart and more. She was tough, but she had a good heart. She genuinely cared about people, a quality I didn't see in many around me. Her all-encompassing empathy balanced out my indifference to people not in my immediate circle.

One of the many things I appreciated about her was that she remained rooted in our Chinese culture and—despite Western influences—preserved her ethnic identity. She embraced traditional values, preferred Chinese cuisine, and honored many cultural practices I didn't know about as an American-born Chinese (ABC). I learned so much from her about where I'd come from. She taught me Cantonese, even though she teased me about my mistakes.

As with all relationships, ours had its ups and downs. Gang culture consumed much of my personal life, leaving little time for my family or girlfriend. Our relationship was on and off. I had other girlfriends during our cool-off periods, but Lian was my favorite. I was authentic around her, without hiding who I was or pretending to be someone I wasn't—a lesson I'd learned from my relationship with Eileen.

Delaying my entry to the police academy brought risks that could jeopardize my big-picture plan. Sometime in 1994, during the peak of my pool hall exploits, my secrets were almost exposed to both the law and my gang associates.

One night Diamond, his teenage brother Lance, and I visited our usual Vietnamese restaurant on Brooklyn's Eighth Avenue. After we finished our dinner and got into my car, I reminded them to put on their seatbelts. I wanted to avoid giving the police any possible reason to pull us over as I had guns in the trunk. However, as I signaled to pull out of my parking spot, I was pulled over by three plainclothes cops in an unmarked vehicle.

Inwardly I groaned. I had taken every precaution, so why were the cops pulling me over? Was it because a Chinese person with two Black companions in Chinatown at ten p.m. looked suspicious? They asked why we were in the area, and I explained that I had just had dinner with my employees. I showed them my business card from the store.

I got more worried when they asked me to open my trunk, telling my friends to stay in the car. One cop kept an eye on them with his flashlight. The other two approached the rear of my car with me as I popped open the trunk.

The cop opened the briefcase inside and found an unlicensed Smith & Wesson 9mm handgun. I had a licensed .38 revolver in my holster at my waist. I presented the cops with my license for the revolver but had no documentation for the other gun.

I explained that I carried the gun for protection because my business was in a high-crime area. They further examined my briefcase. Discovering letters from the NYPD's Candidate Assessment Division, my business cards, and business documents, they saw that my story added up—and I was on track to become a police officer.

The illegal gun was now the issue.

They confiscated that gun but released me, sending relief rushing through me. The documents in my briefcase had likely saved me—not just that night but perhaps for the rest of my life.

Once back in the car, I worried that Diamond and Lance might have overheard my conversation with the cops by the trunk. I could only imagine their feelings of betrayal if they found out I was planning to become a cop. In their eyes, it would mean I was becoming one of the enemy.

A tense silence enveloped the car, with me unable to speak and anxiously awaiting any indication of whether they had heard the conversation. Diamond eventually asked me what had happened, knowing there was the illegal handgun in the trunk. I told him that the cops took my gun but let me go. They both proceeded to criticize the police, discussing the corruption within the system and sharing stories of encounters with police officers.

Whew, they didn't overhear anything.

After dropping off Diamond and his brother, I was left alone with my thoughts. *What if my gang finds out that I'm planning to be a NYPD cop?*

I wanted to be around people who did good in the world, people like Steven McDonald. Why not try the opposite of what I'd been doing? There must be happiness, fulfillment, and peace in committing to a good and lawful life. I had lived a dark, rebellious life, yet it hadn't brought me peace or deep satisfaction.

That next invitation to apply to the NYPD would be my turning point. It would mean giving up everything: my businesses, friends, income, my "family," and life as I knew it. I'd be starting again from the bottom of a hierarchy, and just one of a few Asians on the force—hearkening back to my torturous school years. I couldn't put it off much longer as my next invitation letter to begin the hiring process would be the last before my name expired off the list.

My future path as a cop seemed to poke into my life regularly, as if illustrating the deep dichotomy between my goals and my current life. Law enforcement started taking a deeper interest in the pool hall. One time Lian and I had a little fun with it.

Diamond Billiards's expansive fifty-foot windows provided an excellent view of the whole Junction area from the second floor. On a frigid winter night, after closing the pool hall at four a.m., I counted the day's receipts. Meanwhile, Lian spotted the silhouettes of two heads on the rooftop of a building across the street. They'd duck down every time she glanced their way. I embraced her from behind, wrapping my arms around her tiny waist and resting my head on her shoulder, surreptitiously looking across the way.

Seeing the glint of binoculars against white faces in a Black neighborhood, especially on a cold winter night, led me to conclude our spectators were cops.

I pulled her to the side so that she faced away from the window. "The cops are spying on this place." I gave her a playful smile, arching my eyebrow. "Wanna give them a show and keep them warm?"

With a mischievous grin, she stepped forward and started kissing me. Undressing each other until all our clothes were on the floor, we gave them a show, all right, having sex on the pool table by the window.

Soon after, I found more reasons to suspect that the police were targeting me. One day, I was driving with Diamond in my car, with the windows closed and the radio turned off. Suddenly we heard a brief radio transmission: It sounded like a police scanner. I thought I was hearing things, but Diamond gave me a puzzled and worried look.

I pulled over to see if we'd hear it again. The sound had come from *inside* the vehicle, and we only heard it once. After thoroughly searching the car, we found nothing unusual.

Diamond and I never doubted each other: If one of us were

a police informant, the cops would have apprehended the other long ago. We both knew far too much! Fortunately, we never discussed anything inside the car. Uncle Louie had taught me about "walk talks," and I always reminded Diamond about this. If you want to discuss sensitive subjects, take a walk and talk. Never discuss anything in the car or on the phone. As street-smart as we may have been, however, it was easy to slip up.

Depending on how you look at it, luck was on my side. That week I lost a good amount of money gambling in a card game, and the winner accepted my car to pay off my debt.

One of our young crew members named Chicken Lips also became a source of concern when we began to suspect his loyalty to the gang. He was clever and cunning but primarily looked out for himself. Chicken Lips carried out home invasions using a sinister tactic. He'd approach an innocent child with false charm, slinging his arm over their shoulder.

"Hey, buddy, let's go to your house," Chicken Lips would calmly assert, his words dripping with fake camaraderie. "Tell your mom I'm your friend." Once inside the house, he would ransack and clear out the valuables and leave before any adult realized what had happened.

His manipulative and slimy behavior extended to us, and his true colors surfaced in various instances. Rooster had opened a gambling house in a luxury high-rise condominium in Flushing, Queens, and the crew occasionally provided security. One night, the gambling house was robbed at gunpoint, and all signs pointed to an inside job. Rooster suspected that Chicken Lips was behind the robbery and hinted that he wanted him eliminated for his betrayal. No one stepped up, probably because we just weren't sure.

Chicken Lips also nearly got my fifteen-year-old brother killed. Over the years, I continued to forbid Jason from joining a gang. Preoccupied with running my businesses, though, I had missed the brewing issues surrounding my sibling. I felt guilty seeing him take steps down the gangster path. I felt responsible and knew I would find it hard to forgive myself if something terrible happened to him. Jason was not made for the streets. Unlike me, my brother had a deep capacity for empathy. Physically, he was tall and well built and towered over kids his age, but mentally and emotionally, he didn't fit into the clothes of gang life.

That was largely due to his upbringing, which was very different from mine. During his growing-up years, our family had been relatively well off, and he had not experienced the deprivation I had. In some ways, Jason was spoiled and got whatever he wanted. How could a kid like that make it in gang life, where even minor disputes can rapidly escalate if mishandled?

But Jason had learned that, according to the street's code, threats had to be taken seriously for both safety and pride. So when a Ghost Shadow member named Nick glared menacingly at Jason whenever he saw him at the park, Jason saw it as an unspoken challenge. When my brother shared this with Chicken Lips, he exacerbated the situation instead of defusing the tension.

One evening at the pool hall, Chicken Lips and my brother ran into one of Nick's associates. Chicken Lips provoked my brother, encouraging him to direct his anger toward the associate by physically assaulting him. Word of this incident swiftly made its way to Siu Bo, the *Dai Ma* of Ghost Shadows, a young man around my brother's age who constantly sought recognition and notoriety.

"I'll have Jason taken care of," Siu Bo declared.

Threatening messages from the Ghost Shadow *Dai Ma*, each more chilling than the last, began arriving at our family's home. The ringing phone became a harbinger of dread for my terrified mom.

Enough was enough. I had to take action.

I ordered Chicken Lips to clean up the mess he had created, and he arranged a meeting with Siu Bo in a local park so he could explain the situation. After he'd done that, Jason would arrive, and they'd make peace. But my confidence in Chicken Lips had eroded, especially now that Ghost Shadows were hunting my brother. Diamond and I had a secret backup plan. We drove Jason to the park, then parked at a distance to observe, allowing Jason to walk alone to meet with Siu Bo and Chicken Lips. The plan was for Diamond to kill Siu Bo first, then Chicken Lips if there were any signs that negotiations had failed. Diamond gripped his 10mm weapon, hoping he'd have reason to use it, especially when we spotted eight Ghost Shadows in the park besides Siu Bo.

Tensed, we closely watched the two young men for signs of movement, like a weapon about to be drawn. They talked; then Jason headed back our way. I held my breath until he got into my car and relayed their conversation. Chicken Lips had made it clear to Siu Bo that Jason was not in a gang but that he *was* related to a senior gang member. Chicken Lips admitted to his role in having Jason confront Siu Bo's associate at the pool hall. He persuaded Siu Bo that a war wasn't necessary since no one had been seriously injured.

The matter was resolved, but fate had other plans for Siu Bo. Months later, he was fatally stabbed in Chinatown in an unrelated incident.

Concerned about Jason's life direction, my parents attempted to ship him to Florida, then made him stay at an aunt's house on Long Island. Neither strategy worked, for my brother's association with Fuk Ching had provided him the security and adrenaline high he'd become accustomed to, even if he wasn't a member. He moved back home.

A few months later in the fall, Jason and eight other guys were playing ball in the park. Afterward, they went to a bakery in Brooklyn's Chinatown. A few of the guys had already gotten their food and were outside while Jason was still waiting inside. A commotion caught his attention, and he walked out to see what was happening. A man on a bicycle had ridden up and was talking to the guys Jason was with. The conversation turned into an argument, which then turned into an assault on the guy on the bike. Jason, having no idea what it was about, remained on the sidelines.

When the police arrived, the guys who'd committed the assault fled in a cab. Jason, not having done anything wrong, remained at the scene and cooperated with authorities when they asked for his identification. They then let Jason and the remaining guys go.

A few days later, Jason and his friends returned to the same ballpark. The police arrived and arrested four of them because the guy on the bike had decided to press charges. They were processed through central booking at the Sixty-First Precinct, where their mug shots and fingerprints were taken.

When Jason later appeared in court on that charge, the complaint was dismissed since it was his first arrest. Unfortunately, when he was leaving, cops from the Sixty-First Precinct arrested him on robbery charges related to the incident months earlier when Jason had been in the car, oblivious to the Fuk Ching members' intention to rob the kid they "recognized," and was totally innocent. The victim in that case had pointed out Jason as one of the perpetrators when he saw his mugshot. Jason had to go through the whole booking process again. In central booking, some guys in his holding cell wanted to take his sneakers, but he told them they'd have to fight him for them, having learned our ways in the streets. He held his ground.

He told me later that he'd sat fuming in that cell thinking about how he'd ended up there, with two arrests in a few months' time just for hanging around gang members. He hadn't even done anything wrong!

Jason's attorney advised him to take the plea bargain the district attorney was offering: five years probation with a sealed no-public record case as a youthful offender. If he went to trial, he could serve prison time, so he took the plea deal. It cost $40,000 to sort this out.

After that day in the cell, he left the gang life and never looked back. Despite my efforts to protect him, he'd had to learn that lesson for himself.

Diamond got into trouble once again due to his unwavering belief in standing up for underdogs. Next to Collectibles was a print shop run by Julia, a middle-aged Trinidadian woman who handled our complex printing needs. We'd become so close to Julia that we considered her an aunt. Diamond and I held her in high regard due to her kindness and excellent service.

One day, she arrived at work with a badly bruised face. Diamond asked her what had happened, and she confided to us that her husband had beaten her.

"Do you want me to take care of it for you?" Diamond asked.

The question must have struck Julia, knowing Diamond and what he was capable of. No further words or explanations were needed. Julia must have understood that her husband's fate hung in the balance when she nodded.

"What does he do for work?" Diamond asked.

"He works for a moving company."

"Give me his phone number."

Julia complied.

Posing as a client, Diamond lured her husband to an address. As the husband's box truck pulled in, Diamond swiftly moved to the vehicle, grabbing the side mirror for leverage. He fired nine rapid shots through the open window, all hitting their mark, then retreated, leaving the truck to swerve out of control and crash.

Eager to learn the outcome, Diamond contacted his sister, who lived across the street from the scene. She reported that EMTs were attending to a bloodied man who was now standing on the pavement. To Diamond's surprise, Julia's husband had survived the ordeal—and could now identify him.

Determined to bring Diamond to justice, the husband filed a police report and persistently pushed for his arrest. But the investigation stalled when the police claimed they couldn't find Diamond.

We heard from Julia that her husband was incensed. "What? He's always at Diamond Billiards. Hell, the place has his name on it! Just arrest him!"

Our friends in one of the precincts helped by deliberately slowing down the investigation. They conducted a lackluster search for my Guyanese friend and even tipped us off whenever the victim demanded Diamond's arrest. I advised Diamond to stay out of sight; I'd hire an attorney. He avoided the pool hall and spent more time at his gambling spot on Nostrand Avenue, but that's where the law finally caught up to him.

Diamond spotted a cluster of unmarked cars lurking outside and ordered a swift pack-up, anticipating a raid. But when he emerged from the building, they closed in.

It wasn't a raid. A US Marshal was there with a warrant in hand. Diamond was cuffed for violating parole. He ended up serving eighteen months in prison, then got transferred to

Immigration. During a deportation hearing at the federal immigration courthouse on Varick Street in New York City, several agencies from Florida, Virginia, North Carolina, and Atlanta sought to charge him for prior crimes. They revealed a joint investigation on Diamond, listing all his aliases and accusing him of participating in a criminal enterprise alongside his family. The court ordered Diamond's deportation, sealing his fate. He was deported in 1998.

He called me from Guyana, and we discussed plans for him to reenter the United States. The route would take him first to Venezuela, and from there, he'd head to Mexico. I told him I'd cover the costs noting that he'd need to liaise with Mexican smugglers for the journey across the US border.

"You're going to be the only Black guy stuffed in the back of a truck with a bunch of Mexicans making your way to the border," I said, knowing that would be out of his comfort zone. "That's on top of all the other risks. Are you ready for that?"

"Eh . . . maybe I don't want to come back that bad."

"On top of that, you have all those old cases hanging over your head."

Months later, he got a woman pregnant and decided to stay.

In hindsight, the pool hall was a microcosm of my directionless life. I was a billiard ball, ricocheting off circumstances in the hopes of finding success through sheer luck and determination. But as the haze from weed and cigarettes dissipated, as our glasses emptied, and the jukebox finished its last song, I was acutely aware of the emptiness within the narrow world I'd constructed. By the end of 1994, all the close calls were taking their toll on me.

I needed to make a change.

CHAPTER TEN

THAT COP ATTITUDE?

The feeling of being constantly monitored and the numerous times I'd been in cars that were pulled over by the police made me think they were building a case against me. Now I was simultaneously ducking the police and on constant alert for troublemaking thugs and gangsters who came into my pool hall—at least the ones I didn't know and trust. And Chicken Lips had recently shown me that I couldn't even completely trust some of my own people.

While much of my life remained the same—danger, stress, and skirting the law—the gang life and the Chinatown community were changing. The eventual demise of Chinatown gangs loomed due to the changing social, political, and commercial environment, along with the hard-line enforcement of the Racketeer Influenced and Corrupt Organizations Act, also known as RICO.

Its aim was to dismantle criminal organizations that engaged in activities such as money laundering, bribery, and other illicit actions by pursuing both the high-ranking individuals and the lower-level participants. Getting prosecuted under RICO results in prison time and forfeiture of ill-gotten gains. We had become a menace that society would no longer tolerate. The New York authorities had to end gang violence, so they wielded the full force of the RICO Act against the Italian Mafia and Chinatown street gangs. The fact that BTK gang members had bombed a police cruiser and that an innocent tourist had been caught in the cross fire added additional fuel to their crusade.

Beyond the arrests we'd seen in Fuk Ching, the Tung On and Ghost Shadows suffered similar significant setbacks. In 1994, federal racketeering charges were brought against thirty-three suspected Flying Dragons members. According to the US attorney for the Southern District of New York, Mary Jo White, "With today's indictment of the Flying Dragons, the last of the major Chinatown gangs has been prosecuted and dismantled."[2]

That indictment was indeed the death knell for gangs as I knew them.

The Asian gangs' own actions contributed to their downfall, and their strengths became their weaknesses. These gangs centered around their leaders. Most of the gangs mentioned in this book were led by men who cultivated a cultlike following. They commanded respect, fear, and blind obedience from their followers.

Thus, it demoralized gang members to witness their leaders cooperating with the courts in exchange for reduced penalties or shorter prison terms, especially since Asian gangs placed great

---

2. George James, "33 Suspected Chinatown Gang Members Are Indicted," *The New York Times*, November 22, 1994, https://www.nytimes.com/1994/11/22/nyregion/33-suspected-chinatown-gang-members-are-indicted.html.

emphasis on sacred oaths and vows of loyalty to their groups and leaders. A carefully crafted illusion of invincibility and strength crumbled. Some leaders saved themselves at the expense of their members, leaving *them* to face the consequences of their crimes.

The evolution of crime also rendered traditional gangs obsolete. Territory-based gangs were no longer relevant as turf took on less significance in committing crimes. Technology and more sophisticated criminal methods took over conventional crime rackets.

Just as I felt as though I stood atop a castle looking out at the smoking ruins of a once-thriving empire, a letter arrived from the Candidate Assessment Division inviting me into the police academy. The final lines weighed heavily on me: Rejecting this offer would require me to retest and endure several years for another chance.

It was now or never, a decision with consequences too grave to ignore. I weighed the odds, examined the risks, and faced the truth. Like the revelation I'd had when hearing about Officer Steven McDonald's remarkable forgiveness, I stood on the precipice of accountability, no longer blaming the environment that had molded me.

As I sat in my pool hall office, my deep contemplation muffled the sounds of conversation and laughter and the crack of the balls. I thought about the tragedies that had befallen my comrades: Danny Boy, Little Chicken, feisty Shorty, and my Ghost Shadow friend Kenny Wong, sentenced to long terms in prison; Carrot Head's multiple brushes with death; Cambodian Peter locked up in Rikers; Richard Chan's murder; Dog left paralyzed for life; and Diamond in exile. My group of stand-up guys was gone. I saw the lonely, desolate path ahead, should I continue walking it.

Becoming an NYPD officer meant severing all ties with

my underworld past, and I was ready. But how exactly would I transition from a life of crime to wearing an NYPD uniform?

Throughout the intervening years, Steven McDonald had become an ambassador of goodwill for the NYPD, traveling the world with his message of hope and redemption despite being confined to a wheelchair and relying on a respirator to breathe.

All I'd known in Fuk Ching was violence and revenge, with money as the goal for a fulfilled life. Officer McDonald had changed the way I looked at other human beings and how I looked at myself. I was determined to do a complete one-eighty. The NYPD would supply me with the adrenaline-driven lifestyle I craved while keeping me on the right side of the law, where I could be a help to society instead of a threat. I understood that my decision came with the commitment to survive on my salary by being an honest cop.

I responded to the letter, confirming my entry to the police academy. Little did I know, this decision would force me through a harrowing test before I even set foot inside the NYPD's hallowed halls.

My journey started at the Candidate Assessment Division, a place that demanded every ounce of information about me: birth certificate, social security statements, tax returns, assets, liabilities, medical records, and school transcripts—each document a piece of the puzzle of my character and reputation.

All applicants were assigned an investigator tasked with an in-depth investigation into the applicant's past and present, as well as their family and friends. Who the heck could I put down as character references? Carrot Head? Diamond? A few Mafia types from Avenue U? Yeah, right. I had no one to vouch for me other than gangsters. In desperation, I listed a woman who owned a laundromat near my mom's house.

The office would probe my business dealings, associations, and even the shops I frequented. Investigators would interview my neighbors, delving into the minutiae of my daily existence. I was happy for them to talk to my neighbors. If my parents didn't know what I was up to, they sure wouldn't. Since I'd always been the friendly neighbor who greeted those around him, I hoped my benign persona would shield me from suspicion.

The drug test was an immediate concern. I had recently smoked weed. In a panic, I sought out a Chinese doctor, who gave me a concoction to ingest that would cleanse my body of any incriminating residue for the urine test, and hoped for the best.

Most ominously, investigators could venture into my pool hall or Collectibles branches, all of which might reveal the clandestine life that thrived beneath the surface. If they observed my association with known felons, the consequences would be disastrous on both sides. My gangmates might choose silence if approached by an investigator, but what would they do upon learning my secret?

My journey toward the light hung by a thread.

I participated in intense physical tests, including running for a mile and a half. Since I didn't like running, I dreaded that part. But during the test, an Asian officer named Trish Ormsby offered me words of motivation as I neared her on the track, which helped push me to the finish. I came in last among the runners but fared better than some candidates who couldn't finish at all.

A battery of psychological tests was the final crucible. After a grueling written test covering how I would handle various scenarios, as well as questions reflecting my beliefs and morals, I had to answer them again orally. This was the toughest part of the process, the one which most candidates failed.

When all was said and done, I awaited the verdict.

In 1995, the department finally called me in to reveal the result of my application for the city police. I held my breath as I sat down to await their answer. A civilian police aide and a sergeant informed me that incomplete papers had led to my rejection. I wouldn't be joining the class that began the next day. If I still wanted to proceed, I'd need to retake the entrance exam.

The news hit me hard, but I accepted it. I stood, shook hands with the civilian and the sergeant, and thanked them for the experience. I expressed my willingness to retake the test and left.

That night, my investigator called and instructed me to report to Brooklyn College at a designated time. I smiled as everything became clear. The last interview was probably a test to see how I'd react to rejection and disappointment, and I'd passed. Why else would they declare that they weren't hiring me, only to turn around and announce that I would be sworn in the next day?

As it turned out, my investigator contacted my references but didn't visit the businesses I owned. If they had, things might have turned out very differently. Fortunately, I was accepted and would enter the police academy as a probationary police officer.

My investigator informed me that I could not own or operate any business. I had to give up everything. Of course, I knew that severing ties to my criminal activities was necessary. So, during my academy training, I disposed of the last remnants of my past, using the excuse that I was beginning to feel law enforcement heat. I closed the pool hall and auctioned off my nineteen Brunswick tables for pennies on the dollar. I sold my remaining Collectibles stores and walked away from my past.

I was sworn in as an NYPD police recruit on June 30, 1995, at the Brooklyn College auditorium, along with approximately two thousand other new recruits. At precisely midnight, I raised my hand to take the oath and stepped into my future.

Our gray uniforms designated us as recruits. My training occurred at the old New York police academy on East Twentieth Street in Manhattan. Transforming civilians into highly qualified law enforcement officers was no small task. For this transformation, we had to endure rigorous training and education. We needed to be mentally, psychologically, and physically prepared to combat crime in New York.

At the academy, recruits received instruction in police strategy, which covered legal knowledge and procedures. We learned constitutional law, city ordinances, and local regulations. The curriculum included handling accidents, conducting incident investigations, managing traffic, and operating radios. We received specialized training for driving cruisers, two- and three-wheel scooters, and even vans. Our classes emphasized proper techniques and strategies for apprehending suspects and criminals, as improper apprehension and arrest procedures could result in lawsuits and legal issues for the department—and criminals getting away.

The training program included modules on nonlethal tools such as batons and Mace. I learned the fundamentals of martial arts and self-defense, equipping me to protect myself and engage with suspects in situations where I didn't have to resort to firearms. I couldn't help but think of Carrot Head during my self-defense training and wonder if it would be practical in a real-life situation.

I also acquired skills in aiming, shooting, reloading, disassembling, and cleaning firearms. I thought I knew a lot about guns but now realized why gang members usually don't win in gun battles with the police. We didn't clean our guns or know how to clear a jam. Guns got dusty without regular cleaning.

I learned precision aim instead of the haphazard shooting we had done.

As we were learning to be first responders to crime scenes, our training encompassed emergency procedures, providing first aid, and caring for victims while awaiting medical assistance. It felt like I was back in college as I delved into other subjects including civil rights issues, hate crimes, criminal psychology, negotiation, and de-escalation techniques—also known as verbal judo.

We were sent to the morgue to desensitize us to the sight of the deceased. I didn't need this particular lesson, having been exposed to my share of violence. Seeing death was oddly comforting to me, and I actually looked forward to the morgue visit. Back in my days of being bullied, I'd escaped by watching the *Faces of Death* series.

I vividly remember the moment when the instructor led us into the morgue, along with the overwhelming scent of death. It clung to our clothes and skin long after we left. Inside the morgue, I saw a physically fit African American male on a slab, conspicuously missing his head, hands, and feet, all cut off with precision. The instructor informed us that he was a murder victim dismembered to obscure his identity. Additionally, I saw a middle-aged Latino man with a gaping chest cavity due to an autopsy. It struck me that this strong man hadn't anticipated meeting his demise that morning.

Incidentally, the morgue visits were discontinued shortly after my class graduated, proving too distressing for many recruits and leading some to quit or experience PTSD. It became evident that this line of work was not suited for everyone, and choosing a different career path might be more appropriate for those who couldn't handle the grim and sometimes gruesome realities that often accompany it.

Adapting to a paramilitary lifestyle took time. I wasn't fond of the daily runs and dreaded laps around the gym. Our batch of recruits consisted of twenty-five people from diverse backgrounds. One classmate had a postgraduate degree, another had experience as a former corrections officer, and another was a retired traffic agent. I was the sole Chinese individual in that class and celebrated my twenty-sixth birthday in the police academy.

The facility had around ten showerheads for a few hundred of us. After our gym sessions, we stood in line, waiting for our two-minute shower. Then we had to change into our uniforms and promptly return to class. While I opted to shower after the gym, many recruits skipped showers and continued wearing their uniforms despite their sweat and odor. It was difficult to blame them for avoiding the bathroom as it was filthy and moldy. The locker rooms were so disgusting and foul-smelling that many recruits couldn't bear to stay for long. Having been through worse, I forged on.

I waited a month after being sworn in before telling Lian that I was now a cop. We went to an empty vestibule near her salon, and I gave her the news. She was unhappy about my new career choice, but for entirely different reasons than Eileen had been. Lian and I weren't as serious, and I was also dating other girls. Admittedly I'd kept up my walls with her after being hurt by the implosion of my relationship with Eileen.

Lian was street savvy, and she'd seen a lot, including cops harassing her friends on the street, abusing their authority.

"Why did you do this?" she asked.

"I want a fresh start."

She looked at me with resentment. "I hate cops. Especially their cop attitude. Eventually you're going to get that cop attitude."

I understood her concern. "I promise I won't get the attitude with you."

She wasn't convinced, and she certainly wasn't happy about my change of vocation, but I liked her response better than Eileen's. I appreciated that Lian hadn't given me an ultimatum. Even so, I wasn't surprised when, in the coming weeks, we drifted apart.

Just when I thought my newfound life was going off without a hitch, in December of 1995, I received a beeper message from my mom. Unexpectedly, the last trace of my past threatened to cast a shadow over my new career and possibly put me in prison. Two detectives from the Sixty-Eighth Precinct wanted to question me.

CHAPTER ELEVEN

FORT SURRENDER

Keith, who had bought one of my Collectibles stores, was dead. And it appeared that Detective Donahue suspected me as the cause. I explained that I'd sold Keith the business. He had been making payments, but he still owed me a significant balance.

As I sat in the interrogation room, Donahue's voice grew louder as he continued pressing for information. I could tell he was experienced as he tried to trip me up, asking me the same question several different ways.

After the two detectives couldn't finesse a confession from me, Donahue resorted to a full-on accusation, even pounding on the table in front of me. "He owed you twenty thousand dollars. You have twenty thousand reasons to kill him!"

"Why would I kill a guy who owed me money? That wouldn't make business sense."

Then I recalled a conversation from a few months back when Keith had asked, "Mike, what do you think the best way to die is?" My friend had casually slipped the eerie question into a lighthearted conversation, and I'd entertained it since I was interested in macabre topics.

At the time, I'd thought it was just idle talk, but now, I wondered and suggested, "Maybe Keith committed suicide."

Donahue pounded the table again. "In all my years as a detective, I've never heard of a nineteen-year-old kid committing suicide! Middle-aged guys, yes, but not a nineteen-year-old!"

The detective was so skilled that, for a moment, he made me doubt a nineteen-year-old *could* die by suicide. But of course, someone of any age can when they are in a desperate situation. Keith had become such a heavy sports bettor at the rackets the wise guys ran on Avenue U that he'd incurred a large debt with them. Could the Italians have gotten to him?

As the detectives came at me with more questions, I realized there was something these two cops didn't know about me.

"Look," I told them. "I sold Keith the Collectibles shop because my investigator said I couldn't have a business under my name while I'm in the police academy. I am an NYPD recruit, and actually, I came straight here from my classes to see you."

I pulled my NYPD ID from my wallet, and now they couldn't help but notice my standard department-issued dark-blue slacks with black stripes down the sides. Confusion flashed across their faces during the silence that ensued.

Donahue exchanged glances with his partner, then said in a calmer tone, "You may want to speak to a union delegate and a lawyer."

In the veteran detective's eyes, I had gone from being a suspect to a fellow cop. His tone and demeanor shifted, and it suddenly felt like he was looking out for me. He politely asked me to wait while he spoke with his supervisor, then returned moments later.

"I have no further questions," he said. "You are free to go. I will contact you when we need you to come back."

The detectives solved Keith's case the next day.

He *had* died by suicide.

To delay their discovery at his house, Keith had left suicide notes in clever places: inside the fridge, behind the garbage can, among less-used items, and even in the pocket of a friend's shirt. He mailed notes to a few friends. Unable to pay his debts, my friend had resorted to jumping into the bay.

I identified Keith's body at the morgue and sadly noticed tear residue by his right eye. It seemed he had been crying while lying on the coroner's cold metal bed: a sad ending to a young life.

Before graduation, recruits could choose their preferences for precinct assignments, though nothing was guaranteed. I had no idea which areas the precincts covered, so I selected the Seventy-Second, Sixty-Sixth, and Sixtieth Precincts because they were close to my home. After I graduated, I received my assignment: the Sixty-Sixth Precinct.

When they learned where I was assigned, the other recruits chuckled, as that station was humorously known as "Fort Surrender." Who'd want to work in a precinct with such an ominous nickname?

Giving precincts nicknames had become an unofficial tradition among NYPD officers, often using monikers tied to significant events. Other precincts that had earned their "fort names" included the 112th Precinct (Fort Bagel), Seventy-Fifth Precinct (Killing Fields), Sixty-Second Precinct (Fort Goomba), Seventy-Seventh Precinct (The Alamo), Forty-First Precinct (Fort Apache), 114th Precinct (Fort Souvlaki), Sixth Precinct (Fort Swish), 109th Precinct (Fort Flushing), and the Police Academy (Fort Pencil).

The Sixty-Sixth Precinct was in the Boro Park area of

Brooklyn, encompassing Midwood and Kensington. The precinct maintained a close relationship with the Jewish community, due to their large population and influence. One of my classmates explained that on December 2, 1978, the community's Jewish residents had become outraged about the murder of a man who had been returning home from a synagogue the previous night. It had taken approximately forty-five minutes for law enforcement to arrive at the crime scene, fueling local perceptions of police neglect, indifference, and inadequate protection. An angry mob of protesting Jews stormed the Sixty-Sixth Precinct and took it over, injuring around sixty police officers and causing chaos within the station.

Outnumbered and trapped, desperate police officers had radioed 10-13s to nearby stations. The mob dispersed when additional officers arrived to reinforce the beleaguered precinct, but from that point onward, the department referred to the precinct as Fort Surrender.

It occurred to me that the nickname perfectly captured my current transition. I had surrendered a previous life for this one, and I now surrendered to the path I was on, wherever it took me.

As I arrived at the Sixty-Sixth Precinct on my first day, the sight of the red brick building did little to inspire confidence. It loomed like two huge shoeboxes, one standing tall and the other on its side, with the American flag defiantly unfurling from a rooftop pole. Ascending the steep staircase to a foreboding blue steel door, flanked by signs bearing the ominous 66 PCT, marked a new beginning for me. But I still had a two-year probationary period to get through, and the city could fire me for literally no stated reason during that time. If they discovered my past, they'd have plenty of reasons.

As I stepped inside the building, the heavy air filled the

room with a somber ambience. Columns of plaques adorned the walls, shining appreciation for the precinct's dedicated service over the years. Names of fallen officers and award recipients hung side by side. The memorial was thought-provoking and inspiring. It felt sacred.

To the right, an elevated police desk created an illusion of towering authority, casting anyone behind it as an undisputed enforcer. A doorway that looked like an emergency exit separated the lobby from the office. I stepped inside and encountered cramped quarters and disorderly desks, a stark departure from what I'd expected in a precinct. Small cubicles divided the space, revealing a jumble of aging desks, steel cabinets, telephones, typewriters, and piles of office supplies. All this, and everything else I still had to figure out, overwhelmed me.

I realized I was stepping into a world that, although on the opposite side of the law, had many similarities to my gang life. In fact, I'd heard that the NYPD was the biggest gang in New York. I took some comfort in that. There was a hierarchy, a clear chain of command that I had to follow. There were stated rules, though I was sure there were unspoken ones as well. This was also a brotherhood where loyalty was most important. It took courage to face the unknown every day.

In my former life, I'd been unbound, free to roam, following street rules that, in a way, felt less restrictive —though they actually were not. Now I was stepping into a realm where I'd have to report to the office, be bossed around, drown in paperwork, and don a uniform that initially felt like a shackle.

Despite these negatives, I felt a glimmer of excitement. This new world promised me entirely new experiences. Every day, even every radio run, would be something different. I would be doing good. It felt both strange and satisfying to embark on this uncharted path. Not everyone was granted such a rare opportunity to tread the dark path of the underworld and end up basking in the light of law enforcement.

I approached Desk Sergeant Freeman to report in. He was engrossed in a pile of paperwork on his desk. I knew better than to disturb him, so I waited for him to acknowledge me.

At last, the beleaguered sergeant looked up. He'd obviously had no idea I was standing there and just took me in for a few seconds. "You look like you just graduated from junior high school!"

His comment took me by surprise. At twenty-five, I didn't think I looked like a teenager, but I merely gave him a look that conveyed, *I do?*

I knew I'd have to work hard and make sacrifices to earn the privilege of being one of New York's finest. I had barely settled into the precinct when I spotted the three cops who'd pulled me over as I'd driven away from a Vietnamese noodle house in Chinatown back in 1994. How could I forget them? They'd asked me to open my trunk and found an illegal gun stashed inside: a loaded 9mm Smith & Wesson.

My heart seemed to stop beating. I felt awkward, then vulnerable, knowing these officers would be aware of my past if they recognized me. But as we crossed paths in the precinct they gave me no sign of recognition, and I relaxed a little. Still, the question lingered about whether that incident might come back to them in the future.

Something else hit me: If those cops were here, that meant this precinct covered my old neighborhood. I'd be on the streets among old friends and enemies. How would they react when they saw me? Would they out me to my new police comrades by speaking to me in a familiar, perhaps angry and betrayed way? I was concerned about those possibilities but filed them away in my *worry about it when it happens* mental folder.

I was elated to trade my gray training shirt in for the real thing. "Blue" is slang for NYPD cops or police officers in general since cops wear recognizable blue police uniforms. In the 1970s, the NYPD switched from dark-blue to light-blue uniforms to appear less authoritative and friendlier. However, they later reverted to the traditional dark-blue uniform, which they've retained since.

The NYPD didn't randomly choose blue: Dark-colored uniforms allow police officers to blend in at night and stealthily approach suspects. A University of Georgia study revealed that blue "subconsciously evokes feelings of comfort and security in most people," making it a suitable choice for those in positions of authority.[3]

I came to understand how uniforms can influence perception. Even Asian store owners I interacted with daily during my police foot patrols in Chinatown failed to recognize me during my off-duty hours when I dressed in civilian clothes.

During my time at the academy, I lived with *Po Po*. I recognized a security guard at the nearby mall as a former member of Tung On. I knew Big Head's reputation as a diplomat, and how he'd been shelved by the younger generation of Tung On. *Being shelved* was a term used by the Italian Mafia, meaning that he'd been kicked out and, though he would be accorded respect, he could no longer be involved in any gang or illegal activities. Big Head had no choice but to go straight. He'd lost power by not being as violent as the new generation; plus, he'd been laying low in Hong Kong for two years. We struck up a friendship.

During a day off, Big Head and I were strolling down East Broadway. With a hoodie tied around my waist to conceal my

---

3. Dan Mendelson, "Uniform Color Theory," *Security Management*, September 1, 2017, https://www.asisonline.org/security-management-magazine/articles/2017/09/uniform-color-theory.

firearm, I wore a tank top—exposing the tattoo on my upper arm. A Chinese American police officer from the Fifth Precinct named David Chee and his partner confronted me and were about to pat me down.

"Hey, why are you searching me?" I asked him. "You know I'm a cop."

For a moment, Chee appeared puzzled. As recognition lit his face, a sigh escaped his lips. "Shit." He'd grown accustomed to seeing me in my police uniform, but in street clothes, I resembled an active gang member.

Big Head offered to let me live with him since he was closer to my work, and I took him up on it. But only days in, shots rang out, shattering a window and lodging bullets in his living room wall. I decided to move out.

Becoming a police officer in New York during the mid-1990s was challenging for a rookie cop. Although the crime rate had substantially decreased, we remained overwhelmed in our effort to maintain law and order in the streets. The "broken window" policy compelled us to spend a lot of time targeting low-level crimes, even down to someone urinating in the park or a couple having sex in their car.

Between 1990 and 1999, thirty-six NYPD officers lost their lives in the line of duty.[4] Working in the force carried inherent hazards and risks.

I always reminded myself that I was a public servant to keep myself on track to do the right thing. Aware of my personal responsibility in the fight against crime, I wondered if my prior life as a gang member made me an even more effective cop.

---

4. New York City Police Department, "Fallen Heroes," accessed January 6, 2025, https://www.nyc.gov/site/nypd/about/memorials/fallen-heroes.page.

Would my intimate knowledge of the criminal underworld prove advantageous? It did give me more compassion and respect for the criminals I dealt with. Thinking of my gangmates, and what Steven McDonald had said, I wondered what circumstances drove them to this life. In fact, years later, an armed robber who shot his victim, once released from prison, thanked me for treating him with respect and told me he'd change his life around. Whenever I dealt with victims, I told myself, *What if this was someone you loved? Wouldn't you want them to be treated kindly?*

What definitely helped was how my years amid the dangers lurking in the city's streets had honed my sixth sense for sizing up situations and people.

The precinct assigned me to various high-crime foot patrol posts as the need arose. Out on the streets, I felt a sense of belonging and familiarity. This was the same vicinity where my mom had been attacked when I was four and where my dad had worked in a laundromat when he was seven. I only became aware of this spatial relevance after working at the Sixty-Sixth Precinct. The streets brought me both mundane and eventful moments, and I learned to embrace this unpredictable, unregulated life, especially at night.

Between foot patrol duties, I stood guard over deceased individuals upon arrival (DOAs) or hospitalized prisoners without fuss or complaint. I could eat my lunch beside a dead body, something other officers considered distasteful. For me, it was just a piece of flesh and had no effect on me.

But escorting prisoners from the precinct to central booking, which processed offenders from all corners of Brooklyn, filled me with unease. Anyone greeting me or identifying me as a former gang member could lead to investigations, expulsion from the NYPD, media exposure, and potential charges for past crimes that had not yet exceeded the statutes of limitation. I imagined alarming headlines like, *Ex–Chinatown Gangster Turned NYPD Officer Arrested*.

Each time I entered the central booking facility, my heart raced, and once, the dreadful scenario I had feared nearly unfolded during one of my transport duties. Having come from the Sixty-Sixth Precinct, I escorted a detainee into one of the holding cells, each housing ten to twenty prisoners awaiting hearings before a judge.

As I opened the door for my detainee, I noticed a Black prisoner staring at me, puzzled. It didn't take me long to recognize him as someone who'd bought one of my illegal guns through Diamond. I closed the door and made my way out without waiting to see his reaction. That close call often replayed in my mind, and I became even more anxious each subsequent time I walked in Central Brooklyn.

Despite my nervousness, I maintained my calm facade, a double-edged trait both beneficial and disadvantageous. Keeping my emotions and composure under intense control also meant bottling up my feelings. My enemies, and sometimes even my friends, could not discern my feelings or thoughts, as I have always been a person who speaks sparingly.

Cops hate to wear their hat and take it off whenever they can. Other officers must have found it odd that I consistently wore my police hat inside central booking. Little did they know, this was my way of making myself less recognizable to individuals I had dealt with in my past.

Most detectives I knew back then relished what was commonly known as the "perp walk"—escorting apprehended suspects in handcuffs in front of television cameras and news reporters. It gave them a sense of accomplishment to catch bad guys while basking in the glow of flashing bulbs and the attention of scoop-hungry journalists. Some officers who frequently appeared on television during these perp walks received promotions.

An exception to this trend, I shied away from the media, primarily because I stood out among my fellow NYPD officers due to my Chinese features.

Many people underestimate the physical strain that police officers endure while on their feet. They may assume that standing in the street "doing nothing" is an easy task. However, even seemingly idle moments require effort. Try standing for just one hour under the scorching sun, in the pouring rain, or in the freezing cold, and you'll quickly realize that "doing nothing" under such conditions for eight to ten hours is far from easy. Then add in our uniform and the extra fifteen pounds of weight due to our body armor, guns, munitions, radios, and various police gear hanging from our bodies. These additional accessories strained our knees and sapped our strength by the end of an eight-to-fifteen-hour shift.

When individuals approach police officers on the street, they only witness a brief snapshot of what we experience, often unaware of the toll that extended periods of immobility takes on our bodies day in and day out. Most police officers don't get to spend holidays with their families, who see them less in general because of the long shifts. In the academy, an instructor told us that the average life span of an NYPD cop is seven years after retirement, and the divorce rate is around 75 percent. I don't know if these numbers are accurate or trustworthy, but they sound right in my experience.

Once, during my early days as a rookie, I came close to fainting while patrolling the scorching Coney Island boardwalk on one of the hottest days of that year. After that, I made sure to stay properly hydrated. This incident reminded me of my time at the academy when I was assigned to a stationary foot post in Times Square in our gray recruit uniform to oversee the traditional New Year's Eve celebration.

Icy December weather tormented me for sixteen hours. I only had a thermal shirt under my uniform. It reached the point where I could no longer twitch my face or move my lips. I thought about resigning in that moment. *Is this what being a cop is like?*

But reality came crashing down when I remembered that Keith was dead and I'd sold my businesses—burning bridges to my past. After my Collectibles business reverted to me, I sold all the merchandise and gave Henry, the guy who leased the other half of the space, the entire lease. I had committed to the straight path and would do my best to keep to it.

I survived that night in Times Square by summoning what remained of my inner strength and willpower. I also learned a lesson and dressed accordingly in the future. What they'd taught us in the academy crystallized for me then: *A good cop never gets cold, hungry, or wet.*

Those words would ring in my ears for the next twenty-six years.

In those early days, donning the iconic blue NYPD uniform felt like an otherworldly ritual. Each morning, as I confronted my reflection in the mirror, I experienced a dramatic transformation. I felt a strange sense of gratitude, having made the perilous journey from the shadows of criminality to the light of lawfulness.

As I looked at myself, pieces of my past formed a mosaic of my present self: Police Officer Moy. The clean lines of my crisp blue uniform held a mystique, a world away from the dark garb that had once struck terror into the hearts of the city's denizens. The dragon tattoo etched on my skin had lost its ferocity; it was now a mere whisper of my past and the person I once was.

Did I look the part in the NYPD uniform? To my eyes, I did. In the honeymoon phase of my new career, I strode the streets with newfound purpose and an air of confidence.

(As I wrote this, a humorous memory resurfaced from when *Ah Gung* visited *Po Po* in her East Broadway apartment, where my official NYPD portrait hung on the wall. He confessed to his sister that for many years, he had thought the portrait was just me in a Halloween costume. He never knew or believed I was a police officer until he read about me in the newspapers.)

While I still occasionally had doubts about my choices, I overcame them. The past may have shaped me, but the future was mine to make as I wanted. And what I wanted was to help make the world a little bit better for everyone.

CHAPTER TWELVE

OH WOW, THERE'S A CHINESE COP

During my early years in the NYPD, there were only around five hundred Asians in the entire force in New York, and only a fraction could speak Cantonese or Mandarin. People often gave me a confused look during my foot patrols when they saw me in my uniform, their usual reaction being, "Oh wow, there's a Chinese cop."

In 1996, only three other cops of Asian descent worked in the Sixty-Sixth Precinct. Police Officer Danny Leung retired in 2016 and passed away from natural causes one year later. Police Officer Robert Sung was eventually promoted to lieutenant and assigned to the One-Hundred-Ninth Precinct, where he became entangled in a corruption scandal.

My training sergeant, Philip Lam, later rose to captain. He was a by-the-book guy whose supervisory style worked for me. Somehow he sensed, perhaps from my mannerisms or glimpsing a bit of my tattoo, that I came from the same Chinatown streets he'd come from. He drilled advice into me like "Do everything by the books" and "Keep your hands out of the cookie jar," insinuating that I should never give in to corruption. While I had already committed to never doing so, I appreciated how he ensured that I stayed on track and looked out for me. He inspired me by his example. He retired around the same time as me, and we've remained close friends.

I met many people from various races, opening my mind and expanding my world. Still, the concept of diversity was not as well defined then as it is now, and I observed that even some people in law enforcement found it hard to accept non-whites in the force. They displayed their disdain in subtle but significant ways. Fortunately, there are more good cops than bad ones, and the less-than-ideal officers do not represent the majority.

After spending a few months in the Sixty-Sixth Precinct, my supervisors assigned me to a four- to five-month Prospect Park detail. Rookies without any connections typically end up at the bottom of the hierarchy. As a police officer under supervisors, my new reality was far different from my former life. I had to mentally shift from being the one who moved the pieces to being the pawn who was moved around.

Prospect Park in Brooklyn covers approximately 526 acres. This vast urban park is known for its expansive green spaces, recreational facilities, and natural beauty. For residents and visitors alike, it offers a peaceful escape from the city with walking paths, a lake, playgrounds, and sports fields.

This dull foot post gave me a lot of time alone with my thoughts. I felt like a cork dropped into an ocean, bobbing along at the whim of the current. I watched squirrels come out and play in the trees and the wide span of fields. Though boredom sometimes tortured me, I encountered several robberies and one homicide; no paradise was ever safe from criminals.

On a more humorous note, I also broke up a couple of illicit hanky-panky incidents.

But things were about to get much more exciting—and dangerous. In the middle of the night, a 911 call shattered the monotonous hum of the radio in our squad car. A woman in Chinatown was barricaded in her bathroom. In a distress call to the 911 dispatcher, she whispered her plea for help as two intruders roamed her house. We were among the few units available.

Adrenaline propelled us into action. We tossed our half-eaten sandwiches into the back seat. Our siren sliced through the tranquil air, red-and-blue lights piercing the night. We represented duty and law, a blur of uniformed urgency racing toward danger. To maintain the element of surprise, we extinguished lights and sirens just before our arrival.

As we came to a stop, we saw that another squad car had beat us by a fraction of a second with the same stealthy arrival. Two officers swiftly exited, signaling their intent to enter from the back. We acknowledged them with a curt nod and prepared to cover the front door, our hearts racing.

The front door burst open, and two men with obscured faces rushed out, guns in hand. Gunfire reverberated in the still night, sending us diving for cover. I scrambled beneath the protective bulk of our vehicle, hoping the thin metal shell would be sufficient. The assailants fled into the labyrinth of city streets.

A helicopter chopped through the sky, its spotlight illuminating the fleeing criminals, while the K9 unit sprang into action. As the pursuit commenced, my partner and I stayed behind, securing the scene until the detectives arrived. We looked at each other—a close call. There'd be many more.

This park assignment would be disrupted from time to time by citywide events when the NYPD assigned officers from different precincts as details for certain celebrations. One of these was the celebration of the West Indian parade on Labor Day. Participants adorned themselves with painted faces and exuberant costumes, engaging in wild antics for the street party. The parade kicked off at Grand Army Plaza, proceeding south to Flatbush Avenue near Prospect Park, then heading east toward Empire Boulevard before concluding at Midwood Street.

NYPD officers regarded the J'ouvert Parade as Brooklyn's most perilous event. Rival gangs frequently crossed paths during the celebration. Shootings, stabbings, assaults, and muggings commonly occurred during the festivities. Sometimes revelers indiscriminately fired into a crowd. Drunken people either caused accidents or fell victim to the recklessness of others. Chaos and madness well described the atmosphere, prompting the West Indian American Day Carnival Association and New York City officials to condemn the violence publicly.

Patrolling the parade was a nightmare for New York cops. During the 1990s, the level of violence escalated with each passing year. The city government had not found an effective way to curb the mayhem that occurred during every J'ouvert celebration.

Despite heightened security measures implemented by the NYPD, perpetrators at the festival remained undeterred in their disruptive behavior. I couldn't comprehend why a supposedly joyous and meaningful event seemed to bring out the worst in people.

In 1996, my partner, Officer Tat Mui, and I were stationed along Flatbush Avenue, surrounded by a sea of people. Even as we stood shoulder to shoulder, we could barely hear each other amid the blaring street music. A burst of gunshots erupted in front of us, originating from a man about 150 feet away. People screamed, and the crowd rushed in our direction. I felt a bullet whiz by my left ear, and another ricocheted off a van behind us, bouncing off the heel of my boot.

Officer Mui froze, narrowly avoiding a bullet that passed between his legs. The gunman had fired shots aimed at a rival but missed, and the bullets instead almost claimed our lives. He disappeared into the frenzied crowd. That night, in the locker room, Officer Mui unrolled his pants to show everyone that a bullet had punctured two holes in his trousers. The department issued him a voucher for a free pair of pants.

In another instance, Officer Kelly Beraud and I sat in our patrol car near a high-rise housing development area. As the J'ouvert festivities continued, someone approached us with a severely injured hand, which had swollen to the size of a grapefruit after a bullet pierced the center of his palm. The wound resembled stigmata, a crucifixion wound.

I flagged down a passing ambulance already beset with other revelers needing medical attention. While I gathered information from the injured man, an explosion erupted nearby. Someone had hurled a full soda can at us from the rooftop of the high-rise building, and it had landed and exploded like a grenade just feet from where I stood. It could have fatally injured me or my partner had it hit us. The dangers we faced didn't come only from guns but from objects as seemingly innocuous as a soda can.

Another time, I occupied the driver's seat of a police van, with Officer James Heinrich in the passenger seat. When multiple gunshots rang out, people in the nearby crowd scattered. Heinrich crammed his six-foot-one frame into the leg space of his seat for protection. I dove next to him since the steering wheel obstructed my space. With no true cover, I realized I might not return home from my duties one day. I didn't dwell on that sad thought, though, shifting my focus to the present.

Drawing from my training and all that I'd learned so far on the job, I listened to the noise and screams settling down. With no more gunfire, I gathered that the shooter had fled. No one radioed about any injuries. We sat back up and returned to our surveillance as though nothing had happened. I made a joke about how being a bigger guy was a disadvantage when dodging bullets.

During the many, sometimes tragic, situations encountered by cops, having a sense of humor was essential.

CHAPTER THIRTEEN

CHINATOWN PATROL

A surge in crime incidents in Brooklyn's Chinatown raised urgent concerns within the community. In response, the Brooklyn Chinese Merchant Association (BCMA) articulated their need for a Cantonese-speaking officer to patrol the Chinese community and serve as a liaison between the community and the police department. After searching the database, the department identified me as a qualified officer. Almost two years into my career, this was a lucky break: I'd be assigned a steady foot post with regular hours and days off—a significant shift from ever-changing tours and shifts every week.

Under the Community Patrol Officer Program, my policing would center on addressing issues at the neighborhood level. My duties included patrolling the avenues and handling community security concerns, illegal parking, unlicensed vendors, and issues around public order.

The assignment had both benefits and risks. I'd always felt at home in Chinatown, with access to everything I wanted:

Chinese culture, local food, familiarity with the people, and intimate knowledge of the area. Now I could develop a deeper connection with the neighborhood I patrolled. But it was also home to my former enemies, victims, and past partners in crime, and I was uneasy as I anticipated encounters with both friends and foes from the underworld. I envisioned scenarios and ways to handle potential conflicts. What if a former street associate asked for a favor to secure a racket? Some businesspeople or Tong members in Chinatown might try to pull me into their circle for protection. I relegated these concerns to the back of my mind, ready to deal with situations as they arose.

As I saw the potential for corruption, it also hit me how much power our authority gave us. Some rookies were in their early twenties. That's a lot of power for those whose brains are still developing well into their mid-twenties—particularly the prefrontal cortex, which governs things such as making good decisions. The potential for a misuse of that power was immense.

I resolved to use my power for good, just as I had during my gang days. With my understanding of the criminal mind, I sometimes gave a perp a second chance, letting them go with words of wisdom—or caution.

One time, I entered a bakery that was a known hangout for kids. I saw this kid in the back with a duffel bag who looked kind of odd. Trusting my instincts, I approached him casually and asked what he had in the bag. I didn't have just cause to search him. He actually opened the bag, revealing thousands of cigarettes, which were obviously untaxed, from out of state.

I told him I wasn't going to arrest him this time but if I saw him peddling cigarettes again, I would. I showed him discretion and respect, and he respected me by not coming back into my patrol area.

I was assigned Brooklyn Chinatown's Eighth Avenue, which was in the Sunset Park neighborhood and at that time went from Thirty-Ninth Street to Sixty-First Street. Eighth Avenue had become an alternative settlement for Chinese immigrants looking to avoid the rising cost of rent in Manhattan's Chinatown due to gentrification. An unprecedented number of Chinese shops, restaurants, noodle houses, groceries, dry goods stores, temples, bakeries, and drugstores had sprung up on Eighth. Many of those Chinese businesspeople considered themselves fortunate as eight is a lucky number.

My days patrolling Eighth Avenue might have appeared uneventful, but my foot post filled me with energy. I felt a sense of belonging on those streets, conversing casually with strangers. While I didn't naturally gravitate toward random acts of kindness or assisting passersby, these became integral parts of my duty to serve and protect.

In one incident, a woman with a history of domestic abuse by her boyfriend had broken up with him, and he was threatening to kill her. Getting the call, I recognized the address: a multistory residential building where she lived with her mother and brother. The woman had reported her boyfriend's threats to the police several times in the past.

Under the orders of our commanding officer, our precinct mounted a vigilant watch in front of her residence, watching for the guy. Officers in patrol cars rotated like clockwork in three shifts for a week, but he never showed. Throughout, I worked with Officer George Codd, another young rookie like myself. Codd had police lineage: His grandfather was Michael Codd, who had been NYPD commissioner from 1974 to 1977.

Weighing the ex-boyfriend's persistent absence against the city's stretched resources, my commanding officer finally called off our watch. As soon as our presence lifted, the unhinged guy returned, breaking into his ex-girlfriend's apartment and holding her and her family hostage.

We answered the call to respond, ready for action and fueled by the raw energy of inexperience. We were the first to arrive on the scene, and my heart was pounding as I checked into Central—only to hear platoon commander Lieutenant Belcastro's voice cutting through the static: "Do not enter the building! Form a perimeter and keep a distance from the windows."

We reluctantly obeyed. Lieutenant Belcastro arrived moments later, scanning the scene with a hawk's precision. He pointed at me and Codd and said, "You are the designated shooters."

After a perimeter had been formed and reinforcements and negotiators converged, the media swarmed like blood-scenting vultures. Agonizing hours passed as a tense standoff dragged on with the Hostage Negotiation Team. In a heart-stopping moment, gunfire shattered the silence, and then all quieted down again. The Emergency Service Team surged forward, breaching the perimeter and entering the apartment.

The perpetrator, in a final act of defiance, had killed his girlfriend and her mother, leaving her brother in critical condition. Then he'd turned the gun on himself.

In the aftermath, as the adrenaline faded, the weight of Belcastro's discretion settled on my shoulders. His command to stand down had been a shield against unseen dangers. The perpetrator's violent history and his unpredictability could have turned my haste into a deadly ambush, had we rushed into the building. Lieutenant Belcastro's decision, borne from years of experience, had spared us from walking blindly into a maelstrom of bullets. I'll always be grateful to him.

A chance encounter with my Italian mentor, Uncle Louie, played out like a scene from a movie. I was in my own vehicle on my day off as I waited at the red light near Avenue U in Brooklyn, and his car pulled up beside mine. Our eyes locked, recognition surprising both of us. Uncle Louie had imparted invaluable street-smart advice that I still implement today. We'd also spent many good times together as he mentored me in the car service business.

Seeing him again was bittersweet and somewhat awkward. Old-school guys like him naturally harbor an aversion to cops, and I feared he'd be disappointed in my career choice.

"Hey, how're ya doing?" he called through our open windows.

"I'm good." I owed him the truth; I didn't want him to find out on his own after we'd seen each other. "I'm a cop now."

I was relieved at the smile on his face. "I'm happy fer ya," he said in his Italian accent. And I believed he was, as I know he truly cared about me.

The light turned green. We gave each other a goodbye nod and carried on with our travels. That was the last time I saw him.

A cop must be prepared to fight crime, even off duty. I found myself sometimes chasing perpetrators while dressed like any regular civilian. This was risky: Without the blue uniform, I was indistinguishable from the criminals I pursued. But in the heat of the moment, instinct always trumped caution. Only after the dust settled did the true danger of those situations sink in.

One late night, I was driving along a dark, quiet street in Manhattan's Chinatown, Lian beside me. I needed to make a call and parked near a pay phone. Even off duty, I was always watching my surroundings. I saw two Chinese guys close in on a bigger Chinese man across the street. It looked like they were beating the screaming man. When the man collapsed, I realized he'd been stabbed. The assailants calmly walked away.

I hung up the phone, jumped back in the car with Lian, and drove up beside them, barking in both English and Cantonese, "Police! Don't move!"

They picked up their pace. Seeing that I remained alongside them, they started sprinting. By the time they reached the end of the city block, they were panting and ran in different directions. I hastily parked the car and pursued one of them. I managed to catch him, and a fierce struggle ensued as we wrestled for control of his knife. To disarm him, I yanked his shirt over his head, grabbed his wrist, and wrested the knife from his grip. I tossed it as far as I could, then tightened my grip, forcing him into submission with a headlock.

A police car screeched to a halt nearby, and a white male officer emerged, gun drawn and trained on me from the perilously close distance of three feet.

I shouted, "Don't shoot! I'm a cop!"

The officer wavered, then lowered his firearm, and secured the assailant.

I stood, ready to assist if the guy tried anything. "There's another perp who ran in the opposite direction."

The officer called for backup. Eventually, cops in another precinct found the other attacker hiding in a basement staircase of a building on East Broadway and arrested him.

Lian was still in shock when I returned to her as she waited in the car.

"Did you not hear me yelling at you when you jumped out of the car?" she asked.

"No, why?"

"The car started to move backwards while you ran after the bad guys. You put the car in neutral, not park."

I shook my head in disbelief, realizing the danger I'd put her in.

She went on, "Thank goodness a bystander jumped into the driver's seat as the car was rolling backward and put the car in park."

"Sorry. Instinct just took over. I'm glad you're okay."

She playfully punched my arm. "At least you didn't say you were glad the car was okay."

After my testimony in the grand jury on this case, I ran into the gun-wielding officer in the courthouse.

"Were you going to shoot me if I didn't have my hands up?" I asked.

"Yeah, I would have shot you," he stated.

This possibility seemed inconsequential to him, devoid of any apparent concern. Still, I refrained from placing blame on him, considering the scarcity of Asian-looking cops at that time as well as my civilian attire. Numerous minority cops have gotten shot by friendly fire while taking police action in civilian attire. These incidents made headlines, but that had never entered my mind. This was a reality check.

I hadn't been carrying my gun when I ran after the perpetrators. I acknowledged the foolishness of my actions but harbored no regrets, knowing I had fulfilled my duty. Captain Jin Yee, the executive commander of the Seventh Precinct, was present at the scene and lauded my actions. He commended the quality of my arrest and later inquired whether I would be interested in working under his command. I was flattered and moved by his belief in me but politely declined his offer. I enjoyed my post too much to consider leaving it.

Many unfortunate cases remain vivid in my memory. In one particularly grim incident, a grandmother was pushing a baby carriage between parked vehicles when one of them, a box truck, started backing up. Though she screamed for it to stop, it crushed the baby under its wheels. The infant's remains were scattered over the street, and I took on the grim task of collecting them.

I rescued a child from a burning house, only to witness his life slip away in my arms as I carried him to the ambulance. The image of the lifeless child, his tongue protruding due to smoke inhalation, haunts my memory. Since his family was Cantonese, I had to deliver the tragic news. His father collapsed upon hearing of his child's death, a moment I'll never forget.

Another heart-wrenching incident involved a young girl playing hide-and-seek who accidentally hanged herself with the clothing inside a closet. While I had no qualms about dealing with deceased victims, witnessing harm befalling children affected me deeply.

During my early years as a cop, morale among police officers hit an all-time low. In the first two years of a five-year contract under Mayor Rudy Giuliani, officers' salaries were frozen, and this hit cops who were living paycheck to paycheck particularly hard. This was during a flush time for New York City's coffers, while other local departments still got their raises. Members of the Police Benevolent Association of the City of New York even used the phrase, "Zeroes for heroes."

Given that, most cops did not want to put in any more time than they had to. If their shift ended at four o'clock, they would go into the locker room at three-thirty to allow for the fifteen-minute process of getting out of their uniform. So you can imagine their curiosity when I strolled into the locker room mere minutes before my shift's end when everyone had already changed into their casual clothes, poised to scram the moment the second hand hit the top of the hour. And here I was returning without any extra time to change clothes—time I wouldn't be paid for.

One guy glanced at the clock and chided me with, "What, you like the job so much you lost track of time?"

"Yeah, exactly. I can't believe the city is actually *paying* me to hang out in Chinatown." Telling them this with a straight face and a big smile, I had to squelch my laughter at their genuinely baffled looks.

This happened after every shift when I strolled in close to quitting time.

Another time I shrugged. "I fell asleep while hanging out at a furniture store. That couch was so comfortable!"

The next week I gave them a chagrined smile. "I lost track of time eating at my favorite Chinese restaurant. The owner and I were having such a great conversation. Man, I never laughed so much."

I continued to egg on these glass-half-empty guys. "You know, years ago I was a volunteer auxiliary police officer, right? I actually did the job for free. But it's better now that they're paying me."

They continued gaping at me, and after depositing that lie, I strode to my locker to get ready to go home, all the while trying not to laugh at the constipated looks on their faces. I liked these guys, and, really, I was ribbing them in an attempt to get them to see the light side. It was all in good fun.

It was a common but unproven belief within the police department that the Internal Affairs Bureau (IAB) assigns at least one "field associate" to each command, tasked with monitoring fellow police officers. We heard that rumor during my time at the academy, and most of us grew into our careers aware that a fellow officer could pretend to be a comrade while evaluating our every move, ready to report anything that looked wrong. Because of this, cops took their time to fully trust newcomers.

Officer Zhang was transferred from the Seventieth Precinct to work with me on the Eighth Avenue post. He covered the four p.m. to midnight shift, while I handled the ten a.m. to six p.m. slot, so our shifts overlapped by two hours. On paper he seemed ideal for the job, being bilingual, young, and driven.

In my experience, Zhang displayed a dismissive attitude toward me and seldom engaged in conversation. When we did talk about situations on our post, it was brief and limited. Initially, I found his behavior unusual, as I had done nothing to warrant a cold attitude that bordered on outright contempt.

While he patrolled Chinatown, Zhang stalked Eighth Avenue with a stern military demeanor, always carrying his nightstick. Although serious-looking and uptight, he exhibited a restless and jittery vibe. In my experience observing Zhang, he seemed to adopt a ready-for-a-confrontation approach, keeping his hand over his gun during interactions with civilians. Even the most zealous cops cringed at the way he portrayed himself, recognizing that there was a time and place for employing street policing tactics. His shifty eyes and constant head swiveling created the impression of someone always on red alert. Many people in the community considered him rude and lacking in personality. Still, Zhang maintained his reputation as a formidable enforcer, targeting prostitution houses, gambling dens, street vendors, and thugs with his intense focus. And I continued to receive his curiously hostile attitude.

On top of the lack of raises, our precinct faced a staff shortage, and reassignments had become common. I would be in a police car one day and end up alone on foot patrol in Chinatown the next. This resulted in more officers leaving the force and fewer recruits joining, likely due to widespread demoralization.

I remember seeing graffiti etched on a bathroom door of

central booking during my first year: FUCK THE RAISE; BRING BACK CORRUPTION.

We all had a lot of conversations about the "double zeros from Mayor Giuliani" in the locker room, along with a lot of grumbling. One of the white cops I worked with pointed to his shield. "You know what this stands for to me? White trash."

During this same year, Officer George Codd joined me in a patrol car for the day, a practice when the command was short-staffed and I was called in as an extra body to help. During our patrol, we passed by the office of one of several "dollar van" businesses in Chinatown.

These vans offered transportation for residents, shuttling them from one Chinatown to another at a cost similar to taking the subway. Many Chinese residents preferred the security of riding in these vans with fellow Chinese passengers and liked being able to communicate in their language.

As we parked our police car near the dollar van office, a familiar face appeared at the front passenger window where I was seated: Crazy Wing, an acquaintance from when I operated my gambling house near his territory. Crazy Wing had connections with the Ghost Shadows, and his crew had a history of robbing buses heading to Atlantic City. The expected scenario of encountering a gangster from my past had finally come, and I had an inkling of what was about to transpire.

"Hi, Mike," he said, speaking in Cantonese. "This place is under my watch now."

I understood Crazy Wing's implication, but Codd had no idea what he'd said to me. Then, Crazy Wing produced a rolled wad of cash tied by a rubber band and dropped it onto my lap. I realized I needed to quickly find a way out of the situation.

I glanced over at Codd, whose wide eyes and pale face showed his astonishment. Like me, he was a rookie, and we were both still on probation. Failing to report corruption could result in his dismissal.

I handed the money back to Crazy Wing, telling him in English, "You dropped this. Take it back." My stern expression conveyed a message my partner couldn't perceive. Crazy Wing got it, then glanced at Codd, and took the wad of cash. I turned to my partner, instructing him to drive off.

By "this place," Crazy Wing meant this territory. In the mid-1990s, the dollar van transportation service proved highly profitable. Initially, drivers paid thousands of dollars to secure a route and work for the company. However, drivers realized the significant earnings potential and became willing to pay even more to ensure that they kept their route. Under-the-table payments increased, causing the price to obtain a route from the syndicate to soar to nearly fifty thousand dollars.

Each driver was responsible for transporting fourteen passengers in a van, making a twenty-minute drive to Manhattan's Chinatown, and returning within another twenty minutes with passengers heading back to Brooklyn's Chinatown. Each passenger paid about two dollars for the ride. A driver could net around $500 to $600 at the end of a single twelve-hour shift. Later, operators purchased minibuses to increase profits and efficiency, earning additional revenue per trip with added passengers. The buses also took passengers to out-of-state Chinatowns. Many people, particularly men, worked and lived in other Chinatowns but frequently came home to visit their families.

What helped drivers earn that kind of profit was *not* following the Taxi and Limousine Commission's rules and regulations; they used passenger plates so they only paid regular insurance rates.

Former gangsters or individuals closely associated with them controlled most of this business. By this time, nobody in their right mind would openly declare themselves as belonging to a gang. Thanks to the continued enforcement of the RICO Act, the era of gangs fighting for territory and extorting businesses was long gone, but certain practices of the underworld remained. They transitioned to establishing their own entities wherever they pleased. For instance, a former Flying Dragon member might open a gambling house on Eighth Avenue right across from one owned by a former Ghost Shadow. This was pure capitalism, and for a while their underground economy remained under the government's radar.

Initially, there was little competition in the dollar van business, as most people involved were already part of or associated with the underworld. That changed over time. Ambitious individuals with solid business acumen entered the scene, creating enterprises to compete with the former gang members. Money was there for the taking, and these new entrants wanted their share.

The remaining gang members from my generation learned to navigate the streets without resorting to violence. The Cantonese and Toishanese, who had immigrated to America much earlier, knew how the FBI dealt with crime. Thus, they approached the law with more caution and respect. Being new immigrants, the Fukienese, who had recently started infiltrating the industry and engaged in violent crimes reminiscent of our olden days, did not fully understand the law or the consequences of breaking it.

A distant acquaintance of mine, Tommy Q, had learned the business working as a driver, rising to prominence by employing dirty tricks against competitors. One of the dollar van company owners employed him to harass and intimidate other players. His crew beat up other drivers and sabotaged their operations.

One of these drivers at a legitimate dollar van company approached me for help, but I had yet to learn who was behind these tactics. I told him to make a police report. He did, but nothing happened to his complaints because there was no evidence or witnesses in most of these cases. The complaints piled up and went nowhere.

"What more can I do?" the driver asked me.

"Report it to the FBI."

So, he did. Unknown to me then, the Feds' investigation resulted in the arrest, imprisonment, and deportation of Tommy Q and others.

Word spread to legitimate business owners and savvy businesspeople: Use the Feds to get rid of the Asian underground competition. This driver asked me to go into business with him, but of course I declined. He started from the ground up, doing things the legitimate way, and went on to own the biggest van business in New York.

Times had certainly changed. Years ago, most of these people would have hesitated to make a police report. Business owners who had previously eschewed going to the police were now becoming informants, using law enforcement to eliminate criminal elements and their competition. As word spread, other types of businesses followed suit, including both legal *and* illegal business owners, diminishing the power once held by the gangs.

In a well-documented case, Qian Zheng—who led the violent Zheng Organization—ordered assaults on his competition and those who wouldn't pay extortion money, while also acting as an FBI informant. He used that connection to target competitors of his own illegal business, including prostitution, gambling, and narcotics distribution. Eventually, he was arrested. Upon his release in 2034, he'll be deported to China.

Though I resolved to remain free from corruption, I inadvertently became a pawn to extort money from a house of prostitution. I had become friends with the owner of a restaurant in Chinatown, who often invited me in for delicious lunches. I'd met him while on foot patrol, and we started hanging out during my days off, like any regular buddies would.

One day, about a year after we'd met, he told me of a friend who was planning to open a prostitution house in Chinatown. My friend had a proposal for me: I'd receive money for merely keeping an eye on the establishment and notifying him of any potential police raids. I declined, stating that I couldn't be bought.

Shortly after, I learned this individual had led the prostitution house owner to believe I'd agreed to safeguard his establishment in exchange for a share of the profits. As a result, he regularly collected money from the owner, who believed his business was under my protection. I severed all ties with this so-called friend.

Some might call it a rookie mistake, but it was the last time I made such an error.

From that day forward, I was much more guarded, pushing away most individuals who tried to befriend me. In a way, I was glad this had happened early in my career, as seeing my pitfalls kept me more vigilant and cautious.

While I flourished in my career, my gambling habit worsened. At least I only gambled within my means, using proceeds from the sale of my businesses. I didn't play in illegal gambling dens, but I took regular trips to casinos in Atlantic City. During the dot-com bubble, casinos would fly me out in a private jet, even to international locations. At one point I was in a casino 159 days out of the year.

A common narrative in Eighth Avenue Chinatown was Chinese

people scamming their fellow countrymen. I encountered a complaint from a man victimized by a local syndicate that preyed on Chinese Americans with relatives in far-flung Chinese provinces. Having gathered information about him, including his province of origin and relatives who lived there, the syndicate had one of their people call him and pretend to be one of those relatives. Speaking in their dialect, the perpetrator begged the victim to send money for a medical emergency. The scammer's panicky voice and urgent tone convinced the man to wire the money to the "relative's" trustee via Western Union. Later, the victim discovered it was all a scam.

The people behind this syndicate used various plotlines, depending on the victim's status. Their fabricated stories included a relative being unlawfully detained in China, an emergency hospitalization due to an accident, or being robbed and left with no money.

I held conversations with the victims and their immediate circles to instill awareness and provide remedies for this scam. I advised them that when they received such calls from relatives in China, they must verify their identity by asking detailed questions. I explained that scammers played on their emotions by inducing a sense of urgency and desperation, which scrambled victims' thoughts and made them act on impulse.

Back in my gang days, Carrot Head, my friend I'd brought into Fuk Ching, had introduced me to a woman named Carol Lim, who frequented my gambling den to play mahjong. Back then I couldn't help but wonder how she could afford to gamble with such vast amounts of money. Years later, I bumped into Carol while patrolling Eighth Avenue. After exchanging pleasantries, I discovered that she was the manager of Abacus Bank, and it rekindled my curiosity about her extravagant gambling habits. After that meeting, I sometimes encountered her at casinos in

Atlantic City and observed how she gambled with hundreds of thousands of dollars.

One day, I walked into work, and the desk officer instructed me to proceed to Abacus Bank in Chinatown for crowd control assistance. I arrived to find panicky bank clients forming a chaotic line extending around the block, waiting to withdraw their money. Rumors had spread in Chinatown that the bank manager, Carol Lim, had defrauded clients by skimming safety deposit boxes containing cash, causing distress among the depositors.

According to newspaper reports, Carol had stolen over nine million dollars by accepting money for deposits and embezzling the cash entrusted to her by clients. She'd provided clients with fake paperwork when, in fact, she had not opened accounts for them at all.

She'd also managed to empty numerous safe deposit boxes. Many Chinese individuals stored significant amounts of cash and jewelry in these boxes. Opening them required two keys: one belonging to the customer and the other to the bank. To access the box, you handed your key to a bank employee, who used it to unlock the left side while the bank key opened the right side. When customers returned the box, they gave their key to Carol, whom they'd trusted over the years. By engaging customers in conversation and distracting them, she only created the illusion of locking the box before handing their key back. In the end, she managed to steal the life savings of some prominent businesspeople.

The cash she acquired was unaccounted for, so while the newspapers reported around nine million, word on the street suggested it was well over that, as most of the losses had not been reported for fear of an IRS investigation.

Although I grew up in Manhattan's Chinatown, it retained an enigmatic and unpredictable nature. Unseen dangers lurked around every corner. I'd developed a radar to detect threats and to see the indiscernible in my surroundings. This mindset proved invaluable when I joined the police force. My past as a gang member served as excellent preparation for my career in law enforcement.

This insight was solidified when my brother, Jason, and I caught the attention of Tung On gang members while walking along East Broadway late one winter night. By then, Jason had graduated from high school and was working in a computer career, with no more arrests. Here we were, two upstanding citizens who happened to be walking past a well-known gambling area, and two young gang members began tailing us. They initially kept a respectable distance but gradually closed in.

With my gun and shield concealed on my right side, tucked under my three-quarter-length jacket, I unbuttoned my jacket for swift access to my firearm, if necessary. As the two gang members drew nearer, I whispered to Jason to step aside, allowing our pursuers to pass by. Contrary to my plan, they decided to approach us.

"This street belongs to us," one of them menacingly declared in Cantonese.

I promptly opened my jacket to reveal my badge, simultaneously reaching for my gun. "This street belongs to the government—now bounce off!" I said in Cantonese.

They wisely retreated. My police training and street instincts had both prevailed.

"What were those *gangsters* thinking?" I scoffed in disbelief.

Here they were, the last remnants of once formidable gangs, strutting as if they owned the streets. But they were just a loosely based street gang, no longer supported by the Tongs.

The streets had changed, and so had the game. Compared to the ruthless forces they had once been, these tigers of the past lingered as mere whispers.

CHAPTER FOURTEEN

FULL CIRCLE

My past and present continued to dance together. Sometimes in good ways, like reconnecting with old friends, but also in tragic and tension-filled ways.

In 1997, a shocking newspaper headline hit me like a brick to the head. An assassin had gunned down NYPD Officer Ralph Dols as he stepped out of his car in front of his own house. What a surprise that my high school gym buddy Ralph had become a cop. But the more I thought about it, the more his choice of a career in law enforcement made sense. He'd been the big kid who'd protected me from bullies.

Investigators were quick to link Ralph's murder to Joel Cacace, a consigliere of the Colombo crime family. It was believed Joel had ordered the hit on Ralph because he'd married Joel's ex-wife, Kim Kennaugh. I had no prior knowledge of Ralph's profession as a cop and only discovered it after reading about the murder in the newspapers.

That same year, I was saddened over the news that my

childhood friend, James Niefeld, with whom I'd spent time in pillow fights and wrestling matches, was involved in a vehicular accident with his partner, Christopher Thompkins. The impact of the collision threw him out of the car, and he ended up hanging on a tree. James recovered but later died from an illness during the height of the COVID-19 pandemic.

Rest in peace, Ralph and James.

One night in the summer of 1997, I got involved in another off-duty incident while out with a female friend. We were cruising around Chinatown, feeling lighthearted and relaxed on a pleasant day, windows rolled down. As our car inched along a congested Mott Street, in my peripheral vision I caught a trio of loitering street gang members—remnants of Ghost Shadows. One was perched on the trunk of a parked car, the other two standing on the sidewalk. They looked our way just as my friend and I were laughing. Clearly misinterpreting this as mockery directed at them, the trio's expressions grew indignant.

The guy sitting on the car sprang to his feet and ran into a nearby restaurant. A sickening sense washed over me. Drawing from past experiences, I knew he was retrieving a weapon stashed nearby.

Trapped in a traffic jam on a narrow one-way street, I grabbed my off-duty Smith & Wesson Centennial .38 revolver. Placing my police shield on my lap, I positioned the gun next to it with the barrel facing the window so that if he dared approach my car, he'd spot it immediately.

He came out of the restaurant and headed my way. As his arm shifted with his gait, I saw the edge of a machete. He'd twisted his wrist so that the blade was pressed against the back of his arm, presumably to keep it out of sight.

Our gazes locked, tension filling the air. His previously

arrogant but relaxed expression hardened as he approached, clearly harboring hostile intentions.

I could have held up my badge then, but it was a struggle to shift out of my gang mindset, which was saying, *Keep coming, asshole; you're going to be my next victim.* My police mindset was saying, *It'll be a justified shooting.*

He reached my car window, but before he could shift the machete to hold it upright, he spotted the police badge and gun on my lap. His bravado crumbled when he saw the barrel pointed at his chest. Color drained from his face, and his knees buckled. Gaining his balance, he turned and ran.

The bewilderment on his accomplices' faces was comical, as they had no idea what had scared him off. They watched him run, then turned to look at me with wide eyes. I met their stares head-on. They glanced in the direction their comrade had fled, looked uncertainly at me, and then made a hasty retreat.

Incredibly, I crossed paths with the machete guy again a couple of months later during an undercover mission—the worst possible circumstances. Due to the proliferation of prostitution houses disguised as massage parlors on the south side of Brooklyn, the department assigned me to investigate since I spoke Cantonese. I was working with the three police officers who'd confiscated my illegal gun, men I'd grown to deeply respect.

The mission required me to pose as a customer, gather intelligence, and then signal the raiding team after I made a deal with the woman for a sex act and handed her the money. To transmit audio, I wore a bulky recording device attached to my chest.

Stepping into the dimly lit parlor, I glanced into the kitchen area and recognized a man who appeared to be one of their protectors: the Mott Street guy with the machete. I couldn't believe it. That crazy, random encounter now threatened to blow my cover and the whole operation if he recognized me. My heart raced and my palms turned slick with sweat as I averted my gaze to the girls sitting on the couch who were waiting for me to choose one of them.

Scanning the place, I spotted a restroom at the end of a long hallway. As I headed there, assessing the situation, I passed bedrooms on either side. In the john, I checked through the slightly ajar door to make sure Machete Guy wasn't in the hallway. I surmised that he was in the kitchen, still oblivious to my presence, which offered momentary relief.

I flushed the toilet and ran the water, buying time while considering my options.

Should I abort? How would I explain this to my supervisors?

I needed to exit the bathroom and traverse the hallway back to where the girls were waiting for my return. But the kitchen was across from them, giving Machete Guy a good view of me.

Seconds ticked by, and I anticipated the anxiety growing among my team due to my delayed signal. Could my colleagues at the other end of the device hear my accelerated breathing? My pounding heart? They might storm in at any moment, as they'd yet to hear from me.

I had to act. I left the bathroom, pretending to wipe my face with a towel, and headed directly to an unoccupied bedroom. From there, I shouted through the door's crack in Cantonese, "Bring the girl in white!"

When she entered, I inquired about the price. After I handed her the payment, she confirmed the amount and started undressing. I spoke the code word, signaling the team to initiate the raid. I'd barely finished when the sound of their charge reverberated throughout the building. Officers swarmed in, handcuffing everyone in sight, including me. I was among the last to be led out, giving officers time to escort everyone else out first.

Thankfully, no one asked why I'd been so nervous. Maybe

they assumed it was because it was my first undercover op. I decided right there that I didn't want to do this kind of work. The chances of running into someone from my past life were too risky, and I didn't want to let down my team.

Throughout this time, Lian and I continued seeing each other casually. Though I had kept my resolve to never get emotionally involved, I envisioned being exclusive with her at some point in the future. Our relationship completely changed in 1997 when she told me she was pregnant. This news brought surprise, anticipation, and a huge sense of responsibility. Despite the latter, I was ready to take on parenthood, and in December, a beautiful baby girl named Olivia came into the world. We moved to a one-bedroom apartment steps away from my parents' house in Brooklyn.

Unfortunately, I fell into the same cycle as my parents, focusing on working hard to support us and leaving most of the parenting to Lian. She made it easy because she loved being a stay-at-home mom. I reasoned that I was laying the financial foundation while she gave Olivia the emotional support and affection I simply wasn't capable of—or wired for—giving. Even knowing how difficult things were for my parents couldn't erase the fact that my role models had never shown me love, not even in the few minutes they could spare to spend time with me. Sure, I understood that, like many parents in those days, they had to make a choice: spend time with their children or put food on the table. Still, the fact that I couldn't remember my father hugging me—not one time—left a chasm inside me that I couldn't fill.

I admired that Lian was such a good mother, falling naturally into the role. Raising a child in New York was easier than when I was a kid. Our daughter wouldn't feel like an outcast to be ridiculed as one of only a few Asian kids in her school since the population had grown over the last few years. My job provided money so that she didn't have to wear oversized clothing. And I was relieved that she wouldn't fall into the gang culture since they had diminished. I felt proud that I could give my daughter a better life than either I or Lian had had.

On April 9, 1998, while patrolling the labyrinthine streets of Chinatown, a newspaper article snagged my attention: Wing Keung Tsang had been arrested for a murder that had remained cold since 1977—a shooting at the Pagoda Theater. Eager to read about this, I couldn't buy the newspaper and get out of the store fast enough. The day that Tsang had taken a life, I'd been seated in that movie house with *Kau Fu*.

Chilling memories rushed back, how my uncle had shoved me to the floor and shielded me with his body when the deafening shots erupted from the back-row seats. I couldn't shed the revolting feeling of my limbs brushing against the scum on the floor. I'd watched Tsang leap from the balcony, landing on the horrified people below before vanishing into the shadows. That had been my earliest encounter with brutal Chinatown violence. Unsurprisingly, the murder had been attributed to gang rivalry.

As it turned out, Tsang had distanced himself from gang life after the shooting. He worked as a foreman at a Chinatown noodle factory and had a wife and two children. Yet despite the passing of two decades, justice had finally come for this man who'd taken another's life.

In 1998, Officer Zhang, working solo, grabbed a kid for loitering in an Eighth Avenue Chinatown bakery. Zhang claimed that this troubled kid had retaliated by knocking him down with a punch and then fled. Zhang called for backup. Once the kid's identity was verified, we had an address. I kept the fact that I knew this kid's older brother Turtle to myself.

As a translator, I accompanied plainclothes officers from the anti-crime unit to the residence, and they discovered the kid hiding in the bedroom. My colleagues on this day were again the cops who'd confiscated my gun.

After the incident, Zhang's hostile behavior amped up. Imagine portraying yourself as a tough cop everyone should fear, only to get knocked out by a kid's single punch? Zhang's ego had taken a severe sucker punch.

That he seemed to take it out on me made me wonder if he'd uncovered something that linked me to his attacker, such as my friendship with Turtle. Or the fact that I may have inadvertently aggravated the situation by having an affair with his friend's girlfriend. When this woman left Zhang's friend, it amplified my indirect conflict with Zhang.

He clearly believed he had a reason to wage war against me, but it remained unclear. Our rift went beyond personality differences. We avoided each other and even stopped talking on our shared post. I recall only one instance that broke the silence: when Zhang needed to discuss a job-related matter.

The animosity grew more alarming when a friend working as a police administrative aide in the precinct informed me that Zhang was inquiring about my vacation schedule. He had no authority or need to know this information. At the same time, my Chinese travel agent on Eighth Avenue told me Zhang had demanded to see my itinerary, bombarding her with questions about my upcoming travel plans. His uniform and authority had intimidated her, but when she stood firm, Zhang stormed out of her office.

I remained vigilant, awaiting his next move.

In 1999, I was paired as a fill-in with veteran officer Mike Turcio, and one day we rushed to respond to a distress call from a tenant in a nearby building. After we knocked at the residence, identifying ourselves as police officers, the door abruptly swung open, revealing a frantic woman. But before she could utter one word, a man charged out of the kitchen, brandishing a knife.

In an instant, our weapons were drawn and trained on the knife-wielding man's every move. We demanded that he drop his weapon.

Tension electrified the air. Would we have to use deadly force? We granted him a few crucial seconds before acting, and the perpetrator came to his senses at seeing our guns pointed at his chest. As my finger tightened on the trigger, he dropped the knife a split second before I could fire. Turcio and I handcuffed him, defusing the situation without further incident.

I was glad we'd given him those few extra seconds to register what was going on. In retrospect, when he came out of the room, he probably had tunnel vision, only seeing our faces. Only after that did he register our uniforms and then the barrels of two guns pointed at him.

Another time, a woman dialed 911 to seek help from her knife-wielding boyfriend, who'd just left her apartment. My partner Officer Oranges and I entered the building, coming into a narrow hallway. A man turned the corner from the staircase at the far end of the hallway. He was so blinded with rage that he didn't seem to realize two cops were standing fifteen feet away with guns pointed at him. He stalked toward us, aiming for the entrance behind us.

We commanded, "Put down your weapon."

The man hesitated, escalating the tension. On top of that, he posed a danger to another building tenant, who'd opened her door to see what all the commotion was about. She gasped, frozen.

The man seemed to weigh his options, perhaps including rushing into the woman's apartment and creating a dangerous hostage situation. Instead of resorting to immediately firing, we again ordered him to disarm. Finally, he yielded, dropping his weapon, and we took him into custody.

In many incidents, we could have justified using deadly force, but during my years with the NYPD, the police officers I worked with consistently exercised the utmost restraint. Domestic violence incidents were among the most unpredictable and perilous situations for officers due to perpetrators' emotional and mental instability stemming from personal conflicts. To a certain extent, our training could only prepare us so much. We had to rely on fundamental police skills, quick thinking, sound judgment, and emotional control.

My awakening from my gambling addiction came sometime in 2000 when the dot-com bubble burst and the market crashed. It almost wiped me out financially. While it may be called investing, I was essentially gambling with money in stocks.

I finally acknowledged my addiction and the need for help when I joined Gamblers Anonymous and attended meetings every week for a year. Listening to the experiences of others and the consequences of their gambling habits helped me rewire my mind and attitude. Now, gambling has become a manageable vice that I indulge in occasionally, and I have found better ways to spend my money. I even stopped playing mahjong since 2000.

Around this time, I arrived for my shift at the Sixty-Sixth Precinct and saw officers busily organizing the place while maintenance personnel cleaned. I assumed a VIP was coming to visit. My heart seemed to stop momentarily when I found out we were expecting a visit from NYPD officer Steven McDonald.

Just the mention of his name instantly transported me to my past.

We gathered around the entrance to greet him, and I finally laid eyes on the man who'd inspired my redemption. There he was, Steven McDonald, radiating humanity and quiet glory. He rolled into the precinct amid the applause of his fellow officers. By that time, he had become a national celebrity, acknowledged by President George W. Bush and other national leaders for his courage.

I wanted to tell him how he had changed my life, and I felt bad that I couldn't. Unlike today, the culture then was less open to stories about a gang member turned police officer.

As I came face-to-face with McDonald, all I could say was a heartfelt "thank you" to convey all that I couldn't.

The cops working that day who were not on an assignment accompanied him to a church and attended the service and then lunch. Afterward, I returned to my usual duties, reflecting on my past and the huge changes I'd made along the way.

One crisp morning on Eighth Avenue, Rooster, my former *Dai Lo*, came into view as I sat on my police scooter. Recognizing me, even in my police uniform, he walked over. After initial greetings, he leaned in, his confident demeanor recalling days past when he'd wielded power and influence.

"Mike, you got news on him?" he asked, his voice low.

Even though I hadn't seen Rooster in years, I knew who he was talking about. He didn't like to leave unfinished business with someone who'd wronged him, no matter how much time had passed. Still, I confirmed.

"You mean Chicken Lips?"

"*Hiya*," he said in Cantonese, meaning *yes*.

Chicken Lips. The name brought back memories of our violent past and how he'd nearly cost my brother his life.

His existence obviously remained a thorn in Rooster's side. Rooster's eager tone revealed his continued desire for revenge for conspiring to rob his gambling house. That tone transported me back years to when I took orders from him. Rooster's commanding presence, calm demeanor, and self-control had allowed him to lead our gang through the most challenging of times. I also knew that he trusted his instincts about people.

The clamor of busy Eighth Avenue brought me back to reality. "Believe it or not," I said, borrowing one of Carrot Head's favorite phrases, "he's working for the postal service now."

Rooster looked surprised. "Really?"

"Chances are he's delivering mail to your house," I said with a chuckle. "In the rain, the snow, sleet . . ."

A smile shared in that moment dispelled the bitterness of the robbery. We talked some more, laughter sprinkled throughout our conversation. Unlike back when it seemed we had all the time in the world, we had barely five minutes to catch up. Rooster now owned several nail salons, a tremendous change from the gang days. Our meeting concluded with a firm handshake, sealing an unspoken bond and acknowledgment of the enduring ties of our past.

That same year, Lian found out she was pregnant again. We were both excited and surprised, and we agreed that we'd be happy whether it was a boy or a girl.

The morning that Lian was to get her ultrasound and find out the baby's gender, I was summoned to my first GO-15—when the Internal Affairs Bureau brings you in for questioning as either a suspect or a witness. The IAB doesn't disclose the nature of the investigation until minutes before the interview. Police officers are required to appear and cannot invoke the Fifth Amendment. The department has the authority to terminate anyone caught in a lie or who refuses to answer questions.

I only had a few minutes to alert Lian that I would be in a meeting for a while. I asked her to call my beeper when she found out and send a predetermined code. Then I went into the meeting.

I know they had to do their job, but I still disliked the IAB and considered them rats. Ratting out a fellow officer was considered one of the worst things you could do internally—that was the NYPD culture back then. Of course, I had already embraced that credo when I was in the gang—loyalty is everything.

Soon I found out what the summons was about. Accompanied by my union delegate, Mike Immit, I was being called as a witness in the 1998 case involving Zhang and the loitering kid at the bakery. The kid now claimed that the three arresting cops who later picked him up at his house had manhandled him. I figured the kid's older brother Turtle had coached him to claim abuse for a lighter charge. In reality, the kid hadn't been roughed up at all.

Witnesses I spoke to confirmed that Officer Zhang had lied about the incident. Apparently, when Zhang went to grab the kid, the kid took off, knocking Zhang off balance. He fell inside the bakery as the kid fled the scene. Enraged, Zhang alleged that the kid punched him in the face, which initiated a manhunt for assault on a police officer. From what I found out later, that false claim motivated the kid to accuse the apprehending officers of roughing him up in retaliation.

Back in those days, a complaint against a cop wasn't necessarily considered bad. In the eyes of peers, supervisors, and chiefs, the more unfounded complaints a cop had in their file, the more they were perceived as being active in their crime-fighting duties. It meant they'd made hundreds of arrests, so naturally they'd have lots of complaints and allegations against them.

As I contemplated my response, my beeper went off. I glanced down to see the screen. I had to hide my smile. We were having a boy. Our family would now be complete. I shifted my attention back to the meeting, but my elation made me indifferent to this nonsensical case . . . and perhaps a bit of a smart-ass.

The investigators asked me if I'd witnessed the beating and wanted to know who'd roughed up Turtle's brother.

"I'm not aware of any beating," I said.

"You were there to translate, got them to open the door, and you didn't see the kid get roughed up?" an IAB sergeant pressed.

"I was speaking to the kid's mother. I didn't see anything."

"Could you recognize the anti-crime cops who were in the apartment?"

I shrugged, not giving away that I knew them well. But I resolved not to lie outright, only to skirt the truth. "I work a foot post solo, so I don't deal with the anti-crime unit much."

I didn't feel I was wrong in doing this. Internal Affairs often pressured witnesses to give the answers they wanted to hear rather than the truth. Any officer afraid that their career might be derailed by telling the truth would cave in. I would rather lose my job than go along with their witch hunt of those good cops.

The IAB officers showed me a photo array of white cops and asked me to identify the three who were in the apartment. I perused the photographs, then shook my head. "It's hard to say. All these white guys look the same to me."

Mike Immit shot me a look that screamed, *What are you doing?*

I continued with an emphatic tone, "Let's see how well you guys can pick out someone if you worked in a police department in China and you saw a bunch of Chinese cops running around."

Not expecting this sarcastic response from a rookie, Immit called for a break. While I faced intense pressure, even as just a witness in a GO-15, I emerged from this interview unscathed.

And I got to go home after my shift and celebrate the coming of our son with Lian.

Zhang was promoted to sergeant and left the Sixty-Sixth Precinct. Unfortunately, about six months later he came back, assigned to the Vice Unit in Brooklyn's Chinatown. I found this odd since getting a cushy position right after a promotion was rare. Was this reason enough to conclude that Zhang was indeed working with the IAB?

Zhang continued his aggressive raids on prostitution and gambling houses on Eighth Avenue. I heard on the streets that the targeted business owners alleged he disregarded standard operating procedures by trashing his way through the targeted establishment and flinging objects, perhaps as a way to intimidate suspects. After shutting them down, he arrested anyone he could charge with a crime, then personally herded his suspects—business managers, staff, pimps, hookers, and gamblers—to the station for interrogation.

Once, while he questioned people in the massage parlors and gambling houses, I issued him a summons for double parking in Chinatown: His department vehicle did not display a placard. He sought me out to resolve the summons; otherwise, he would have to do paperwork to address it. Because he hadn't talked to me since 1997, my actions forced him to make a request from me, and he was none too happy about it.

What happened next was unsettling. Multiple people approached me on the street, even those I didn't know, and expressed concerns about Zhang. The operators of several establishments and their customers cautioned me with, "Beware of that cop. He's targeting you. He's been showing people your picture and asking if you're involved in corruption."

Even more ominously, others confided that during his raids, Zhang isolated individuals away from his team. Then he'd show them my photo, press a gun to their heads, and ask whether I frequented those places or received payments from them.

Could I believe their stories? Given the behaviors I'd witnessed, it was entirely—and terrifyingly—plausible. Was this possibly connected to my affair with his friend's girlfriend, or was Zhang an IAB associate assigned to target me? I may have been clearer about the latter scenario if that tryst hadn't muddled the situation. I just couldn't be sure. With each passing day, my suspicions deepened, fueled by his escalating efforts to unearth nonexistent incriminating evidence against me.

Even when off duty, Zhang's fixation persisted. He once jumped into the passenger seat of Turtle's car, demanding information about me. This answered the question about whether he'd found a connection between us.

"I know you're Michael Moy's friend! Tell me what he does and who he associates with!"

"I don't know you, so get out of my car!" Turtle told him.

"But I know who *you* are, and I'll be watching you!" Zhang shot back before exiting Turtle's vehicle.

Zhang seemed to illustrate his vendetta by making my friend Tommy, who'd bought the car service from me, a target of selective enforcement, which eventually resulted in the shutdown of his karaoke bar in Chinatown.

This harassment reminded me of an odd incident during the time when Zhang and I were beat cops on Eighth Avenue and a string of bank robberies occurred in Brooklyn South. The precinct provided the suspect's description, which I remained aware of while on patrol.

I spotted a non-Asian male on the other side of Eighth Avenue who matched the suspect's physical profile standing in front of a bank after hours. I felt his eyes on me, arousing my suspicion. Was he an IAB officer? I radioed Central and informed them that an individual at my location matched the description of the person wanted in the Brooklyn South robberies, and I requested backup.

My backup arrived: three anti-crime cops, two of them the cops who'd confiscated my gun years earlier. I watched them pull over in front of the suspicious-looking man across the street, exit the vehicle, and question him. I started crossing the street, but before I reached them, they'd released him and were walking back to their vehicle.

I got into their car's back seat. "Who was the guy?"

"Mike, he's from the dark side," one of the cops answered. "I think they're after you."

The officers seemed nervous. I could only speculate what was going through their minds: *Is it because the IAB is conducting operations in the Sixty-Sixth Precinct as a whole, or do they think Mike's doing something illegal?*

Knowing a bit of my past may have fueled their suspicion that I was engaged in something illicit. But I wasn't doing anything wrong. Still, I admired these great cops, and I didn't want them to suspect me of corruption. I exited their vehicle and watched the unit drive off.

Even before this incident, I noticed IAB undercover associates trailing me and parking near my house to monitor my movements. How could I not be aware of the methods the IAB used for conventional surveillance? They went to great lengths to perform their duties, and in some instances, I heard they'd even search through the garbage of those they were investigating. Many clues could be discovered in the trash.

Was I perfect? Of course not. I am a human who made mistakes as a cop and committed minor infractions, but after my probationary period ended, the department would have a hard time terminating me if there was no criminality involved. As a penalty for minor errors, they could deduct vacation days, delay a promotion, or transfer me to a precinct far from my home—known as "highway therapy." Perhaps Zhang saw my downfall as a necessity in his quest for another promotion, but his efforts were in vain. I was clean of corruption.

As I dealt with all this daily turmoil, my son was born. I worried about another innocent, sweet child coming into the cruel world I saw every day, but I would protect and take care of both kids as best as I could. I took my role as a father very seriously, but still mostly in the financial aspect. Lian continued to be home with the kids, giving them all the love and attention they needed and deserved. I worked hard to support them and was always there for them.

It's typical in the Asian community for fathers to seem stoic and unaffectionate, but this doesn't mean they don't care. Given my own upbringing, I continued that aspect of the stereotypical Asian dad, unable to turn on that switch and become the father who goes to all the plays and games and gives them spontaneous affection. Although I could understand why my father was cold, I couldn't find a way to connect emotionally with him, and that deficit made it hard to connect with my kids too.

As sergeant of the Vice Squad, Zhang possessed more clout and authority that he could use to destroy me. His actions indicated to me he was likely to escalate his efforts. In theory, all he needed to do to pin me down was compel one person he'd arrested to falsely testify against me in exchange for a lighter sentence.

This possibility grew into my biggest fear. He could ruin my career, my reputation, and my pension. I felt that it would come down to him or me, so I knew I had to make a move.

Incidentally, around this time Turtle sought my advice regarding Zhang's continued harassment of business owners in Chinatown. I told him that the police must follow protocol to enter and search private property.

In those years, when using CCTV and data storage backup were uncommon practices, I advised, "Tell your friends to install security cameras. Hide one recorder and leave the other one for him to find."

The owner of a massage parlor heeded this advice passed through my friend. Zhang raided his establishment on suspicion of prostitution and arrested several female suspects. Angry, the owner taunted Zhang by claiming he had evidence on tape that could prove there was no prostitution in the parlor, only massage therapy. Zhang and his team returned to the building to carry out a raid on a nearby business, then broke into the massage parlor and stole the surveillance system.

The owner followed the advice provided to Turtle by me and submitted the backup tape showing the police officers stealing evidence directly to the district attorney and filed a case against Zhang. I wasn't surprised to hear that Zhang was later arrested in a forty-count indictment that included felony burglary. A lieutenant who was also charged in this raid admitted that he'd lied about the women offering sex for money in the initial raid but later recanted. During the investigation, they even found property that had been confiscated from one of the raids being used for police business in the vice department and at the lieutenant's home, according to legal documents.

Though the case against the raiding team was dropped due to evidence mishandling, the charges for what prosecutors called a flawed raid were consistent with what I'd heard about and witnessed with Zhang. The case led to his suspension and then reassignment. I'd had to do something to stop Zhang, not only from harassing businesses but from sabotaging my career. Most concerning, I could have served jail time for something I hadn't done—ironic, given my past. As the chapter on Zhang ended, numerous other IAB cases opened against me. I felt as though I were in a never-ending fight to prove my innocence.

People impersonate cops more often than you'd think. Their reasons can be many: gaining respect, getting freebies at restaurants, going on a power trip, or more nefarious reasons. With my experience, I got good at differentiating between "true blue" and "buffs" as I encountered a number of police impersonation cases, with two incidents standing out.

Once I was driving with my young children in the back seat when two white guys pulled me over. It looked like an unmarked police vehicle, but I wasn't sure. I was in Brooklyn's Chinatown when they pulled up alongside me, and the car's passenger gestured for me to pull over.

I complied but remained cautious, my phone at the ready. As they approached, I kept my window partially rolled up and waited to see what they wanted. They asked for my license. I asked them who they were. The one who peered through my driver's-side window told me they were the police. I inquired about where they worked, but neither answered.

At this point, I mentioned that I was a police officer too, after which they hastily retreated to their vehicle and sped off. I followed them for a few blocks, jotting down their license plate number, then reported the incident over 911.

Unfortunately, backup didn't arrive in time, and they managed to elude capture as they sped onto the highway. I had the license plate number, which led to an investigation that traced the car's registration back to someone related to another person with a prior arrest record. From a photo array, I identified the individual who'd presented as a cop.

The department issued an active investigation card for his arrest, but he'd fled to Florida. Months later, the police apprehended him when he returned, putting him in a lineup, where I identified him. He was charged with impersonating a police officer. I found it ironic that the perpetrator looked more like a stereotypical NYPD officer than I did.

The second time this happened, I entered a Chinese convenience store and noticed a middle-aged white man with an NYPD badge and ID hanging from his neck. In my casual clothes and being Asian, he would have no idea I was a cop.

I walked over to him. "Are you a police officer?" I had to get him to state it before I could arrest him for impersonating a cop.

"I am."

I nodded, as though I'd taken him at his word. "Where do you work?"

He told me his precinct.

I started to ask questions that only real police officers could answer. Unable to answer, he got nervous and asked who I was.

"You are not a cop," I continued. "I am a cop."

The man wilted under my assertion. "This was my Halloween costume yesterday," he admitted.

I detained him, and officers arrived to arrest him a few minutes after I called 911.

A police uniform is powerful, wielding an immediate influence and impact on people. It builds a presence of authority and influence. Business owners sometimes offer cops small freebies like donuts or coffee; the guy I'd just collared was likely looking for that. But it's still a crime, no matter the motive.

On September 11, 2001, I was driving across the Verrazzano Bridge with Lian and the kids in the car when I looked over my shoulder and saw the North Tower of the World Trade Center in flames. Seventeen minutes later, another airplane plowed into the South Tower. I told Lian I needed to go into work immediately and would drop them off at my mom's house.

Like most Americans, I was shocked when I saw the Twin Towers of the World Trade Center crumble after hijacked airplanes hit them. Reporting to the precinct for duty, we were enveloped by a grim shadow as we assembled, awaiting our orders. Grief muted us, and I felt shattered in a way I'd never experienced before. Nothing had prepared the police force emotionally or physically to handle this level of destruction and terror.

"Did this really happen to America? Right in the heart of New York City?" I whispered to myself amid the crowd of fellow police officers as we watched the news, sadness etched on our faces.

The two 110-story towers of the World Trade Center had soared to over 1,300 feet high. This iconic Manhattan landmark of nearly ten million square feet of office space housed 430 businesses and 35,000 people, welcoming around 70,000 daily visitors and commuters.[5] Those amazing buildings and the thousands of people who couldn't get out in time were just . . . *gone*.

"Your job is to secure the inner perimeter," our sergeant said somberly. "This is a rescue and recovery mission. Pick up and recover anything unusual." When the sergeant mentioned "unusual," he was referring to body parts, personal belongings, jewelry, clothing fragments, et cetera.

I, along with eight other police officers, rode in a van to Ground Zero in a mournful mood. No one spoke, and an overpowering sense of dread came over us as we neared the World Trade Center site. Seeing the utter devastation and chaos up close felt like I was witnessing the end of the world.

A cloud of dust permeated the air, darkening the site, and

---

5. 9/11 Memorial & Museum, "World Trade Center," accessed January 6, 2025, https://911memorial.org/learn/resources/world-trade-center-history.

floodlights streaming from the ground made everything surreal. The first thing that hit me was the odor that arose from the ground: an indescribable smell that clung to my uniform, face, nostrils, and every part of my body. Masks weren't available yet, and I knew that the fumes in the air would affect my lungs. I did not have to be a medical expert to conclude we were breathing in poison as soon as we got out of the van.

The deformed steel bars and mounds of concrete and debris scattered all over the site looked like a studio set for an apocalyptic movie. Together with my fellow officers, we scoured the area, inspecting every inch as the shadow of death hovered above us.

Thousands of lives were buried under the rubble or had disintegrated in the explosion. How could I be stepping on it? I had always believed myself to be stoic, cold, and detached, but the 9/11 site affected my emotions in unimaginable ways. It felt as though I were in the aftermath of a gang war, but involving countries, leaders, and soldiers, with hundreds of innocents caught in the cross fire. That last part affected me more than anything else.

There was no "selfie culture" then, and mobile phone cameras produced grainy photos. Several police officers, our own and from out of state, brought digital cameras to get pictures of themselves posing in different areas. It felt disrespectful to me to take photos during a rescue and recovery in which thousands of people died.

I toiled for twelve to sixteen hours daily amid the fallen debris and toxic materials, securing the inner perimeter of Ground Zero. I often wore the same dust-covered uniform for days since there was hardly time, or even a care, to do laundry. Before bed I'd hang my worn police uniform in the cabinet and in the morning put it back on for the next day's duty.

First responders suffered significant losses when the

buildings crumbled, particularly in the fire department. For the NYPD, the aftermath pushed us to nearly breaking point due to unbearable exhaustion. It's hard to imagine how we survived when we barely slept. The psychological impact of death, destruction, and despair added to our burden.

In a bittersweet irony, an attack meant to break our spirits kindled the purest sense of patriotism among Americans. The people of New York City united and showed a determined resolve to rise from the catastrophe. Many people in the United States and worldwide regarded the actions of government responders in the aftermath as heroic. The public offered overwhelming support and appreciation to firefighters, police officers, medical personnel, and emergency responders. They clapped when they saw us in the streets, stopped to shake our hands, or paused to hug us. Food and refreshments poured into our temporary stations around Ground Zero.

Newspapers, magazines, and news websites featured photos of first responders working day and night during the recovery operations, though no image or newsreel could accurately portray the gruesome work we did at Ground Zero.

I felt a genuine connection with the city as it grappled with this unspeakable disaster, one I still often think about. My heart ached for the lives buried under the rubble and the families who'd lost their loved ones. Yet something rare and unheard of emerged from the ashes. Amid the collective grief of post-9/11, I awakened to an unexpected reality, one that instilled a deep sense of belonging. Strangers became like family, and the bond between colleagues strengthened with empathy and unity.

During that period, no one seemed to notice the ethnicity or racial differences of the people in uniform working at the WTC. The color of our skin didn't matter; we were all embraced and lauded as Americans. People saw a cop first, then a Chinese guy, rather than the other way around. On that day, when a part of humanity died, it arose in another form and embraced a city in pain. It took a tragedy like 9/11 to make people realize the folly of division and the value of our intrinsic connection as human beings. Never in my life since 9/11 have I experienced such openness and acceptance from those whom I had come to expect rejection and prejudice from.

The Ground Zero cleanup officially concluded on May 30, 2002, more than eight months after the terrorist attack. Unsurprisingly WTC rescue and recovery responders developed 9/11-related illnesses, and I was among the thousands who acquired a respiratory condition due to the toxins breathed in during our work. Several of my colleagues from the Sixty-Sixth Precinct, Detective John O'Reilly, Lieutenant Marci Simms, and Detective Vincent Galeno, succumbed to 9/11-related illnesses.

The World Trade Center left scars, from both the loss of friends and the harm it did to my health. Since 2001 I've also suffered from recurring flashbacks stemming from the Ground Zero recovery work.

The James Zadroga 9/11 Health and Compensation Act was the silver lining in our nightmarish saga. This US law provided health monitoring and financial aid to survivors of 9/11, the volunteers, and the first responders, including the NYPD officers who served at Ground Zero. James Zadroga, an NYPD police officer, fell victim to toxins from the debris of the World Trade Center, and Congress fittingly named the law after him.

To be compensated, the September 11th Victim Compensation Fund required us to show proof of our participation in the post-9/11 operations. The police officers who had indiscreetly taken pictures had evidence of their involvement, but I had none.

Fortunately, I received a letter of acknowledgment and

gratitude from a two-star chief for being part of the rescue and recovery teams. I submitted affidavits from fellow officers who attested to my participation in the work, in addition to my detailed notes in my memo book that I found in my locker. Many cops discarded their memo books and had a hard time proving they were at the site.

During my police career, I survived violence in the streets and made it through numerous near-fatal encounters. Bullets whizzed by me so close that I felt the wind pass by my ear. It would be an unfortunate twist of fate should my illness one day cause my demise—that terrorists got me, not the gangs or criminals in the streets.

Returning to my foot post provided a respite from the traumatic experience of 9/11, even with the typical challenges in Chinatown.

Mr. Hong was a familiar face who often visited my post and conversed with me about trivial matters. One day in 2002, our talk took a big turn when he proposed a plan to open a prostitution house. Mr. Hong offered me a bribe of around a thousand dollars a month in exchange for keeping an eye on the operation.

"Just give me a heads-up if there's a raid or anything," he said. "And you can have your pick of any girl."

"I'll need to consult with my sergeant," I replied. "He can help us and might be interested in getting a piece of the action."

I followed protocol and informed my supervisor, Sergeant Philip Lam, about the bribe offer. The by-the-book sergeant contacted the Internal Affairs Bureau. As part of a planned sting operation, the sergeant and I agreed to meet Mr. Hong at Jade Palace Restaurant on Sixty-First and Eighth Avenue to discuss the offer under IAB surveillance.

We wore concealed wires on the evening of the meeting to

allow the IAB to record the conversation. We captured him on record discussing his intention to open an illegal prostitution house and reiterating his offer to Sergeant Lam and me for our protection.

Once the IAB determined they had enough evidence, I alerted them to Mr. Hong's location in Chinatown, and they apprehended him for attempted bribery.

The department commended my actions, and the bribery arrest was held in high regard as it demonstrated that the NYPD valued integrity over corruption. It also demonstrated my character. While I'd been skeptical about rumors of the department taking care of officers who made significant bribery arrests, I was in fact offered a choice of positions and assignments.

Not long after, I received an invitation for an interview by the police board to determine my preferences. I expressed interest in community affairs work, given my involvement in community policing. I was informed that I would be interviewed for a position working for the deputy commissioner of community affairs at headquarters.

The lieutenant conducting the interview lived across the street from where I'd been living for the last ten years. My neighbor had been unaware of my police background until the clerk pulled up my file. That's how low of a profile I kept!

A few days later, I received a call from the Community Affairs lieutenant, who informed me that I could start working there on Wednesday. This offer was gratifying, but after careful consideration, I chose to stay at the Sixty-Sixth in Brooklyn. I believe that when you enjoy your work, it hardly feels like work. And I truly enjoyed my work in Chinatown.

In the early 2000s, gang-related crimes experienced a resurgence in New York City's Chinatowns. During this period, the NYPD

Intel Division was in the process of forming an Asian gang task force under Captain Michael Lau to gather information and combat the criminal activities of Asian gangs. My commanding officer, Inspector Steven McAllister, recommended I join Captain Lau's team tasked with dismantling these gangs.

This was a full-circle moment. At one time my gangmates and I had tried to avoid Lau, who'd arrested some of our friends, and now I was being offered a chance to work with him. I was honored.

At a meeting at headquarters, I met with four-star chief Joseph Esposito; my commanding officer, Inspector McAllister; the commanding officer of the Intelligence Division; and Captain Michael Lau. I provided insights into the escalating violence among Fukienese gang members who were vying for control over bus routes and the dollar van business.

It was surreal to find myself at a meeting with Chief Esposito. I felt gratified to be called upon by a high-ranking officer to consult on crucial policy matters. I couldn't help but wonder how they would react if they knew I had once been on the other side of the law, running criminal operations under their noses from the late 1980s to the early 1990s.

Aside from extorting bus and dollar van drivers and imposing control over karaoke bars in Chinatown, Asian gangs were now committing home invasions, street robberies, and other crimes reminiscent of their past. This growing concern for the department was exacerbated when these gang-related crimes began making headlines.

Many old-guard gang members were being released from prison around this time. Those who didn't want to or couldn't find a way to go straight had resorted to making money the only way they knew how: illegally.

During the meeting, headquarters proposed that I engage

in undercover work using a new identification card, a fabricated name, and an address. To gather vital information, my mission would involve befriending gang members in karaoke bars, massage parlors, pool halls, and known hangouts.

They considered me ideal for the job because of my ethnic background, physical appearance, and proficiency in Cantonese. But I could not accept this position. Word had circulated in the underworld that I'd become a police officer, so my cover was already blown. On top of that, after my first undercover op, I'd resolved never to participate in another.

I now faced a dilemma, unsure how to decline the offer without causing offense. The high-ranking police officers awaited my decision as my prolonged pause amplified the room's silence, and my mind raced for a way to handle this the right way. All of this transpired in seconds, yet it felt like an eternity.

I respectfully declined the offer, stating my desire to focus on my family, particularly my two young children. I recommended another Chinese cop I had previously worked with, asserting he was the perfect fit for the job. Shortly after, this officer joined the intelligence unit and quickly ascended the ranks. Eventually he became a deputy inspector and the commanding officer of the Asian Hate Crime Task Force. By turning down a position in front of the chief, I'd sealed my fate and might never receive a similar offer again. But I could in no way jeopardize the mission or my own life by joining the task force.

I ran into Captain Lau approximately a month after this high-level meeting. He extended an offer for a position on the Queens Robbery Squad, emphasizing that it was an opportunity for me to earn my gold shield. I was taken aback by the on-the-spot offer, especially considering my refusal of the chief's offer. Some higher-ups take it personally when officers decline positions or promotions, but not Lau. Nor was it a case of "Chinese helping Chinese" for promotions; I could tell that he genuinely believed I was well suited for the role.

I shook hands with Captain Lau, once the nemesis of gangs in Chinatown. As a police officer, I fully comprehended the reasons behind his actions during my time on the streets. He remained unaware that my crew used to extort businesses on his turf. If he had known about my gang affiliations at that moment, he might have thought life was playing a joke on him.

I respectfully declined Captain Lau's offer, content with my role as a police officer in Chinatown, without immediate aspirations to become a detective. I explained to him that the commute wouldn't align with my family life. Over time, Captain Lau continued to climb the ranks, eventually achieving the rank of deputy inspector.

While on my scooter patrolling Chinatown in 2003, I encountered Kenny, the Ghost Shadow who'd bought a gun from me when he was sixteen. At the time it had seemed nothing more than a casual business transaction. But some people turn from friend to brother, and although we'd been in different gangs, Kenny and I had clicked. Later his imprisonment and my police career kept us apart.

I spotted his familiar face and felt a surge of emotion: *my long-lost brother.*

He took me in with a wry grin. "You're not going to arrest me, sir, are you?"

I fell into a hug with him, shook hands, and spent a moment just basking in his company. I shook my head, still overjoyed by the reunion. "I'm so happy to see you."

Kenny had been released from prison and was starting life anew. He was unsurprised to see me in my police uniform since he'd already heard about me through the grapevine. He said that he'd kept his distance from me to avoid the risk of jeopardizing my job. Active police officers were not allowed to be identified with felons, and the Feds were monitoring him. Hearing that confirmed this guy was a true brother.

I shook his hand again. "I appreciate that. Stay out of trouble, you hear? I'll reach out to you after I retire."

Some months later, while I was wearing my police uniform inside a local cell phone store, I spotted Shorty, my feisty former comrade, coming in, and it struck me that he hadn't changed, even after years of imprisonment. When I approached him, he shared my surprise at seeing him. I hugged this old friend, with whom I'd shared countless adventures. Shorty spoke with the same accent and carried himself with the same spunk.

I'm not given to strong emotions, but that meeting stands out as one of the most joyful and memorable days of my life. I was genuinely happy for him to be released from prison finally. I couldn't help but imagine his incarceration, a time when his world had crumbled and his young life had been forever changed by cold steel bars and bare walls.

He'd been unfairly charged as an adult for a crime he did when he was fifteen, and had been given no dispensation for having killed another person in self-defense. Still, Shorty hadn't allowed his circumstances to defeat him. After taking responsibility for his actions, he had seized life once more.

When he suggested grabbing a bite, I considered that rule about hanging out with felons, but I found myself saying yes anyway. Over dinner, he told me that he'd learned many valuable lessons in prison, including a deep appreciation for life and every moment that came with it. I told him he seemed happier than most people, and his smiling eyes confirmed it.

The joy of seeing my old gangmates turn their lives around

balanced out the frustration of dealing with those who continued to commit petty crimes and be involved in sketchy schemes.

One of those sketchy crimes included the thriving counterfeit goods business in Chinatown. Tags and brand logos were churned out in clandestine sweatshops and smuggled in from China. Assembling the bags took place on American soil. Shrewd buyers were discreetly directed to hidden malls tucked away along Canal Street and neighboring areas that offered counterfeit bags, high-end brand apparel, watches, and accessories.

One standout counterfeit product was imitation Rolex watches, attainable for a mere $300 or less. Counterfeiters in the US clandestinely imported specialized equipment from China, enabling them to craft the Rolex crown, the brand's distinctive logo. These watches were impeccably designed to deceive an untrained eye.

In another devious ploy, a criminal syndicate duped a department store through a "return-the-merchandise scam." A member posed as a well-heeled shopper, purchasing a genuine high-end bag worth thousands of dollars. Days later, the impostor returned a counterfeit version of the bag to the store, and a clerk would unwittingly refund the fraudster's money. It took a while for store managers to discover that ruse.

While on my foot post, I once crossed paths with a fellow I knew who'd previously had no job. Now suddenly he owned a big granite business. He'd amassed a fortune by peddling counterfeit Duracell batteries, making a profit of $400,000 per shipping container. He'd buy cheap batteries in bulk from China and Duracell labels separately, affixing the labels here in the US, and then off-load them to discount stores as genuine products. Though illegal, it nevertheless amazed me how an immigrant who spoke no English could make so much money.

In March 2003, my supervisors offered me a position in the Sixty-Sixth Detective Squad. Accepting it would allow me to stay in the same precinct, earn a promotion to detective, and work under Lieutenant Manfredi, the squad's commanding officer. Having served as his driver for a short time during my patrol days and knowing him well, I liked the idea of Manfredi as my boss.

The precinct covering Chinatown had never had a Chinese investigator, having to call in Chinese police officers from other areas to translate. Since these translators weren't detectives, they lacked interrogation skills and could only pass information back and forth. This also prevented investigators from establishing a true rapport with suspects and victims. The best way to continue serving the people in Chinatown was to accept this new role. I would be the first Chinese detective in this precinct.

This offer, I accepted.

Mr. Yi was a Chinese acquaintance who organized shows at the Mohegan Sun casino in Connecticut. He asked me to bring a couple of buddies to work for two days on a security detail for a Hong Kong celebrity.

Cops were allowed to take off-duty employment by observing proper protocols, one of which was completing the required forms. I chose not to file an off-duty employment form, as this was just a one-time, two-day gig, not regular work.

Our task involved securing the singer before, during, and after his show, which included crowd control and ensuring the star's safety. I enlisted the help of three of my Sixty-Sixth Precinct Detective Squad buddies: Hallowell, Russo, and Bianchi.

Hallowell, an African American, displayed an earnest drive to make arrests. Whenever he investigated cases in Chinatown, he asked for my assistance since no one would open the door for him. Bianchi specialized in handling domestic violence cases, while Russo, our union delegate, was an old-school cop who remained calm under pressure.

At the casino, we carried out our duties. I wore a backstage pass labeled SECURITY. While I was guarding the show entrance, a Chinese man in a suit introduced himself as an FBI agent and inquired about Yi's whereabouts. I didn't know where Yi was and told him he might be in the stage area. I replied casually, assuming he was a friend or acquaintance of Yi's who was attending the concert.

I became suspicious when he pulled out his notepad and asked more questions, jotting down notes. Upon learning that I was a cop, he asked if I was armed, and I said no, even though I had a gun concealed under my jacket. Once the man left, I discreetly handed my gun to Bianchi to store in the hotel safe to avoid any trouble with the FBI, as I was unaware of the legality of being armed within an Indian reservation.

I called Yi and discovered he was at home. I went to his house after the show, informed him about the FBI agent, and pressed him for more information. Yi revealed that the FBI was investigating him due to his connections with casino executives who were suspected of taking kickbacks. He had partnered with these execs to bring Asian performers to the Mohegan Sun in Connecticut. I was upset that Yi hadn't shared this information earlier, as I might have declined the gig had I known about his issue with the FBI.

Yi wouldn't cooperate with the FBI, so they were building a case against him. An informant claimed he'd seen Yi playing poker at a friend's house in Connecticut, violating Casino Gaming Commission rules. His business license and role as a show organizer were in jeopardy. He stood to lose significant money, and the FBI threatened to shut down his Mohegan Sun operation unless he testified against the two executives. Yi remained silent, so they charged him for participating in a poker game, resulting in the revocation of his license.

Upon learning of Yi's predicament, my buddies and I anticipated being called by the IAB for a GO-15 after the FBI filed its report. My friends grew anxious at the possibility of an investigation, but I reassured them that I'd take all the blame and responsibility for anything the IAB might charge us with.

The worst that could happen was they'd deduct my vacation days, block my promotion, or transfer me to another command. None of these potential consequences bothered me too much. At that time, I was a white shield in the detective squad, working toward my gold shield. If they denied my promotion, returning to patrol seemed like a good "punishment" since I missed being out on the streets. My only concern was the possibility of a transfer, but it didn't keep me up at night.

Eighteen months later, the IAB contacted me to inquire about our off-duty security gig in Atlantic City. Hallowell was devastated, and Russo and Bianchi were uneasy. I never lost sleep over it. It wasn't a criminal matter. I reassured them with, "Just direct any questions at me during the GO-15. Tell them the truth. I was the one who organized it and brought you there."

I walked into the GO-15 prepared for any outcome. After over three hours of questioning, I told them to take vacation days from me since I was the organizer. I would give up one hundred days to protect the three guys I'd brought.

In the end, they wanted to take twenty days from me, but I got cocky and said, "Take thirty if you want." They did, and the charges against my buddies were dismissed.

Hallowell earned his promotion to second-grade detective and decided to retire shortly after. Just days before retiring, he confided in me that a reliable source had informed him that

Zhang was an IAB associate. The mystery behind the sergeant's relentless pursuit of me, which had puzzled me for years, was finally solved. It all made sense. And since Hallowell owed me money, this info might be his way of paying me back.

During my eighteen months of detective training in 2003 and 2004, I was assigned to the BRAM unit: Burglary/Robbery Apprehension Module. Due to a string of robberies committed by a masked gunman, we were tasked with staking out pharmacies. Two other detectives and I sat in a nondescript van with no windows, parked on a street a good distance from a pharmacy, using a periscope to scan the high-crime area. I would sometimes be there at three a.m., trying to get a little of the moving breeze from a tiny fan while waiting for armed robbers to appear so we could nab them. Random people banged on the sides of the van or tried to peer in through the front windows to see why our suspicious vehicle was parked there.

Sitting in a vehicle from evening until dawn and adjusting to a drastically changed schedule of alternating weeks of all-night and all-day shifts took a toll. Physically and mentally fatigued, I asked myself what the hell I had gotten myself into. The hardest part of my foot patrol had been deciding what to have for lunch. I had given up steady days off, regular hours, and enjoying my job for *this*? Not much more pay but the prestige of being called a detective?

One night I was returning home at one a.m. Before parking my car, I performed a cautionary scan of the area. This neighborhood was notorious for car break-ins and muggings, which often occurred as unsuspecting victims stepped from their vehicles. Bits of shattered car windows regularly glittered on the pavement.

After parking, I secured my belongings in a plastic bag, which I intended to stow in the trunk, ensuring nothing of value was in sight to tempt thieves. As I approached my open trunk, a glance behind me revealed an unsettling sight.

Across the dimly lit street about two dozen car lengths away, a hulking, bald Hispanic man, much larger than me, sped toward me on a mountain bike. No doubt he'd intended to sneak up from behind, but I'd blown his element of surprise.

In a fluid motion, I drew my gun, concealing it against the side of my leg with my finger on the trigger. I stood still, my face devoid of emotion.

Trying to intimidate me as he closed in about twelve car lengths away, he bellowed, "What you got?"

I could never defend myself from a guy that size without using my firearm. In that instant, I made a choice: If his feet touched the pavement, he'd meet his demise. In the academy, we were taught to shoot at center mass. In real life, there was no shooting to disable. It was far too difficult to try to shoot a moving target like running legs.

His voice echoed once more as he came within five or six car lengths. "What you got!" he yelled even louder this time, his eyes locked on to mine.

A game of nerves ensued, a test of wills to see who'd chicken out and move at the last second to avoid a collision. Unwavering, I stood rooted to the ground like a tree.

He must have caught a lethal glint in my eyes and understood my intent. There was no way he could have seen my Glock 19, ready to fire with 98 percent accuracy within seven yards. Just as I was poised to raise my weapon and take aim, he executed a sharp right turn about one car length away from me and rode off as fast as he'd ridden toward me.

That man had teetered on the precipice of possible death, and I'd had no hesitation in defending myself. If it had come to that dire point, shooting him would have been my sole recourse, for in our department, we were taught it is better to be judged by a jury of twelve than be carried by pallbearers of six.

Months before my official promotion to detective, a bitter detective ratted out Lieutenant Manfredi for playing video games on his department computer while on duty, and he got transferred back to patrol in uniform.

Sergeant Macuso stepped in as his replacement, and from our earlier interactions, I pegged him as a narcissistic office bully with an inflated sense of self-importance.

I approached Macuso after completing my eighteen months of detective training and requested to return to foot patrol in Chinatown. "Detective work is not for me; it's not my passion." I didn't add that it wasn't my passion to serve under someone like him. Understandably, bullies were a trigger for me. I anticipated a future filled with endless trivial tasks while being closely monitored by my boss—this, as opposed to working on my own on a foot post with little or no supervision.

If I accepted the detective position, going back to patrol would be a complicated transfer. I wanted to avoid that entanglement.

Macuso spent an hour emphasizing all the benefits of accepting the promotion, determined to keep me in my detective position. I knew this was not for my benefit but his. Macuso would have a sticky situation to explain to his chief: After all, why would an active investigator in his BRAM with the most felony arrests in the unit during eighteen months of training not want to work with him? He assured me that he'd address my concerns about his micromanagement style.

I had doubts, but I wasn't someone who would shy away from a challenge or hinder my growth in a new environment. I chose to pursue my detective career and accept the promotion.

CHAPTER FIFTEEN

DETECTIVE MOY

After eighteen months of eye-opening, information-filled training, in October 2004, I became an NYPD police detective. I had gone from criminal accomplice to detective in a suit and tie tasked with solving crimes. Detectives are the relentless hounds of the urban jungle, chasing elusive perpetrators. We are architects of truth, piecing together the puzzle of each crime by identifying suspects, unraveling motives, and deconstructing the choreography of criminal acts.

That meant determining whether suspects were innocent or guilty. I understood the responsibility of getting justice for the victims and their families, but I found equal satisfaction in clearing a suspect of a crime when they were innocent.

I also saw how easy it was for a detective without integrity to frame someone just so they could close the case. Our words could send someone to prison. Sometimes we knew a person was guilty, but would we bend the rules to imprison that person if there wasn't enough hard evidence? If we didn't, what if a guilty person got away? Even worse, what if they continued to commit their crimes? Good detectives must always do the right thing: find evidence to either arrest or clear.

In my new job, my senses sharpened even further. Every object, every placement held a narrative: a shattered glass, a soiled shirt, a missing kitchen knife, and a muddy footprint were clues. Even a hair clinging to a garment could unlock a crime's secrets. In the chaos of crime scenes, we left no stone unturned.

My ears became my allies, capturing subtle nuances in the human voice. A quiver, a stutter, an anxious tremor, or an overly animated pitch all provided information. I mastered the art of reading between the lines and fostering an environment where people felt free to reveal their inner selves. I wielded verbal judo when needed—employing words, tone, and emphasis to dismantle emotional barriers.

A sense of smell was also in my arsenal of tools, offering a storehouse of clues to the story unfolding within crime scenes: the acrid odor of drug concoctions, the smoldering remnants of burned documents, the lingering fragrance of spilled perfume, the nauseating pungency of rotting food, and the stench of refuse.

While honing investigative skills was paramount, intuition also played an integral role. Some detectives possessed an innate sixth sense, an uncanny ability to chart their course through a maze of crimes, often with eerie accuracy. Like bloodhounds on a scent, they unearthed secrets with a finesse that defied explanation. I'd been relying on my sixth sense since my childhood and then through my gang days; my years as a cop had honed these instincts, and I trusted them implicitly.

Long before I joined the force, I believed that detectives were the cream of the crop. However, some, despite being lackluster, obtain the position through connections and nepotism. "Detective Do-Nothings," we call them.

When paired with a lackadaisical partner, I became a lone wolf in pursuit of justice. Perhaps my fellow officers perceived me as overeager, an untested newcomer outshining them and overshadowing their abilities. My diligence had a downside, transforming me into a repository for cases no one else wanted. Still, the weight of the caseload mattered little, for I embraced the responsibilities of my calling. *Bring it on*, I thought.

At that time, the old and new generations of detectives were divided, and the chasm grew more evident with each passing day. Some seasoned officers struggled to keep pace with swiftly evolving technology, while others stubbornly resisted change. They clung to typewriters while the rest of the world embraced computers and printers. The battle-hardened detectives who had faced gunfire without flinching now found themselves intimidated by modern machines. They couldn't accept a reliance on the younger generation to navigate this digital terrain, and many chose to retire rather than adapt to new ways.

Watching them, I resolved to be flexible and learn new technology so I didn't get left behind.

Lian and I had discussed getting married over the years, but it was never something we felt we had to do or even wanted to do. I've always questioned anything considered "required," pushing back on what society tells me I must do. The idea of marriage is something society created, and we don't need to follow societal norms to prove anything to anyone about how we feel about one another. I question everything, such as why people buy a diamond ring for marriage. Why not a ruby? Why even a ring? Why not a necklace? Or a fucking shoe? Who created these norms for society? That's how my mind works. I'm not the person to buy flowers on Valentine's Day because the herd does it. If flowers make Lian happy, I'll surprise her with flowers any other time.

She understood my rebellious mindset, and she didn't seem to want or need that certificate to put value to our relationship or our family. Besides, she had very little family here in America, so an elaborate ceremony didn't seem necessary with so few people to attend.

But we came to realize that getting married made sense because of the benefits, including the transferring of assets and social security and tax considerations. I wanted to take care of Lian and my family should anything happen to me; I didn't want to burden her with financial issues beyond the grief she and our kids would experience. Admittedly, it was more practical than romantic, but I asked her to marry me. In truth, I cared deeply for this amazing woman and mother, so we tied the knot at city hall.

One day, I stepped into my office and caught sight of a familiar face on a wanted poster: Monkey, Shorty's younger brother, was now being sought for a string of ruthless home invasions.

During the waning days of my gang life, Monkey and Shadow, our gang's enforcer, were arrested and sentenced to ten years in prison. I visited Shadow soon after he was locked up, during the twilight of my gang days. The sight of him behind bars tugged at my chest. While the world deemed him a criminal, in my eyes he was a brother.

Once released, Shadow was deported to Cambodia. Monkey, a legal immigrant, returned to the US and plunged right back into home invasions. For him, there seemed to be no other path to make a living.

I worried that Monkey and I might cross paths. Could I look the other way? I would decide what to do if or when such a moment confronted me.

One of my most unforgettable cases brought me to a living room where a man lay bathed in blood, his body riddled with over thirty stab wounds, a samurai sword beside him.

Entering the fourth-floor apartment, I scoured the scene for vital evidence: the weapon, security cameras, signs of forced entry, and potential witnesses—initial steps in such cases. The front door and the fire escape window showed no signs of forced entry, which made unauthorized entry unlikely. An undisturbed layer of dust on the windowsills suggested they hadn't been opened for some time.

My inspection led me to a bookshelf stacked with occult literature, which raised intriguing questions. Was this a straightforward murder, or were darker forces at play?

I turned my attention to the exterior security cameras. Contrary to popular belief, detective work is far less fast-paced than depicted in TV dramas. I painstakingly reviewed hours of footage, yet to my surprise, no one had entered or exited the building since the victim's phone call with his girlfriend around midnight.

The dead man's grief-stricken parents came to our station from out of state, driven by frustration over the sluggish progress of the case. The notion that anyone harbored malevolent intentions toward their son bewildered them. The idea of suicide seemed ludicrous, considering the savagery of the stabbing. His parents demanded answers, and I offered reassurance, emphasizing the time required for a thorough investigation while outlining our procedures.

To glean more insights into their son, I broached the topic of his interest in the occult, referencing the books found in his apartment. Their shocked expressions indicated ignorance of his potential involvement in such matters. I stressed the necessity of delving into his life to unearth potential leads. I confiscated his computer and dispatched the hard drive to our computer crimes unit, revealing a trail of dark-web searches related to drugs and connections to the occult. This case demanded a comprehensive approach, necessitating the meticulous assembly of every available fragment of information to unveil the truth.

During the autopsy, I scrutinized the man's body, documenting each stab wound that marred his left upper torso and right leg. Considering the victim's right-handedness and the absence of defensive wounds or signs of a struggle, the medical examiner arrived at a chilling conclusion: suicide. The scars on the upper torso and left side bore the hallmark of wounds inflicted by a right-handed individual. Most of his wounds were superficial, except for the fatal one that had nicked his heart.

With the chest opened in the customary autopsy procedure, I studied the exposed heart and discerned the minuscule perforation responsible for his demise. A similar nick on my finger would have healed within days, but such an injury occurring within the heart transformed into a fatal wound.

The next day in my office I met with the victim's parents. His mother shook her head, her expression conveying both disbelief and shock. "How could it be *suicide*? How is it possible for someone to stab himself thirty times?"

I explained the concept of the hesitation wound. Those attempting suicide typically harm themselves incrementally, gradually mustering the courage to ultimately end their own life. When the autopsy results were unveiled, we learned that the victim had been under the influence of drugs before his demise, providing a rational basis for my account of hesitation wounds and suicide.

Ultimately, they couldn't argue with science and sadly accepted the cause of death. In truth, they really didn't know their son or his proclivities. This case stuck with me, and in hindsight, I understand why. Every parent thinks they know their kids, but my job revealed that this was the opposite of the truth. "Not my kid!" is a refrain I often heard, even when they were caught in the act.

Another chilling case peeled back the layers of hesitation wounds, revealing the grim tale of a Chinese man who'd brutally murdered his wife. The investigation drew the precinct's attention to my skills as a translator, bridging the language gap between another detective and the perpetrator.

"Why did you decapitate your wife?" I grilled the Chinese man with cold, flat eyes. Bandages circled his wrists, the aftermath of a harrowing act of self-harm.

The man softened as his eyes filled with tears, and out spilled his horrifying narrative. He had enlisted the services of snakeheads to smuggle his wife into the country from China. His desperate move cost an insurmountable $30,000 debt owed to the human trafficking syndicate, to be paid with years of bondage, an unrelenting grind in a restaurant, where he toiled day and night seven days a week.

Fate took a cruel twist when his wife, upon arriving, found love in the arms of another man, forsaking him. Overwhelmed by a maddening fury at her betrayal, he unleashed a savage barrage of stabs upon her, severing her throat and leaving her head precariously hanging by a slender thread of flesh.

During our interrogation, his wrists and forearms bore the undeniable evidence of hesitation wounds, a testament to his suicide attempt. Slashing at his wrists, he'd lacked the resolve to carry out the act decisively.

I understood the crime of passion committed by the perpetrator: Betrayal is the catalyst for many murders.

But in my former world, true gangsters don't hurt women. We'd had females in our circle who felt secure with Fuk Ching, knowing we would not take advantage of their vulnerability. Some of them had been runaways, rape victims, or homeless.

This man could only blame himself for his poor judgment in trusting such a woman and making such a drastic commitment without discretion. The victim was a woman who had wanted to reach America and had used her husband to achieve that goal. Every crime scene told a story, raising difficult questions that compelled me to seek answers.

My next focus was a series of cases that happened in all the Chinatowns in New York City, orchestrated by cunning Chinese scammers. A friend's mother, victimized by the "Buddha blessing" scam, suffered a staggering loss of $350,000. I told my friend to have her come in and file a police report.

Betty Wang was embarrassed, but she relayed her story. She was at a tea shop mentally grappling with an issue around her son's health when a woman sat down at her table, a sympathetic expression on her face. Without preamble, the woman said, "I feel that you are worried about your son's health." She took Betty's hand. "I know this is hard to believe, but I have a gift of knowing. And I feel such pain in you right now."

Betty was shocked, but the stranger's sympathy compelled her to say, "Yes, he has cancer."

The woman shook her head sadly. "And you and your husband . . ." She looked up, as though tapping into the ether. "You are in the medical area, but you cannot heal him. And this is very frustrating to you."

Again, Betty's eyes widened. "My husband and I own pharmacies here in Chinatown. We have given him many things, but nothing has helped."

Again, the woman shook her head in deep sadness. "The place where I get this information, it's telling me that someone placed a curse on you, long ago. The curse has brought about this cancer."

Being superstitious and religious, Betty began to think about other misfortunes that had befallen her over the last few years. Yes, it made sense. She could even think of a woman who could have done it. "How do I get rid of the curse?"

"Simple. You get a Buddha blessing."

A second woman *happened* to be passing by just then, and she inhaled in surprise and turned to them. In a hushed voice, she asked, "Did you just say Buddha blessing?" When woman number one nodded, the second woman dropped into the available seat at the small table. "Getting a blessing saved my marriage. We went from almost getting a divorce to being the happiest people in our family. All that bad karma was gone. It's truly a miracle!"

The first woman nodded. "I hear many stories like that. Relationships mended, financial windfalls, and . . . health restored." She turned to Betty. "I can arrange, if you'd like."

Betty's heart swelled with hope. "What do I do?"

"We ask for a blessing to clear the curse. To show your faith, you must bring all of your valuables to the ceremony. Put everything in a black bag like this one." She dug in her large purse and pulled out a cloth bag. "Here, you can take this one."

Betty shook her head. "I can't just give away—"

"No, you don't give it away. It's just as a symbol. I do the ritual, and you take your bag home again. I don't charge you for the ceremony. I just want to help"—she looked up again—"Mark, right? I want Mark to get better."

Hearing that the woman even knew her son's name convinced her. Betty went to the bank and pulled out $350,000 and jewelry from her safety deposit box, then met the woman at a designated place. Just out of the bank camera's view, right there in the street, the woman held up the bag and chanted a prayer to Buddha, with both women supposedly closing their eyes. Then she handed the bag back to Betty—who later said it felt as heavy as it had before.

"Now, you must go home and wait two days before opening the bag, to show Buddha that you are patient and faithful." She patted Betty's shoulder. "Go, and be well."

Betty waited the prescribed two days before opening the bag, only to find some bottles of water and cut-up newspapers bundled together like cash. She was devastated.

I explained to Betty that these scams are run by syndicates, who choose a suitable target. They send their people to shadow them, listening to their conversations and noting life details they can use later to "*supernaturally know*" when they put their scam into action. A "random" passerby corroborates the effectiveness of the blessing, further convincing the target.

These scams go on to this day, targeting people who have more hope than they do skepticism. Because of the time between the crime happening and the victim's discovery of it, rarely do these criminals get caught. Even worse, because victims of these types of crimes are often too ashamed to report them, the authorities don't know how many actually occur. When they do report them, they'll say, "They must have blown drugged smoke in my face that made me not think straight" or "They had to have slipped me some kind of drug." In hindsight, even they can't believe they fell for the scam.

Our small office accommodated twelve detectives and two supervisors. I had to adjust to thirteen people's personalities, moods, habits, and attitudes, which was sometimes challenging. I kept to myself, minding my business and only engaging when someone sought my help or interaction. Despite this, over my first two years as a detective, the power struggles in the precinct intensified, and my relationship with my supervisor became a daily burden. The tension reached its climax in January 2007 when Sergeant Macuso coerced me into a court hearing despite me not feeling well.

A reaction to an antibiotic had left me dizzy, with a headache and fever. I was scheduled to testify in court about one of my arrests. I called Macuso the night before to advise him that I would be unable to come in because of my condition.

He told me, "Lieutenant Zark from the court section has called for you to testify at this court appearance numerous times. He's going to give you a CD [Command Discipline], and since you already have pending charges in that casino case, that CD will automatically be upgraded to charges and specs. I'm just looking out for you. After court, you can call in sick."

I reluctantly agreed to attend court, requesting transportation due to my dizziness.

The next day, at the court sign-in desk, I saw Lieutenant Zark and introduced myself.

"Sir, the only reason I'm here is because you threatened to give me a CD if I didn't show up, and that CD would be upgraded to charges and specs because I already have charges pending. I want you to know that I had a reaction to an antibiotic and I'm dizzy and nauseated."

Lieutenant Zark looked confused. "Your CO never told me you were sick. Other arrangements could have certainly been made."

As suspected, Macuso hadn't been looking out for me at all. And I doubted that Zark had been calling all those times.

Zark promised to expedite my release and managed to get the assistant district attorney (ADA) to drop everything and meet with me. I handed over copies of my paperwork and awaited my partner, Detective O'Reilly, who would drive me back.

As O'Reilly and I started to head out, dizziness and nausea overcame me, and I tumbled down seventeen steps at 350 Jay Street. Bruised and in pain, I suffered a hairline fracture in my ankle. An ambulance took me to the hospital, where my blood pressure registered at 100/60, with a fever of about 100 degrees.

During my hospital stay, I learned of Sergeant Macuso's furious reaction to my accident. He suspected I'd staged it for a lawsuit, venting his anger in front of the other detectives and saying how he would crush me. As things settled, he realized his blunder in ordering a sick person to work and feared potential legal repercussions.

Upon my return to the office, Sergeant Macuso's attitude took a complete turn. Gone was the arrogance, replaced by a caring facade that aimed to dissuade me from pursuing a lawsuit, which could tarnish his reputation. He reassigned me from the Burglary/Robbery Apprehension Module to work with a team, resulting in a lighter workload. This new assignment allowed me to work independently without his constant oversight, lifting a weight from my shoulders.

Meanwhile, the court contacted the precinct to inquire about my intentions regarding a lawsuit for the staircase accident. I informed them of my lack of interest in suing; it wasn't in my nature. The facility administrator then renovated the staircase by building a landing platform in the middle of the long flight of stairs for safety. At least something good came of it for all the people who traversed that staircase in the years to come. And my accident freed me from Sergeant Macuso's grasp. But if I *had* planned this, as he suspected, I would have ingeniously outsmarted him.

CHAPTER SIXTEEN

SKILLS OF A FORMER GANGSTER

For nine years in the gang world, I navigated the murky waters of criminality, honing a methodical approach to unlawful endeavors. The many illegal acts I orchestrated involved meticulous planning, always including exit strategies.

Clumsy criminals relish crimes of opportunity and leave breadcrumbs for detectives to follow, while the cunning and disciplined ones erase their footprints and sever connections to their dark deeds. Yet a criminal's trail is seldom hidden entirely. As a detective, I would piece together these fragments to form a picture of each crime.

According to the FBI's Uniform Crime Report data, as scrutinized by the Murder Accountability Project, a staggering 345,613 cases of homicide and non-negligent manslaughter from between 1965 and 2023 remain unsolved out of a total of 1,029,984. The FBI's Criminal Justice Information Services (CJIS) reveals a troubling trend: an escalating percentage of unresolved murders in the United States. In 2022, the clearance rate for homicide cases plummeted to a record low, with a mere 52.3 percent of the nation's estimated 21,156 crimes solved.[6]

The police needed to demonstrate their crime-solving prowess to deter criminals, who only grew bolder and more resolute in their illicit pursuits when they believed they could evade capture. Detectives like me aimed to send a clear message: "We will find you and bring you to justice."

My role as a police detective was a small but vital cog in the machinery of justice, overseeing a slice of New York's Chinatowns under the Sixty-Sixth Squad's jurisdiction. Each case I cracked contributed to America's law enforcement tapestry. During my early years in the Sixty-Sixth Squad, the NYPD wielded technological tools for crime prevention and investigation, but compared to today's arsenal, they were primitive and limited.

Detective methods have since evolved, including satellites, innovative surveillance systems, computers, artificial intelligence, and state-of-the-art communication systems. However, for all its might, technology is merely a tool in the hands of detectives. Success hinges on the skills, talent, and unwavering dedication of those who wield it. Instincts can never be replicated by technology.

Throughout my seventeen-year tenure as an NYPD police detective, I juggled over three thousand cases and made hundreds of felony arrests. I filled my detective notepads with notes about crimes from petty thefts to homicides. In our world,

---

6. Thomas Hargrove, "Uniform Crime Report for Homicides: 1965–2023," Murder Accountability Project, updated September 25, 2024, https://public.tableau.com/app/profile/thomas.hargrove/viz/UCR1965-2019/HomicideClearances; "America's Declining Homicide Clearance Rates: 1965–2023," Murder Accountability Project, accessed January 6, 2025, https://www.murderdata.org/p/reported-homicide-clearance-rate-1980.html.

multitasking was the norm, with several cases demanding our attention simultaneously.

In each investigation, I assessed the crime scene and pieced together our experts' findings, building a case that would stand up in court. I called in helicopters to track homicide suspects from above and surveillance teams to shadow their every move. Tools like facial recognition, photo analysis, and forensics were at my fingertips. Even though we had access to the best tools and training available, it still boiled down to good old-fashioned detective work. A detective's dedication is crucial; without it, all resources are wasted. These were some of the cases that stand out in my memories . . .

On the early morning of June 30, 2007, a Chinese gypsy-cab driver named Stephen Chen stopped his vehicle in Manhattan's Chinatown to pick up three Vietnamese male passengers. Upon reaching their destination in Brooklyn's Chinatown, one of the passengers seated in the back looped a bicycle chain around the driver's neck. Chen fought desperately, clutching at the chain that threatened to strangle him. Meanwhile, the passenger in the front seat rifled through his pockets and snatched his belongings. Once the ruthless trio had seized what they desired, they ejected him from his own vehicle and sped away toward Ninth Avenue, leaving him robbed and shaken.

Stephen Chen walked into the Sixty-Sixth Precinct approximately an hour and a half after the crime had unfolded. As a gypsy cab, his vehicle lacked the protective partition shielding licensed taxi drivers from unruly passengers. He also had no video camera footage of the incident.

His account of the incident detailed the loss of $200, a bank card, a credit card, a New York State gold ring with a white stone, a driver's license, and a cell phone. Most notably, Chen described the assailants as Vietnamese, a detail that would prove crucial in the investigation.

After reading the report and consulting with the responding officers, I arranged a face-to-face interview with the victim to corroborate his account and clarify specific details. Chen claimed he could identify all three perpetrators if presented with the opportunity.

I showed him the precinct's extensive photo database of individuals with previous arrests near the Sixty-Sixth and Chinatown precincts. Unfortunately, no matches emerged.

Undaunted, I devised a plan for the victim to accompany me in an unmarked police car equipped with tinted windows as we scoured Chinatown and known hangouts frequented by Asian suspects. This canvassing also yielded no leads. This second setback did not deter me, as I knew even the smallest detail could lead to a breakthrough.

To heighten our chances of locating Chen's stolen vehicle, I entered its details into the police database to alert fellow officers to be on the lookout. If they discovered the car unoccupied, they were to maintain surveillance in case the perpetrators returned to it. If they didn't, the police would tow the car to the precinct, enabling us to dust it for fingerprints and conduct a meticulous DNA analysis.

We initiated notifications to pawnshops in New York, alerts for the described jewelry, a call to the victim to verify any unauthorized card usage, and a subpoena for records of the victim's stolen cell phone for the next thirty days. In addition to notifying bridge and tunnel police to watch for the stolen vehicle, I scrutinized robbery patterns and delved into UF-250 reports (Stop, Question, and Frisk worksheets) to see if any of my fellow officers had stopped anyone matching Chen's description of the suspects.

Just one day after the initial incident, another victim called 911 about a similarly horrifying ordeal perpetrated by a trio of individuals. It wasn't merely the modus operandi (MO) mirroring the earlier case that got my mind racing, but it happened at the same time and location. In this instance, the victim had been dealt a harsher hand: He had lost a hard-earned $1,000, a cherished gold ring, a credit card, all his keys, his cell phone, and his New York driver's license. The pieces pointed to the once-dreaded, remorseless Vietnamese group: the BTK.

The situation called to mind a case from my distant past, in which a person afflicted by Alzheimer's had gone astray. In that instance, the person's cell phone was a lifeline. We collaborated with the phone company, and they used the signal to lead us to within fifty feet of the lost individual.

I navigated the bureaucratic maze for a subpoena from a judge to obtain the second victim's cell phone's International Mobile Equipment Identity code so I could track it. Once activated, it would reveal calls, text messages, and the phone's precise location.

I cast the net wider, looping in the Brooklyn robbery squad, taxi robbery unit, gang division, and the NYPD's Auto Larceny Unit.

The bridge and tunnel division joined the hunt too, alerted to the stolen vehicles roaming the city's arteries. In those days, the city's surveillance was rudimentary, fixed primarily on bridges and tunnels. Cameras designed to capture license plates would sound an alarm if a stolen car passed. I entered the stolen car's license plate into the system, hoping it had incurred a parking ticket or committed a traffic violation.

But the trail remained cold, devoid of Vietnamese suspects, stolen vehicles, witnesses, or a scrap of surveillance footage. In that void, a flicker of intuition began to take shape.

I maintained that the culprits had once belonged to the notorious BTK gang, individuals who were likely old-school gangsters around my age. Their pasts and lengthy prison sentences had seemingly left them with no choice but to turn to robbery as a means of survival.

I could still recognize my kind, understand their thought processes, and anticipate their moves as only a former gangster could. I imagined them operating in tight-knit, covert groups while navigating the intricate streets of Manhattan's and Brooklyn's Chinatowns. I scoured arrest records going back a few years, aiming to uncover any prior arrests in a similar vein. Unfortunately, without a name, the computer yielded no results.

The case took a significant turn when I received notification that the perpetrators had tried to use the ATM card at a bank on Bowery Street in Manhattan, suggesting they were holed up in the heart of Manhattan's Chinatown. Though this was out of my jurisdiction, I could go into any other districts to investigate, should leads send me there.

I had little expectation for the bank's CCTV footage. I was sure the culprits had obscured their identities by donning caps or some other disguise. Still, I requested the footage from the bank manager, recognizing its potential as additional evidence should a court trial follow an arrest.

In Chinatown Manhattan, I turned to the cops on foot patrol. I knew firsthand they had extensive knowledge of their assigned areas and were acquainted with everyone from street urchins and the homeless to petty criminals, business owners, and community leaders. Approaching one of the patrol cops, I shared details about the perpetrators and my suspicion that they might be former BTK gang members.

"Leave me your number," he replied. "I'll get in touch if something comes up."

A few days later, that call arrived. "Mike, I've got something for you. My informant mentioned that he had a drug session with the individuals you're looking for on the rooftop of a building on Grand Street. Their ringleader is a Vietnamese named Vu, and just like you suspected, he's a former BTK member out on parole."

Yes! I had been correct.

I went back to our Records database, going year by year for any reference to Vu as a nickname—and there he was. Looking at Tam Vu's long-ago mug shot rekindled a memory: I suspected that he'd been an accomplice to the gang member who'd stabbed my friend Carrot Head during the party in Brooklyn. Anger surged within me, for we'd been unable to exact revenge for our friend that fateful night. Tam's crew could have also ended my life had it not been for Viet Jim's warning as we were about to drive into that ambush planned by the BTKs.

A mix of spite and anticipation welled up within me. My ultimate revenge would be to see recognition in Tam's eyes as I handcuffed him. Luckily, my better judgment prevailed as that could unearth my past to my superiors and jeopardize my career.

The informant had described Tam as well dressed and fluent in Vietnamese, English, and Cantonese. He traveled with the other two males. They'd all arrived from Philadelphia eight days prior, with plans to depart New York shortly to conduct their criminal activities in another state.

According to the informant, during their drug session, Tam had brandished a knife, an electric cord, and a cab driver's license.

Bingo.

We heard the rooftop of that Grand Street building was a regular hangout. With a backup team of plainclothes cops, I went up to the roof but found no sign of the suspects. I escorted both complainants to the Fifth Precinct in the heart of

Chinatown, which had additional photos of the criminals. Unfortunately, most of the pictures of them were from when they were teens, too outdated to be useful.

Undeterred, I continued making moves in this figurative chess game, confident that something would eventually surface. And it did. The patrol officer who'd provided me with information about Tam caught sight of the perpetrator in the heart of Chinatown, and he wasted no time in calling for backup. The Vietnamese suspects were apprehended seventeen days after the first robbery transpired.

The Fifth Precinct even reached out to me in recognition of my dogged pursuit of this case.

I summoned my partner, Detective O'Reilly, to transport the carjacking complainants to the precinct. Per standard procedure, Tam joined a lineup behind a window alongside five other individuals, some of whom were cops in plainclothes while others were civilians compensated ten dollars to participate.

The complainants identified Tam as the man who'd robbed him. Tam had been on parole when he committed the crime, so he now faced the prospect of serving ten to twenty years for his malevolent actions.

Curious to learn more about the suspect, I ventured into a few Vietnamese restaurants in Chinatown and inquired about Tam. One owner recounted an interesting encounter: Tam had entered the restaurant, introduced himself as a BTK member who'd just gotten out of prison, and asked for money. Moved by pity rather than fear, the restaurant owner had handed Tam $1,000.

This noodle house held memories for me, as it was where I'd dined with my friend Diamond in 1994, only to be subjected to a stop-and-frisk by the police.

I was happy about the arrest and all the work we'd done, but I had a dilemma. Processing Tam would mean hours of face-to-face time, and he might recognize me. I chose not to pick him up and instead asked my partner, Detective O'Reilly, to undertake the task. He happily accepted it. That loss was worth avoiding the risk of being recognized—nothing good could come from that.

Detective McGrath accompanied Detective O'Reilly in the vehicle to assist with the transport. From what McGrath told me later, during the cruiser's journey across the Manhattan Bridge, Tam Vu was asking the detectives questions about his arrest.

McGrath, who was a talker, entertained those questions until O'Reilly shouted at Tam, "Shut the hell up, you yellow Chinaman, or I'll toss you right off this bridge!"

"I'm no Chinaman, old man!" Tam said. "I'm Vietnamese. I'll knife your eyes out!"

That silenced the car for a while.

In the world of crime solving, a crime is never dismissed as minor. Every case demands diligence, whether it's a robbery or a murder. I approached each case with equal gravity, marshaling the NYPD's vast resources to track down culprits and lawbreakers.

On November 3, 2007, near the intersection of Forty-First Street and Ninth Avenue in the heart of Chinatown, two men approached an unsuspecting victim engrossed with his cell phone.

"Got some money for beer?" asked one of the perpetrators.

Startled, the victim couldn't even respond before the assailants grabbed him and launched a pocket-pilfering assault. In the struggle, a gun went off, sending a bullet through the victim's cheek and out the other side.

Fortuitously, a passing police patrol car saw what happened. Officers pursued the fleeing perpetrators while the victim ran off. He was found exhausted and bleeding not far from the initial attack site and was rushed to a nearby hospital for medical attention. Meanwhile, the cops caught one of the assailants.

Upon my arrival at the precinct, the responding officers briefed me on the incident. While one of the officers positively identified the arrested perpetrator as the shooter, the identity of the second assailant remained a mystery. Finding him became our goal. Once the victim was stable enough to communicate, I went to the hospital to interview him, hoping to glean further insights.

Remarkably, despite losing several teeth, the victim could still communicate. According to the doctor's assessment based on a CAT scan, the bullet had traversed from the left side of his neck to exit through his right cheek, narrowly missing a major artery. The police had not recovered the bullet.

The victim had unwittingly made himself the perfect target for these criminals. He'd strolled through a robbery-prone area of Chinatown oblivious to his surroundings. I didn't chide him about his poor choices. I only wanted more information about the assailants.

"They were Hispanic teenagers," he said. "The shooter was tall and thin, while the other was shorter and stocky. It all happened so quickly that I couldn't get a clear look at the one who shot me."

"Where did you run to after being shot?"

"In shock, I ran from the Ninth Avenue to a store in Eighth Avenue and asked a friend there to dial 911 because my English is not very good."

Detective work diverges from the immediate response of patrol officers; detectives need to conduct thorough preparatory work before confronting a suspect. Before I approached the suspect for questioning, meticulous groundwork was imperative.

As a rookie detective, I'd learned this important lesson from senior members. Coming from patrol, my first instinct had been to pursue perpetrators as soon as they were identified. However, the old-timers would rein me in with, "Hey, kid, slow down. Before you leave this office, make sure you conduct all the checks and gather as much information about the perp as possible."

So, I took my time doing due diligence. First, I needed to do all the computer checks to piece the story together. I did a complete background check on the apprehended perp and checked the UF-250 log to see if anyone fitting the description had been stopped in the confines of the Sixty-Sixth Precinct and its adjoining precincts. I also checked to see if anyone fitting the description was on parole in the area of the Seventy-Second and Sixty-Sixth Precincts or if anyone had been arrested for similar cases and made bail. I particularly paid attention to any complaint reports of robberies.

I checked the 911 log and verified the victim's account of seeking assistance from a friend. Then, I cross-referenced the information provided by the responding officers, and one of them corroborated the identity of the shooter.

Moving forward, my partner and I undertook a canvass operation. We knocked on doors, rang doorbells, and interviewed potential witnesses. Additionally, we scoured the area's CCTV footage, hoping in vain to capture the crime on video, but we needed more eyes and hands to gather clues and leads. Alongside the crime scene squad, we scoured the vicinity for the firearm. Despite thorough searches under cars, in sewers, and nearby establishments, the weapon remained elusive.

Armed with the first suspect's name—Ramos—and his address, we proceeded to his residence. Given his history of arrests, our inquiries extended to individuals associated with him as we sought to identify codefendants or accessories from his prior criminal record. Once armed with this information, I interviewed the suspect.

Ramos's account unfolded. "I was just about to exit the cab when my friend Fernandez beckoned me over. He signaled for me to approach this guy who was distracted, so I did. In an instant, he lunged at the Chinese man, robbing him at gunpoint before firing a shot. I never expected him to resort to robbery, let alone shoot the poor guy. When those shots rang out, I made a run for it."

"Can you provide Fernandez's first name?" I pressed.

"I only know him by his last name."

"Did you witness Fernandez discharging the firearm?"

Ramos affirmed with a nod.

"What type of firearm did he use?"

"It was a silver .380 handgun."

"Are you absolutely certain?"

"Yes."

"You were found in possession of a loaded magazine," I pointed out. "Can you explain why you had it?"

"It's mine, but I don't own a gun."

Right, I thought, *you just carry around a magazine for a gun you don't own.* During our conversation, I couldn't help but notice minuscule blood specks on his arm, shirt, and shoes. Ramos said that these had resulted from minor lacerations sustained during his altercation with the police. I took a swab of his mouth and arranged for his clothes to undergo DNA testing.

I was sure Ramos had disposed of the gun after firing it. His lies fortified my determination to bring him to justice, especially as he'd thrown Fernandez under the bus to divert focus away from himself.

Ramos provided details about Fernandez's residence and favored haunts. My partner searched the park and other locales in the surrounding area, but our efforts yielded nothing. I ran the name through our database to identify any individuals residing in the vicinity. I contacted the youth offender unit, hoping to find any record of Fernandez, but that also produced no results.

I enlisted the assistance of the gang division in my investigation, exploring their knowledge of individuals named Fernandez among known gang members. I also cross-referenced the list of parolees, but again, Fernandez failed to surface.

This pursuit of Ramos's codefendant resulted in a list of twenty-three potential suspects matching the profile and name. I narrowed the list down to five known members of the Mexican gang *Niños Malos*, one of whom had a prior arrest for robbery and had recently been released from jail.

I conducted a comprehensive background check on this particular Fernandez and visited his listed address to speak with family members and relatives. To my dismay, he was absent, and his relatives claimed no knowledge of his whereabouts.

When I finally obtained a photograph of him, I arranged for the victim to view it alongside five other images of individuals resembling the suspect.

"That's him!" the victim exclaimed, pointing to Fernandez's photo.

The image corresponded precisely with the description the victim had given during our initial interview. Armed with this identification, I promptly issued an active investigation card, indicating there was probable cause to arrest and requesting law enforcement officers to detain him and notify me. Regrettably, our informants relayed the disheartening news that the fugitive had fled to Mexico.

Despite Fernandez's escape, Ramos remained within our grasp, and I was determined not to let him slip away—especially since I suspected that he was, in fact, the shooter.

A few days later, I received a phone call from the patrol unit, delivering news that they'd recovered the silver .380-caliber automatic handgun. A tenant had inadvertently stumbled upon it concealed in the bushes, prompting an immediate call to 911. Forensic analysis and the crime scene unit confirmed that the blood I'd seen on Ramos's attire matched the victim's. Ballistic testing, examination of the magazine clip, and scrutiny of the handgun all pointed to Ramos as the perpetrator. With the mounting evidence, he was formally charged and arrested.

About a year later, I received notification that his partner in crime, Fernandez, had been arrested and deported by the border patrol in Arizona while attempting an illegal return to the United States. I found myself powerless in this situation, as New York arrest warrants held no sway over federal offenses. At the very least, Fernandez's deportation meant he wouldn't be around to commit further crimes on US soil.

Another case resolved.

In 2008, I could see that Lian was getting restless and bored now that the kids, Olivia, who was eleven, and Brandon, who was nine, were in school. I encouraged Lian to get a part-time job. She'd been a stay-at-home mom for years, and I thought getting out in the world would be good for her.

An anonymous benefactor had created a fund for police precincts across New York City to hire sixteen interpreters from various ethnic backgrounds to assist people who spoke no English. I suggested she apply for one of those positions, working at the front desk. Because she was fluent in Cantonese and Mandarin, she could assist people from our community. At that time, there weren't many Asian police employees, and those who spoke the language were sent to work the streets. Though she didn't like cops back when we first started dating, she'd matured from that nineteen-year-old mindset. She got the job.

I liked that she'd get a sense of what I dealt with on a daily basis and why I worked long hours, often coming home late. I'd never revealed the issues I endured with some of the more difficult personalities I worked with, shielding her from the pressures and dangers I faced. Besides, I wasn't the kind of person who dumped my day on her.

She ended up liking the position because she was able to advocate for and help those in distress. Otherwise, victims had to wait for a translator, with no one who could comfort them in their own language. She also learned to be alert for scams and dangers by hearing victims' stories.

Once she was settled into the job, it occurred to me that we had had similar life journeys, going from the criminal world to law enforcement. Like me, she had been scrappy and resourceful when she'd needed to be, and now we both served our community in satisfying ways. Looking back, it made perfect sense that we ended up together.

CHAPTER SEVENTEEN

CRIMES OF THE HEART

The early 2000s birthed a new predator: the cybersex criminal. In the shadowy world of cybercrime, the web's freedom morphed into a trap for the unsuspecting. The NYPD had to develop new skills to track down hardhearted thieves taking advantage of the lonely and lovelorn.

This next case began with a knock on my office door.

A patrol officer stepped in. "Mike, there's a university student outside, desperate to talk to a Chinese detective."

"Send him in."

A young man stumbled into my office, the picture of anxiety. His complexion was ghostly; his eyes darted around, unable to settle on mine.

I nodded to the chair. "Take a breath. Then tell me your story."

An online encounter with a girl had spiraled into an explicit exchange. As he recounted his actions, I could almost see the digital noose tightening.

"She asked me to record myself masturbating. She said it

got her off." He rubbed his face with trembling hands. "After I sent it to her, she threatened to unleash it to my friends and family on social media unless . . . unless I p-pay her five thousand dollars," he stammered, terror heavy in his voice.

"How did you connect with her?" My question was sharp, cutting through his panic.

"A *friend's* recommendation," he said, a hint of betrayal creeping into his tone.

"You never met her in person?"

"No. But I trusted his judgment. He works out with her in the gym."

I leaned forward, my instincts kicking in.

"Listen," I insisted, "you might be book-smart, but you're not street-smart. She doesn't go to the same gym as your friend. I'd bet that your friend is also a victim. He introduced you to her because this same person blackmailed him. She threatened to post his videos on social media if he couldn't get her more victims. Your friend was not only scammed out of money but is being coerced into helping her."

His face, a canvas of confusion, fell with the dawning of truth. He curled up into a ball of despair. "What should I do now?"

"These syndicates are not in the US. They work overseas and victimize people all over the world. Chances are, they're in a place where I have no jurisdiction."

When the poor guy looked like he was going to cry, I said, "I can start by doing a computer forensic and try to get the girl's IP address."

The kid said that he would think about other options and left.

The next day he returned, resignation slowing his steps and stooping his shoulders. "You were right, Detective Moy. My friend admitted that he got caught in the same snare."

"I wouldn't call him a friend anymore, if I were you," I said.

"He sold you out to save his own hide. Are you ready to proceed and provide me with all the information I need?"

He shook his head and made a hasty retreat, despite my prodding for him to make an official report. Fear had made its decision for him. He chose silence over action.

He might have decided to pay off the girl, yet there was no assurance that the syndicate would not demand additional money. Some Chinese syndicates bleed their victims dry. In his wake lingered a harsh truth: The monsters of our digital age can be even more terrifying than those lurking in the shadows of our streets.

Lust and the promise of pleasure never failed to trap victims. Lust can blind even rational individuals, who often realize too late that they have been scammed.

A Chinese man responded to an advertisement online for hiring an escort. He texted the number, and a woman quickly replied. After a brief exchange, a pimp took over and directed the man to a specific motel to await further instructions. Once the man was in the room, the pimp called and demanded an initial payment via a $300 iTunes card.

"Why should I do that?" the man asked.

"It's assurance money, so we know you're serious," the pimp explained. "Go to the store across the street and buy the iTunes card."

The man complied and sent the iTunes card's number to the pimp. Soon after, he received another call and was told to send another $300 iTunes card. He protested, but the pimp insisted the extra money was refundable after the service. It was merely a precaution in case of a police raid, as well as to ensure he was a serious customer and not a cop.

Having already paid for the motel room and the first iTunes

card, the man felt compelled to pay the additional amount to salvage his investment.

Now the pimp concocted another excuse to extract a further $300. Realizing he had been scammed, the man cut his losses and ceased communication. The pimp persisted with calls and messages with threats to notify his family if he did not pay, but the man ignored them until they stopped.

Lust can cloud judgment, leading to costly mistakes.

In some corners of Chinatown, a sinister racket known in the underworld as "*deng bofai*" preyed on the heartstrings of unsuspecting men, using the lure of romance to extort victims. Like many of these scam cases, victims were usually reluctant to make a report, but they often came in for my advice.

In one instance, a man named Joe relayed his story to me. He described being in a Chinatown club, and amid the clink of glasses and the hum of conversation, his gaze locked on to "the kind of woman who makes your heart race, you know? I approached her, and sparks ignited. Mei and I started a whirlwind romance. You have to understand, it was intoxicating, enchanting, a dream come to life. The only shadow, which also made me feel protective of her, was her story about her abusive ex-boyfriend, Frank. But she told me how safe and protected she felt with me, and that made me feel so good."

One day when Joe was alone, Frank cornered him, and indeed he looked like a scary guy.

"You're dating Mei," he'd growled. "She was mine for years, and you owe me for every penny I spent on her. I will find you later, and I expect you to pay me fifty thousand dollars."

Joe shook his head. "I couldn't believe it. I told Mei what had happened, and she was scared."

She'd wiped her eyes. "Please, you have to pay him.

Otherwise, he'll never leave me alone. Leave us alone. He's . . . killed people."

"So, I paid," Joe said, "every bit of money I'd saved to buy a house."

I tensed, suspecting what he was going to say next.

"And now . . . she's gone. I'm worried he did something to her anyway."

I shook my head. "He didn't do anything to her, other than hand her half of that money for doing her part."

Joe blinked. "I . . . I don't understand."

"I'm afraid you were taken in by the *deng bofai* scam. Mei, if that's even her name, is working with a gang associate or hustler who's the puppet master. She seduces her target, a caring man who buys her story about her cruel ex, and sets him up as her protector and true love. But this love story comes with a hefty price tag, this so-called break-up fee to untangle her from her past. It's emotional blackmail, a test of your devotion measured in cold, hard cash."

Desperate for love, countless men have fallen into this trap. Some pay astronomical sums, believing it's the price for true love. The highest known fee I came across was a staggering $150,000. For these gullible men, it isn't just money; it is a sacrifice for the woman they yearn to save. Her manipulative pleas—"I thought you loved me. Why won't you pay? Am I not worth it?"—seal the deal, tugging at the heartstrings and wallets of smitten suitors.

I looked at the devastated man across from me. "Do you want to file a report?"

He pressed his fingers against his forehead, clearly reeling, and stood. "I . . . I have to think about it." Then he rushed out.

I guessed that I'd never see him again. The *deng bofai* is a cruel dance of deception with love as the bait and extortion as the catch. In the tangled web of Chinatown's underbelly, love doesn't just hurt—it costs both money and dignity.

One of my earliest encounters with transnational crimes happened when a patrol officer ushered a distressed Chinese man into my office. From his slumped shoulders and teary eyes, it was evident he had just endured a harrowing experience.

"Mike," the officer began, "this guy just lost twenty-five grand."

I perused the report and initiated the interview. "What happened?"

"I saw this advertisement on a social media messenger for a money transfer company. I, um, wanted an alternative to Western Union and the banks for sending money home."

What he left unsaid was that he didn't want a large money transfer to alert authorities to his income. Some people had to take cash-paying jobs so they didn't lose their government assistance.

"So, I called the company and asked how much they charged for the money transfer."

"One hundred dollars for every ten thousand dollars," was the response from the other end.

Encouraged by the lower fee, the man had asked, "How will you transfer my US dollars from here to China?"

"Where in China are you sending the funds?" the operator inquired.

"Fujian," the man replied.

"To whom are you sending it?"

"My grandmother."

"How much are you sending?"

"Twenty-five thousand dollars."

"That's an easy transaction!" exclaimed the operator. "That

will cost just two hundred fifty."

"So, how do we proceed?"

"Bring the money tomorrow at one o'clock to our office in Chinatown. Instruct your grandmother to visit our cooperative bank, where one of my associates will meet her. We will establish a teleconference call between us, your grandmother, and our associate, who will hand her the equivalent yuan amounting to twenty-five thousand dollars. Once she receives the money, you will give me your twenty-five thousand dollars, along with the remittance fee."

The proposal seemed safe and practical as the exchange of currencies would occur in real time via teleconferencing. This manner of transferring money was common, usually conducted by legit middlemen who made a living doing just this. Chinatown's underground economy was based on trust and efficiency.

Convinced by the arrangement's feasibility, the man agreed to meet the remittance operator the next day. As instructed, he arrived at the building, going through the entrance and into a vestibule. Beyond that, he entered another room and waited for the remittance operator's arrival. The victim sought reassurance regarding the transaction's safety when the man arrived.

"You don't need to worry," the perpetrator assured him. "Call your grandmother now at the Fujian bank. My associate is already there."

The man initiated a video call through a social messaging app and, to his relief, saw his grandmother in the bank standing next to the remittance operator's associate. The victim conveyed that he would hand over the money only after his grandmother had received the yuan.

"Grandmother," the man spoke into the app, "do you have the money yet?"

"We're still in line, waiting to withdraw it."

Upon hearing this, the remittance operator requested to see the man's US money for his own reassurance. The man showed him the twenty-five thousand dollars cash neatly stowed in a small bag. The remittance operator snatched the bag, ran from the room, and slammed the door shut behind him.

The shocked man intended to pursue the thief but found the door locked. When they'd entered the room, the perp had left the door ajar. As soon as he fled, the door closed, and the lock required a pin number to open it. With no way to unlock the door, the frustrated man eventually sought help from others and was able to get out. By then, of course, the remittance operator had vanished with his money.

Meanwhile, after learning of the theft, the victim's grandmother grabbed the associate in Fujian. Chinese authorities intervened, detaining the associate and questioning the victim's grandmother. However, as the crime had transpired in the United States, the Chinese police could not press charges against the criminal associate, who, in actuality, hadn't done anything illegal.

Powerless in China and confined by jurisdictional constraints, I still commenced an investigation. I conducted a comprehensive canvassing of the building, identifying residents with prior arrests or criminal records. I examined CCTV footage, which revealed the perpetrator's familiarity with the building, enabling him to avoid areas covered by cameras. The individual behind this scheme had been meticulous, leaving no trace.

Under mounting pressure by the police in China, the criminal associate there provided the Chinese authorities with a picture of the perp who was in the US, and the Chinese police officer sent it to me. It was a single image, but it held immense value. Armed with this, I felt confident I could apprehend the individual.

An unexpected hurdle arose. I had to report the matter because cases exceeding specific monetary thresholds required notification to the Grand Larceny Division. Upon learning of my case, they contacted my boss, wanting to transfer it to their jurisdiction.

The sensational nature of this crime prompted the Grand Larceny Division to assert jurisdiction. My boss did not contest their decision, and the case was handed over. Such were the challenges I faced when detectives from other units, hungry for publicity, sought to make a name for themselves. They wrested the case from my grasp, despite the painstaking effort I'd already invested. But at least I had the satisfaction of taking the case as far as I did because that's what was important to me. I didn't want the publicity anyway, nor did I do my job for recognition, fame, or a pat on the back. I saw it as a challenge to see how far I could take a case and test my limitations. There were many arrests I never took credit for, passing it on to my colleagues.

On March 12, 2013, an Asian woman was walking home around eleven o'clock at night in Chinatown. A man lunged from the shadows, grabbing her mouth from behind while wrapping his other arm around her body. Another perpetrator rushed in front of her and rummaged through her pockets and purse. During the struggle, he punched her in the abdomen. The assailants took her jewelry and cash before fleeing on foot.

I was assigned the case and interviewed her when she reported the incident at the precinct. She was still shaken, but it helped that we shared the same ethnicity. I asked her to describe the perpetrators—face, hair, eyes, complexion, body marks, height, clothes, and distinguishing features or accessories. She described the first perpetrator as approximately five-foot-seven, thin with big lips, while the one who took her possessions was the same height with a medium complexion.

My partner and I led her to the photo manager, where we asked her to view dozens of mug shots to identify the attackers. Nothing came from that, so we produced a composite sketch of the suspects. The next day I canvassed the area, starting from the crime scene, checking CCTVs, and knocking on doors to speak with possible witnesses. Unfortunately, we found nothing, and the CCTVs yielded no useful footage.

Initially, the case seemed like a typical one-off robbery, but within a few days two more similar cases occurred in the vicinity. In one, another Asian woman was attacked in the same manner. This time, the assailants got a cell phone and $600 in cash.

Interestingly, the perps grabbed everything valuable inside the bag, not realizing the value of the bag itself. At least the victims were able to keep their fancy bags.

After following the investigative process, we monitored the signal of the stolen iPhone, hoping the perpetrator would turn it on since it had a built-in tracker. Unfortunately, they didn't. Despite our efforts, the photo array and CCTV again yielded nothing. I conducted a meticulous canvass of the area in Brooklyn where the crime had occurred, not far from the first robbery.

I concluded there was a robbery pattern, suggesting this might be the work of the same individual or group. Similarities can include the type of victims targeted, the locations, the time of day, and other specific details.

One key aspect we analyze is the modus operandi, which includes the method of operation. We look for similarities in where and how the robberies are carried out, such as the type of weapon used, the approach to the victim, specific demands made, and the escape route. We note and compare any unique behaviors or quirks exhibited by the suspect during the robberies.

Geographic profiling plays a significant role in our analysis. Using Geographic Information Systems (GIS), we mapped out the robbery locations to identify clusters or patterns. Identifying hotspots—areas with a high concentration of similar robberies—can indicate a pattern.

The three previous robbery cases targeted Asian women with the same MO, within the same vicinity, same time frame, and with the same general description of the perpetrators, so I classified the case as Robbery Pattern No. 2013-33. The number three in Chinese means "life," so thirty-three stands for "staying alive." Once this classification was set, our precinct notified other nearby precincts to be alert for similar patterns.

Many of these same types of crimes were also happening in the Sixty-Eighth, an adjoining precinct with a decent-sized Chinese population, so we worked with them. When the department puts a case into a pattern, we're given more resources and manpower.

In reality, we didn't know how many of these robberies actually happened. I suspected that many women didn't report the crime at all. Some who did then resisted cooperating afterward—for example, not returning to the station to look at a lineup.

Still, I was determined to find the culprits. We had a sense of urgency, considering that there had been a series of robberies throughout March, and failure to crack the case would taint our reputation.

The perpetrators must have gained confidence, if not arrogance, after their successful robberies. Another robbery spree occurred over a few days around the crime scene areas in Brooklyn, with three more Asian females suffering the same fate of being attacked from behind by the first perpetrator while an accomplice took their possessions. Two victims reported that the perpetrators escaped using a black van with sliding side doors. Later, our surveillance team returned with photos from CCTV showing the vehicle stopping at an intersection, but the license plate was unclear.

I subpoenaed all the stolen iPhones so that I'd be notified if they sent out a signal—and luckily, one of the mobile phones did, but not for long enough to get the final address. Still, that information helped tremendously in my next step: using Entity Analytics (EA) technology. "EAs" refers to a search result from an Entity Analytics system, often used in law enforcement to analyze and correlate data about entities—such as people, organizations, and locations—from various sources.

I used our precinct's EAs to list people with arrest records out on parole who had a history of robbery within a certain radius of the crime scene areas, including where the signal from the stolen iPhone was last transmitted. I narrowed the search by filtering the general description of the perpetrator. The short-listed names provided a photo array of their faces that the victims could look at.

Success! Three victims identified one common attacker. I pulled out the file, and there he was: José Sanchez. He'd been released from prison eight months ago and had a history of robbery. *Got you.* I went to the perp's known address with my partner and police officers.

Sanchez did not resist arrest, and I charged him in court with sixteen counts of robbery. The other perpetrator remained at large.

Detective Mark Leonard from the Sixty-Eight Precinct and I worked three days straight in the field and at the precinct without going home. We had to process the arrest, locate the victims, prepare the lineup, do paperwork, and present the evidence to the assistant district attorney. In a big case like this, the district attorney's office generally sends an ADA to the precinct to "ride the case." In police jargon, that means they assist the detectives with capturing the interview on video, charging the perp with the correct charges, reviewing the evidence, and anything else that will ensure the case is tight and done right to keep it from being thrown out on any technicalities.

My partner and I were exhausted to the point of physical breakdown. We were meeting with the ADA to record a confession from Sanchez —incidentally in the same room where I'd been interrogated by Detective Donahue at the beginning of my journey. While we were waiting for the ADA, sitting shoulder to shoulder, my partner Leonard, who was more than three hundred pounds and over six feet tall, was so tired that he fell asleep and slumped onto me, a skinny, five-foot-seven detective.

The case should have been classified as a hate crime, not just a robbery. It was evident that the perpetrator had exclusively targeted Asian women. But because hate crimes must contain an element of a racist verbal assault or identification, it didn't meet the qualification. I thought there was a gray area in classifying crimes, and the criteria must be more circumspect. If this case had been classified as a hate crime, Sanchez would have served a lot more time.

I ended up with sixteen cases of robbery to pin on the suspect, giving me sixteen arrests on my police record. Some jealous detectives in my precinct claimed that because all those arrests were committed by the same perp, they should be counted as one arrest. I wasn't petty like that, nor did I brag about "all my arrests." This was one of the reasons I kept to myself, did my job, and went home. Still, I *was* proud that I'd solved that case through a lot of hard detective work.

In 2016, I took a six-month leave of absence, needing a break from the job and wanting to find the perfect place to spend time when I retired. I was in the Philippines in early January 2017 when I opened my phone to read the news and saw a stomach-sinking headline: "NYPD Officer Famous for Forgiving Shooter Passes Away at 59."

Steven McDonald—gone. It hit me hard: sadness for his loss but also the inspiration I'd felt during all those times I asked myself, *What would he do in this situation?* He had helped me make decisions throughout the years. I sadly couldn't attend the funeral, as I was in the process of purchasing a condo for my retirement.

But I spoke these words to him: "Goodbye, Steven. Wherever you are, thank you. I wish you had known that in your suffering, you redeemed a life—mine. And perhaps many others too. During all those years you spent in your wheelchair, you gave my legs the strength to patrol the streets and do the job your paralysis prevented you from doing. I should have shared my secret past with you when I had the opportunity and told you how profoundly you changed my life."

In 2018, while just outside the premises of the Sixty-Sixth Precinct, a Chinese sergeant I didn't know approached me. He'd been recently promoted and had transferred to the Sixty-Sixth Precinct. I stopped to give him my respectful attention and waited for him to speak.

"You're Michael Moy, right?" he asked.

I nodded.

His tone remained low, and he glanced around to make sure our conversation was private. "I heard a lot about you before you became a cop."

I kept quiet, but my mind raced.

He continued, "I was in the park when your brother settled his issue with Siu Bo. I used to be with the Ghost Shadows."

I waited to hear more before speaking. He told me he'd

become a close friend with my brother, Jason, in the years after the incident, which I later confirmed. He understood what I'd gone through to get into the police force, as had he. Still, he was aware of the rules of our game, and he left as soon as he finished speaking.

What a revelation that another former gang member had made it into the NYPD, someone who, like me, had a secret to keep. We'd both escaped the streets' underbelly and gone from being gang rivals to members of law enforcement. It made me smile with pride.

That same year in October, a patrol cop from the Sixty-Sixth Precinct approached me. "Did you know a guy named Jack?" The name took me back twenty-five years: The most consequential Jack I'd ever known was Chinatown Jack. I had a gut feeling he was now out of prison, and this cop had come across him.

"What happened? Did you collar him?" I asked.

The officer told me Jack had threatened someone with a metal pipe. When he approached Jack and asked about the pipe on the ground next to him, Jack took off running. The officer called for backup and initiated a pursuit. He finally caught up to Jack and grabbed him.

Jack looked at his brass collar. "Oh, man! If I knew you guys were from the Sixty-Sixth, I wouldn't have run!"

"Why's that?" asked the officer.

"'Coz, you guys are soft! I thought you were from the Seven-O 'coz those guys fuck me up every time they get me!"

As they made the arrest, Jack said, "You guys know a Michael Moy? He's my friend."

After hearing this story, I asked, "Do you have a picture of him?"

The officer pulled out his phone and showed me a photo.

Yes, it was Chinatown Jack, his face now a pitiful reflection of someone who'd endured much hardship, including prison, drugs, and street life. My mind drifted back to my pool hall, where he'd played billiards with hustlers, the nights we practiced target shooting, and the countless times he and my gangmates played cards with drinks and cigarettes.

The police officer said Jack had started mumbling about conspiracy theories and nonsense while driving to the precinct. Showing signs of an emotionally disturbed person, the police sent him to a hospital for evaluation. I neither denied nor affirmed that I knew him. Let them think Jack was a raving lunatic. *Me*, friends with a gangster? No way.

Deep inside I knew drugs had got the better of him. I missed those days when he was that carefree fifteen-year-old soldier to Cambodian Peter, with whom we'd had so many laughs together in the pool hall. Now we were all a bunch of middle-aged guys with different issues and challenges to deal with.

A happy reconnection occurred with my old loyal friend Jordan Rini at our twenty-five-year high school reunion. He was the study partner I'd left behind when joining the gang. At the time, our friendship had been significant because this white kid hadn't minded being associated with me, a Chinese American, even though it could have made him a target for bullies.

After I joined the gang, guilt had consumed me for a while, and I'd felt sad for abandoning him. I knew he missed our time studying together before a test, sharing our comic books, and enjoying the simple, happy things friends do.

Seeing him now took me back to the days when we studied after school and then walked to the Triangle pool hall. Like most people, he was surprised that I'd become a cop. He had become a teacher and was married to a Chinese woman.

Meeting these people from my past provided nostalgic moments for me to ponder about how my life could have taken such a different direction. I could have continued to hang out with Jordan and never joined a gang, for instance. Maybe I would have been a dissatisfied pharmacist. So many things would have been different, including who I was. Every decision I made at every juncture had determined the events and the people in my life.

By July 2021, I faced another decision about my life path. Was it time to retire? While my work gave me immense satisfaction, I had the unfortunate luck of working with some people who didn't exemplify what being a member of the NYPD meant. I don't want to weigh down my story here, so I'll simply say that retiring was the cleanest way for me to cut ties with that short-but-toxic part of my career. People said I'd know when the time was right, and I knew that, yes, this was the time. After filing my retirement, I went from "detective" to "mister." This gave me a happy feeling and the anticipation of opening a new chapter in my life.

As someone who seldom attaches emotions to life's events, my first day at the Sixty-Sixth Precinct stands out as quietly joyful, especially considering the challenges I had overcome to become an NYPD officer. Retiring from the service after twenty-six years and nineteen days marked another fresh beginning.

What a life I've led. From bullied to empowered, from bad to blue, from street kid to detective, husband, father, and fighter for justice. I appreciate all the events that led me to where I am now: satisfied, fulfilled, and proud of who I've become.

EPILOGUE

After twenty-six years as an NYPD officer, I retired in July 2021. My career tied up the loose ends of my life, bridging the gap between past and present. I'd like to believe that nearly three decades as an NYPD cop somehow atoned for the misdeeds of my youth.

Becoming a cop was a rational choice, and I'll never regret it. The NYPD's pragmatic goals gave me a purpose every morning: to help maintain order in society. In my earlier years, my recklessness caused chaos in the streets. Being a cop balanced the scales, bringing peace and order to my small world within New York City's Chinatowns. I added my drop to the bucket of social change and order.

Of course, the NYPD isn't perfect; no place is. Being an American-born Chinese cop in the NYPD came with challenges, but I owe a debt of gratitude to the department for allowing me to become one of New York's finest. The badge offered me the redemption I had sought.

The saga of my parents as Chinese immigrants found its culmination in me. Despite America's flaws and failures, it's a land of opportunity for those who work tirelessly. Immigrants are an integral part of New York and the country as a whole. In law enforcement, I proudly represented my rich Chinese heritage. My transformation story speaks to everyone's abilities to evolve and reinvent ourselves. No one is lost or irretrievably broken if they can see their faults and the path those faults will lead them down and are then willing to change.

Both my daughter and son took entrance examinations for the NYPD and passed. However, only my son decided to pursue a career in law enforcement. My daughter came to realize that this life was not for her.

My children grew up in a different era, one in which the Asian gangs in Chinatown had ceased to exist. They didn't know about or understand my involvement in the underworld during their childhood. To them, my dragon tattoo was a fashion statement. I made a point to shield them from the vices that had once trapped many of my friends, particularly drugs, alcohol, and gambling. I ensured that their childhood was vastly different from mine. My children didn't need to join a gang for protection and belonging or to run rackets so they could buy the things they want. They didn't participate in high-risk activities. Their concerns revolved around how and where to watch Black Pink and BTS concerts.

My biggest regret as a parent is that I, like my father, put more emphasis on ensuring my family's security than spending time with them. Looking back, I wish I'd instigated more heart-to-heart conversations with my kids and gotten involved in their activities. The lack of those kinds of exchanges with my own father hurt me the most, and sadly, I replicated that behavior. If I could turn back time with the wisdom that the years bring, I would. If I could miraculously mend the past and erase the pain I caused them, I would. But I have no Chinese herbs or mystic rituals that would accomplish that, so I am a human doing what I can to make up for the past. Because I can see my faults and am trying to atone for them, I have hope that we will build that bridge. Unfortunately, I have been unable to mend the rift between me and my father.

Realization is the first step to change. When I realized I needed to get out of the gang environment, it was easier because that was a road only I was driving on. I can control my own journey. But for the disconnected relationship with my dad, that change represents two drivers on the road who need to align. I can't control the other driver, only myself. In that regard, I offered olive branches in the form of invitations to go fishing, and he came, but our tepid relationship remained the same. I can only control my own actions, and I must accept that I cannot control his. I wish I could restore our relationship, but I don't have the answer as to how.

Writing this book has helped me see my relationships more clearly. I hadn't even thought about the fact that my father had never hugged me until I was digging into this section, and the shock of it brought a heaviness to my heart. What I did take away from my childhood was to always give my kids hugs and kisses when I came home from work, even if it was more out of respect than a true sense of connection. If I could give parenting advice, it's to give your kids a hug. They may not realize how important that gesture is to them at the time, but someday they will. And isn't it better for them to look back and cherish those hugs than to feel the gut-wrenching loss of not having them? But what's most important is to really connect with your children, to look them in the eyes and listen to them. That will make the most impact on you and them for all the years to come.

Two events stand out among the instances featuring significant individuals in my transition from a troubled past to a law enforcement career.

The three cops who chose not to arrest me when they caught me with an unlicensed gun in 1994 cleared the path for my journey into law enforcement. Had they arrested me, it would have closed the door to the NYPD, and who knows where I would be today?

When I met them again in the precinct, none of them asked if I was the young man they'd almost arrested outside that Vietnamese noodle house. The topic remained untouched, even after we became close colleagues.

Over twenty years later, as I approached retirement, I sat beside one of those officers during a training session and decided to bring up that old memory. The other two cops had already retired by then.

"I'm about to retire now," I said, "and I've always wanted to ask you: Do you remember when you pulled over this Chinese kid over twenty years ago—?"

Before I finished my question, he cut in with, "Yeah, we knew it was you," in a casual, reassuring tone.

I extended my hand for a handshake, overwhelmed with gratitude. My longtime curiosity and unanswered question had finally been resolved.

"I want to thank you," I said sincerely. "And the other guys too for deciding not to arrest me that night. Otherwise, I wouldn't be here today, preparing to retire."

He clasped my hand, and we never discussed it again. Being able to thank and shake the hand of the officer to whom I owed so much brought a sense of closure.

An unexpected reunion with Ian Einhorn, the kid I had bullied in sixth grade, was a more humbling but still gratifying experience. While working in the Sixty-Sixth Precinct as a detective, I noticed a name tag on an auxiliary police officer: *Einhorn*.

He stood outside the precinct with five other auxiliary officers. Seeing that name transported me back to my school days, and memories of how I'd made life difficult for Ian Einhorn nearly forty years ago rushed back.

Back then I didn't want to be at the bottom of the food chain, so I became a bully. I took Ian's lunch money almost daily. Acting tough, I didn't cut him any slack. Approaching him now, I wasn't sure how he'd react upon seeing his former tormentor.

"Are you Ian Einhorn?"

"Yeah," he replied with hesitation. He gave me a puzzled look, and I knew he didn't recognize me.

"I'm Michael Moy."

His eyes widened. "What? This is crazy. You popped into my mind out of the blue a week ago, and now you're standing right before me!"

My stomach sank. "Did I traumatize you so much that you're *still* thinking about me after all these years?"

"You sure did."

"I'm sorry for putting you through that. Can I take you for dinner sometime?"

He nodded without even hesitating. "Yeah, that would be nice."

"How long have you been working here?"

"Seven years." He still looked bewildered by the synchronicity.

"I've been here over two decades."

"Wow, we've worked in the same precinct for seven years and didn't recognize each other."

I chuckled. "Well, we've both aged a lot after almost forty years."

Being the good guy he'd always been, he got so excited that he called his mom and told her about me as soon as she picked up. Ian handed me the phone, allowing me to talk with her on the spot while his colleagues watched a slice of my life unfold. I apologized to her for all the terrible things I did to her son. Later, I invited Ian to join me for dinner at a Malaysian restaurant in Chinatown to catch up. Apologizing to him for what I'd done to him, we shared the happy moment.

I still saw the eleven-year-old boy in his face, even though he was in his fifties. It seemed like yesterday, and I felt like a schoolboy again. This unexpected reunion with someone from my past brought with it nostalgia that's hard to put into words.

Meeting Ian raised questions. Why on earth was he happy and excited to see me? I stole his lunch money, made him go hungry, and caused him daily distress. Perhaps he was just a genuinely good person who quickly forgave and moved on from the hurts I'd inflicted on him. Heck, he even called his mom and asked me to say hello to her! Ian and I hadn't shared pleasant times in school; he'd been my victim. Why had he treated me like a long-lost best friend instead of an enemy?

If a person from my past had come up to me and introduced themselves as one of the bullies who'd hurt me in school, my reaction would have been different. Who knows how many of them might have recognized me but didn't approach?

These episodes revealed a deep sense of humanity. They enriched my understanding of how life should be lived, as demonstrated by the empathy of the three cops and Ian's gracious attitude toward a former enemy.

I've harvested life lessons from my experiences and the people I've encountered, both the good and the bad. My life consists of three chapters: the day I became a gang member, the moment

I was sworn in as an NYPD police officer, and now, as a retired detective attempting to fulfill a new purpose.

Years before my planned retirement, I looked forward to retiring in a country far from New York, where I could start again with a clean slate. The Big Apple battlefield during my police career had left me scarred. I needed to step away from the city's hustle and bustle in retirement.

Throughout my career, I had the opportunity to travel to various countries in Europe, the Americas, and Asia. I was always assessing potential relocation options.

In late 2015 I was visiting friends who had served their time and been deported to Hong Kong when I decided to spend time in the Philippines. I experienced the warmth of the people and their hospitality. Most Filipinos are fluent English speakers and well educated. The country boasts a rich history and has been a US ally for over five decades. I had access to some of the best resorts and beaches across its seven thousand islands.

The Philippines is a wonderful country to live in. The virtues of its people make up for any shortcomings in public utilities, bureaucratic processes, and infrastructure. While Metro Manila struggles with horrendous traffic, I found plenty of reasons to be thankful for being there.

So, after careful consideration, I took a giant leap. In 2016, I bought a condominium in a pleasant urban township in Metro Manila. Later, I obtained a Special Resident Retiree's Visa (SRRV) for foreign nationals seeking to establish the Philippines as their second home or investment location. The SRRV allows me to make multiple entries and have an indefinite stay in the country.

In parallel with my retirement plan, a profound restlessness began to stir within me. I recognized the importance of preserving and sharing the history of Asian gangs, a crucial part of the story of New York's Chinatowns. While there was a plethora of literature about Italian mobs and other organized crime groups, there was a significant gap when it came to Asian gangs in New York. Few literary works on this subject existed, and even those needed to be revised or corrected. I hoped that telling my story in a book could be a humble contribution to history.

The stories from that era might be violent, reflecting the consequences of moral breakdown, but they also highlight how society fails to address the problems and situations that push people into lawlessness. These stories were on the brink of being lost forever. I felt that if I didn't take it upon myself to document and preserve this history, it could vanish.

Former gang members, especially those from my era, often prefer to remain silent, and there are various reasons behind their choice to keep their stories untold, a fact I've come to understand during my efforts to reach out to them. Some are embarrassed because they cooperated with the authorities and incriminated their gangmates to help their own prison sentences. Others simply desire a peaceful life without the shadows of their dark history haunting them. Some fear the consequences of their children discovering the troubled path they once walked, while others have not fully grasped the complexities of the statute of limitations.

Still others live as fugitives, adding another layer of complexity to their silence. And of course, many expect monetary compensation in exchange for sharing their stories with me, wanting to know what is in it for them.

Despite the challenges, I felt compelled to share my story, shedding light on the struggles of minorities during that era so that their experiences could become part of the annals of New York history.

In line with my commitment to preserving the history of Asian gangs in New York's Chinatown, I launched my YouTube channel, Chinatown Gang Stories, in June 2022.[7] Through my content, I share glimpses of my experiences in New York City's Chinatown gang life. I also feature former gang members, retired NYPD officers, and other individuals with significant insights into the world of gangs. These interviews provide perspective on Chinatown gang culture through the eyes of insiders. Interestingly, victims and their families are still reluctant to come forward, perhaps still afraid of gangs.

Ironically, my grown children discovered details about my life as a gang member from people who'd watched my YouTube channel. My audience had more knowledge about my past than my children did.

My channel evolved into a historical program, offering narratives from people who had either fond or traumatic memories of Chinatown—sometimes a mix of both. I delved into how Asian gangs engaged in organized crime, drawing from my dual perspective as a former gang member and detective. My aim is to provide a unique outlook from both sides of the coin.

History has a remarkable way of unveiling the truth, no matter how much time passes—decades, centuries, or even millennia. Future generations might find something to learn from an average person like me. Perhaps, in the future, I'll become part of a case study on the impacts of bullying and racism.

Survival has been baked into the DNA of Asian people by the persecution and hardships they've endured for generations. We innately tap into our strength and fortitude to adapt to whatever situations arise. When we adapt, we grow stronger still. Because of this, in the face of chaos and catastrophe, I assess and look for solutions.

---

7. https://www.youtube.com/@chinatowngangstories

Every tombstone has a story; I've ensured mine has one for people to know clearly. I want to share our stories before I reach my final resting place. This book marks a fresh start, a world of new possibilities. And many more stories are still waiting to be told on my YouTube channel.

My circle of acquaintances, friends, and followers has grown in ways I couldn't have imagined as a scrawny kid in oversized clothes back in that hostile school building. No life is beyond repair, and no tunnel is too long and dark to find the light at its end. I turned my life around with determination and purpose, and I can only hope my story inspires others to do so as well.

ACKNOWLEDGMENTS

Writing this memoir was one of the most rewarding endeavors I have ever undertaken. While I knew it would be difficult, I did not expect the extent of the time and effort it would demand, which included countless sleepless nights, as well as long hours of meeting with my writer and editors. The completion of *Bad to Blue* was due to the help of several people.

Marilyn Kretzer of Blackstone Publishing showed exceptional patience and understanding while we struggled against deadlines. My book agent and editor, Tina Wainscott of the Seymour Agency, went above and beyond her role. She took a chance on me by accepting my manuscript. Tina had no prior knowledge of the Asian gang genre, but she believed in my redemption story, giving me the opportunity to share my story with the world. Her outstanding editing skills and storytelling improved the manuscript to make it worthy of publication. I acknowledge her relentless effort and expertise as a book editor and agent who genuinely wanted me to succeed in this project. Thank you, Tina.

ACKNOWLEDGMENTS

Dana Isaacson was the editorial wizard who lent his expertise to further polish, refine, and bring this memoir into its best version. He patiently went through every detail to ensure that *Bad to Blue* was print-ready. Dana's help was invaluable for the fruition of this project.

I acknowledge the inspiration and motivation from the subscribers of my YouTube channel, *Chinatown Gang Stories*. Their overwhelming reception to my videos strengthened my belief that my memoir has value and is necessary to preserve the history of Asian gangs in New York Chinatowns. My interview guests were brave enough to tell the stories of their dark pasts and affiliations with the underworld. They came out in the open despite the advice of others who discouraged them from being guests on my channel.

I am grateful to the late NYPD officer Steven McDonald, who sparked the change in my life from a gang member to a police officer and detective. He never knew that his heroic act of forgiveness solidified my decision to be in law enforcement. Had I not encountered his story, I would have spiraled downward and ended up like most gang members.

Lastly, I acknowledge Leo Almonte, a writer and book development consultant from the Philippines who started working on this memoir in 2015. He had the unenviable task of gathering and archiving tons of narratives, information, data, and references related to my life story. On two occasions, I flew him to the United States, where we worked on the first draft of the book. He interviewed my friends, family members, relatives, and former gangmates to get firsthand stories about me and my former life.

In the course of this book project, Leo lived with me for a total of four months between my Brooklyn house and my condominium in the Philippines, where we formed a bond like comrades-in-arms holed in the same trench. Admittedly, Leo and I had chaotic moments when the project seemed to go nowhere. We were sometimes at odds, argued, and voiced our differences. Until the end, Leo remained committed, humble enough to admit his limitations, but at the same time bold in using his strengths as a writer. I acknowledge his invaluable help and thank him for his dedication.